YOU BET YOUR LIFE

YOU BET YOUR LIFE

My Incredible Adventures in

Horse Racing and Offshore Betting

Dave Stevenson

With Laura Morton

Skyhorse Publishing

Skyhorse Publishing books may be purchased in bulk at special discounts for sales promotion, corporate gifts, fund-raising, or educational purposes. Special editions can also be created to specifications. For details, contact the Special Sales Department, Skyhorse Publishing, 307 West 36th Street, 11th Floor, New York, NY 10018 or info@skyhorsepublishing.com.

Skyhorse® and Skyhorse Publishing® are registered trademarks of Skyhorse Publishing, Inc.®, a Delaware corporation.

Visit our website at www.skyhorsepublishing.com.

10 9 8 7 6 5 4 3 2 1

Library of Congress Cataloging-in-Publication Data is available on file.

Cover design by Tom Lau
Cover photo credit: Michael Burns Photo Ltd.

Print ISBN: 978-1-5107-2078-7
Ebook ISBN: 978-1-5107-2081-7

Printed in the United States of America

CONTENTS

In memory of my great friend Henry "Jerry" MacDonald, whose insistence, dedication, and support was mainly responsible for the creation of this book. The stories told on a golf cart, and on many other sojourns, seemed to buffer his pain and allowed many laughs along the way.

To Barbara, whose indefatigable love and dedication shone through in the midst of the burdens of Canadian farm life; love of her children; and the angst of many perilous journeys in the back seat of a screaming Mitsubishi plane at 29,000 feet over a stormy Caribbean.

And to my children—David, Dianna, Rebecca, and Aaron—who all shared the highs and lows of a rigorous racing life at various times of their lives and managed to grow into wonderful and responsible human beings.

"In 2016, the approximate value of the billions of underground transactions around the world is close to $12 trillion . . ."

FOREWORD

I have known Dave Stevenson since 1980, when he changed the tempo of the Thoroughbred industry in Saratoga Springs by utilizing the famed Oklahoma Training Track for several months outside of the annual summer race meeting. Before his innovation, marked by an innate sixth sense that guided him through a career of making such moves, the track was used only during the short summer racing season. Stevenson's advocacy of Saratoga Springs as an off-season center for training racehorses ushered in a period of sustained investment in the small historic city that continues to pay substantial dividends. It was but one example of Stevenson's skill in recognizing the potential gains to be made by broadening the relationship network of tracks, communities, breeding farms, betting parlors, and entertainment venues.

His remarkable career, which includes life-threatening encounters with criminals, could only have happened, in the opinion of this writer, in the world of Thoroughbred racing. Stevenson's life experience ranged from jobs with no pay in the darkest of conditions, to executive positions with major league racing organizations that enabled him to conceive and promote racing events of world class importance. His inner drive, guided by a self-confidence honed by numerous tests of survival, enabled him to move forward in a business marked by intense competition on a daily basis.

He managed, despite a brief career in the irons, to win the Queen's Plate, the most important race in Canada, aboard Canadian Champ at Woodbine in 1956. This was accomplished despite a long-standing and increasingly bitter feud between Stevenson and Canadian Champ's trainer. Disagreement among trainer, jockey, and horse is a recipe for failure in the Thoroughbred game.

With respect to Canada and the United States, while a racing official for the Ontario Jockey Club, Stevenson worked with political leaders to eliminate an onerous import/export tax, with the goal of improving the quality of racing at Woodbine. The result, like that of the aforementioned Oklahoma Training Track, continues to help the industry on both sides of the border.

When Secretariat, the Triple Crown winner of 1973 and considered by some as America's greatest horse since Man o' War, was nearing the end of his career, Stevenson again produced a terrific idea for racing. He envisioned Secretariat racing at Woodbine in the Canadian International in order to elevate that race in importance. In race track parlance, the idea of Secretariat racing in Canada had no shot.

But we are talking here about Stevenson latching on to an idea and not letting go. He discussed the idea with Secretariat's owner Penny Tweedy (Penny Chenery at that time) and his trainer, Lucien Laurin, who just happened to be a Canadian. Secretariat came to Woodbine, put on a phenomenal show under adverse conditions, and put the Canadian International on a path to a succession of participation by top class horses.

Racing in unlike other sports in many ways, and the life of Dave Stevenson is a prime example. Every fan of the Thoroughbred sport will appreciate this story.

Michael Veitch has covered Thoroughbred racing as a turf writer since 1979. He is the author of two books on the history of racing in his native Saratoga Springs, a member of that city's History Hall of Fame, a trustee of the National Museum of Racing, and a nominating committee member of that institution's Hall of Fame as well as the Canadian Horse Racing Hall of Fame, Thoroughbred division.

INTRODUCTION

Miami Lakes, Florida, 1991

Collecting money is the bane of nearly all businesses, but when you deal with questionable characters from mostly third-world countries that trade in multiple currencies and the underground economy, collecting can be a real bitch. My business was simulcast horse racing and offshore betting—specifically with wagers placed on American transmitted horse races throughout the Caribbean, a territory covering 1.63 million square miles, including parts of Central and South America. My company offered an arsenal of signals from various tracks around the United States. I created the system of offshore simulcast racing, pioneered it actually; and for a while I was the only source to make it available. We didn't just sell signals; we brought years of expertise to the trade that could only be learned about racing from the inside out. But more on that later.

For years, I tried to work on alternate ways to get our money out of the various countries we provided service to without having to fly there and collect it myself. I never came up with a better or more reliable solution. They couldn't wire it. There were no foreign transfers allowed on U.S. currency earned from simulcasts or anything else. Perhaps I could have hired someone to be a money courier, but, given the large dollar amounts I collected on a monthly basis, I didn't have anyone I could trust with our cash. Besides, my clients weren't exactly white-hat-wearing good guys. I once had a client, Cecil Charlton, the Mayor of Mandeville, Jamaica, ask if he could fax me his check. At the time, fax machines were new, especially in third-world countries, so he didn't understand it didn't work that way. We were dealing in six different currencies, and, in a way, our business was primitive, and so were many of the people we were dealing with. The only logical solution to our money collection problem was for me to fly to each territory and collect it myself.

From the day I started working in simulcast racing, I was never hesitant to involve my kids in the family business. In fact, aside from my wife, Barbara, my children were the only people I knew, without a doubt, I could trust. My daughters, Rebecca and Dianna, ran the office. My son, Aaron, a financial consultant for a large bank, counseled us on money management. Barbara and I made perfect partners; she was more than willing to accompany me on my professional endeavors, enjoying royal gatherings as well as enduring the depths of uncertainty that came with the territory we covered.

I owned twelve planes over the years, but my favorite by far was the pressurized MU2-10, an upgraded, multiengine, jet-powered aircraft fully equipped with 1,000 horsepower on each side. The MU2-10, or "Mits" as I liked to call it, is very complicated to fly but ideal for the frequent trips I made to the Caribbean. I also had to make domestic trips to more than two-dozen states to meet and consult with our host racetracks. Fellow pilots and controllers referred to the Mits in communications as the "rice rocket." Flying over mountainous terrain and thousands of miles of ocean—say nothing of dealing with rapidly changing weather patterns—posed lots of challenges, but none that this jet couldn't handle. It was able to land on short 2,400-foot runways, fly nonstop for over 1,200 miles at 30,000 feet, and comfortably cruise at over 300 knots. It topped any other million-dollar aircraft in the air. It's very much a pilot's airplane with no room for error. These trips took a lot of planning and preparation, especially ones involving complex routes to avoid uncertain weather, heavy air traffic, and unnecessary security risks.

I usually filed my flight plans out of FXE, the Executive Airport in Fort Lauderdale, Florida, which served as our home base. This time I wanted to make a quick stop in St. Croix for fuel before heading on to Trinidad, where I was due to meet with clients and pick up our monthly receivables. My son Aaron had made these trips with me dozens of times. In his younger days, he was a badass brawler who loved going into bars and picking fights. He was a real son of a bitch but was always an asset, especially when it came to collecting what we were owed and delivering decoder boxes (programmed to allow the reception of racing signals off of the satellites). I'm not saying

Aaron ever had to get physical with anyone, but it was sure nice to know he was there just in case. Aaron wasn't a big guy, but he had a certain presence and was very aggressive when he needed to be. He was a street fighter by nature. On one trip, he even saved Patrick Troutman, the simulcast coordinator for Churchill Downs, from drowning off of Buck Island in the U.S. Virgin Islands.

On this particular trip, however, my daughter Rebecca was going with me. She wanted to meet the people on the other end of the phone with whom she dealt on a regular basis. As the president of our company, she hoped to foster a better rapport with clients by meeting them in person. Although Rebecca weighed ninety-five pounds and stood only slightly more than five feet tall, everyone she talked to throughout our regional client base imagined her to be six-foot-two. Rebecca's primary responsibilities in the company included accounting, so, naturally, she was the money handler. She may be short in stature, but she is tough as nails, especially when it came to collecting the tracks and our share. She is famously remembered by her friends for jumping on a bouncer's back to keep him off of Aaron after he had decked a smart aleck for insulting his sisters. At S&A, the name of our family business (which stands for Stevenson and Associates), she took her job extremely seriously, and, as a result, our clients really respected her. If they had only known her actual size, I'm sure our losses would have been far greater. Thankfully, she is unafraid to ask for what she wants, and she doesn't take crap from anyone.

Three hours and forty minutes after taking off from Miami, Rebecca and I touched down in St. Croix. My sister, Ginny, and her husband, Larry, owned and operated St. Croix Marine and Caribbean Sea Adventures, an exotic scuba-dive shop, which at the time had the largest railroad haul-out for boats in the islands and the only full-service boatyard in the Caribbean.

We taxied into Bill Bohlke's FBO in St. Croix, and while the airplane was being refueled and serviced for a quick turnaround, I met with some local horsemen who raced at Doc Randall Park on the island. They had hired me to consult on the purchase of some Thoroughbreds they were interested in. Over the years, I had successfully sold about two hundred head of horses in the islands, so my opinion and services were in demand. Normally, I would have stayed the night to visit with Ginny and Larry, but Rebecca and I had business to do on a few islands en route to our final destination. We also had about a dozen new decoder boxes to deliver to customers. Rebecca had files of data detailing who owed us money and in what amount. The files also noted any discrepancies or other matters to be discussed with various clients and governments along the way. The numbers Rebecca held were the figures we operated by and the sums we were there to collect. We weren't open to negotiation regarding unpaid bills. Overdue accounts lost signal service.

Our "clients" included anyone with a betting shop, whether it was a local bodega in a city, town, or village; an office operation; or just a lone receiver strung up in a tree somewhere in the jungle next to an old tube television set powered by a single outlet and a hundred-foot extension cord. The poorer districts we dealt in were higher security risks. They had a tendency to invite more violence, especially when losses were reported or counterfeit hundred-dollar bills were used for payment—a common attempt by many overdue clients. Most of our customers were bookmakers who allowed their clientele to bet on credit, while others were small, local racecourses that took our signals to air at their location. We liked to deal with the tracks separately, because they were pari-mutuel (a form of betting in which those backing the first three places divide the losers' stakes, less the operator's commission) and therefore had a different mentality than the others who leased our signals. We also dealt with the national government agencies over local laws every bit as much as did the local businessman trying to make a buck—or whatever currency he was dealing in.

When we first started doing business in Trinidad, using American currency was illegal on the street. You couldn't have it, bank it, or transfer it. You had to deal in what was referred to as "TT"—Trinidad and Tobago dollars. To operate, I would have to meet with the Minister of Tourism or the Prime Minister, so they were aware of what type of business we conducted and why we were there. What we were doing wasn't illegal. However, the transferring of American currency was—unless you were an American. Since I could possess American currency, I made my clients pay me in U.S. dollars as often as possible. That softened my losses and enabled me to move the money off of the black market. In Trinidad, we had ten or fifteen outlets, ranging in size from large to small, that were all owned by independent proprietors from a vast array of backgrounds. Some people weren't into racing, but they understood the money to be made in wagering. Trinidadians are some of the most brilliant gaming and gambling handicappers I've ever dealt with throughout all my years in the business. They studied the racing forms like they read their Bibles. They grew up with racing when England colonized the island. Wherever the English went, cricket, soccer, and all-things-English followed, and the local people soon became invested. Horse racing was no exception.

What was unusual about this particular visit to Trinidad was that we had agreed to meet a dozen people, eleven men and one woman, to collect our money—together. I was completely unaware that they called the meeting in an attempt to barter collectively for better rates from us. Signal pricing was based on which tracks the customers wanted to receive. A premium track, say, any of those associated with NYRA (New York Racing Association), demanded a premium fee. A smaller track, one that operated seasonally in an outlying area, cost less. The decoder boxes we provided could be programmed to receive multiple signals from as many tracks as the customer had purchased. The more business the client did, the better price they could ask for and generally get. This didn't sit well with the clients who couldn't compete. By asking to meet us all together, in their own way, they were trying to unionize their stake in our gaming business.

Even though they were operating independently of one another, they were fiercely competitive, especially in downtown Port of Spain. They weren't buddies, and by no means were they friendly in their pursuits. The wagering wasn't illegal, and the money made and moved wasn't considered to be a part of the $14 trillion worldwide underground or what is commonly referred to as the "subterranean economy." Sure, it was fringy—I assume most, if not all, of the bookies neglected to declare what they earned or handled on a daily basis, but I was always aboveboard and accounted for every dollar—in all six currencies in which I was dealing. I thought I knew every customs agent from Fort Lauderdale to New York City. When I showed up carrying brown paper bags filled with money, they'd say, "Oh, it's just Dave. Let's get counting."

On this particular day, when I was traveling with Rebecca, we were twenty miles out of Piarco International Airport when we received our clearance down to 3,500 feet. The Mits fell like a stone as I eased the condition levers full forward, pulled the power levers back to just above idle, and set up for the letdown to runway 10. Once we were on the ground, the Mits screamed over to the number 12 parking ramp. Upon shutdown, I popped open the door. Rebecca was stirring from her nap on the plush gray leather bench. When she realized we were in Trinidad, she sat bolt upright and gathered her purse and briefcase in an unnecessary spurt.

"We're not going to meet in the parking lot, dear . . . slow down," I said, humored by her eagerness.

When we deplaned, Leonard, my longtime driver, immediately greeted us. He had barged his way through the nine bureaucratic stations that demanded everything from flight data, licenses, fees, and manifests to passports and his mother's maiden name for clearance—with a badge and an old .45 caliber automatic. He had what I wanted and I had what he wanted. My relationship with Leonard was a long and uneventful partnership that had minimized my concerns through the dark narrow corridors of Port of Spain. All lean six-foot-two of him was cordial and combat-ready. He was a policeman and a fireman, though I never knew which I would need or when. Leonard knew the city and the bookmakers and had handicapped our customers down to their childhood.

Leonard momentarily froze in place when he saw Rebecca. His concern needed no explanation. We both knew where we were going.

"No Aaron this time?" he asked.

He had provided a good point man for Aaron and the occasional guests who came along to experience Trinidad's noisy dance halls and frivolity of the nightlife, long after my day on the island would come to an end.

The introduction between Leonard and Rebecca was brief. I raised the boot door of the airplane, retrieved the bags, and Leonard spotted the transmission parts I'd flown in for his old green Datsun. We had almost rebuilt the damned thing over the years. Auto parts were not easily available in Trinidad, and they provided good barter for our partnership. Leonard clamped the pieces under his right arm. His left arm and shoulder blade had been shattered in a gunfight years ago and had limited movement. Still, he was strong and agile. He was right-handed, and he often joked that his aim was not impaired.

The three of us headed right to our meeting, which took place in a local restaurant that looked like a ramshackle building from the outside. The awning over the entry was torn, and the sign was half missing. The chef prepared an assortment of East Indian cuisine, common for the area and none of which smelled good to me. The floors were worn wooden planks that looked as if they had been there for forty years. The ceiling fans swirling above kept the dirt and dust circulating so you could see it in the beams of light that shone through the paned windows. Despite the presence of these fans, the air was thick, hot, and still. It matched the climate, which, to me, was disgusting.

Rebecca and I made our way into a back room where the rest of the betting proprietors had already gathered. Several of the men were smoking thick Cuban cigars. There was no embargo on them in Trinidad like there was in the United States. The room was full of silvery-blue smoke that filled my lungs and made it hard to breathe. Rebecca stood out in the room like an ice cream cone in the middle of a desert. She was young, blonde, and dressed in American attire—jeans and a soft, flowing top. Rebecca doesn't like to dress down, but it was important that she not show up looking too feminine.

I knew everyone in the room, except for the sole woman. She wasn't a Trinny, as I called the locals; she was African and new to the game. The assembled group represented every walk of life on the island. Some were dressed in shorts, T-shirts, and sandals, while others wore clothing that represented their culture—whether African or Asian, as both cultures were predominant.

There were a lot of Chinese people throughout the islands who were very strong business leaders. One of the largest players in Trinidad was a Chinese man named Phang. His older brother, a British bookmaker, had actually pioneered the method of sending telegraphed results and payoff prices for British racing to Trinidad. Phang didn't join in on the meeting that day because he didn't think he should mingle with that crew. There was a lot of animosity, and he knew their gripes. Phang ran a much bigger operation than those gathered together that day, so we had worked out a pretty substantial deal with him that we could justify separating from the others.

When I walked into the room, I made a point to say I didn't want to see any weapons. I was concerned because my daughter was with me. Even so, the atmosphere was charged. You could cut the tension with a knife—an appropriate analogy, since one of the men at the table had an intimidating ten-inch blade prominently displayed next to him. It wasn't a dagger, but a butcher's knife. The blade was tapered and had serrated edges that could, no doubt, make a nasty cut if necessary.

At the start of the meeting, everyone was civil, shaking hands and making introductions. Some were even drinking whiskey, but I wasn't falling for the niceties. They had a lot of talking to do, and we were there to listen. And then, there was great shock and surprise when I introduced the young woman I was with as Rebecca. Many simply couldn't believe the petite girl with me was the *same* Rebecca they had been dealing with over the phone for several years. Until that moment, she was the intolerable, larger-than-life ogre always demanding payment or shutting down signals by controlling the decoder boxes from the uplink source in the United States. Although Rebecca's presence heightened the tension even more, there was an unusual and unexpected amount of respect being shown.

We each took a seat around the circular wooden table. It was like a Mafia family meeting—only worse because this was tribal. The Trinnys liked to talk—often and fast. They were sometimes difficult to understand, but it was obvious they knew the ropes and the politics. Most of them didn't steal from their competitor, but they certainly understood how to undermine him and his business to advance their own. It was clear from the moment we entered the room they had all compared notes about who was paying what price for the same service. We didn't necessarily disclose that information on a regular basis, so if anyone knew what his or her neighbors were paying, the information didn't come from us.

Anxious to get to down to business, Rebecca and I started the meeting by asking for the money we were owed. She had records of each account and would be the one to clear the debt. They each had brought their currency in suitcases, pouches, and even brown paper bags. Some wanted to pay in private so nobody could see how much they were handing over, while others didn't really care. Rebecca took each parcel to the ladies' room, a roughly built addition with a loosely fitting yellow door and a wooden bobbin for a lock. It was the safest place for her to do the counting, and as things began to get heated around the table, I was glad that she was out of the room. If someone was short, she'd let me know. Otherwise, I was there to answer whatever questions they had, get our money, and head out.

Two hours had come and gone and many thousands of dollars were exchanged before tempers really began to flare, fueled in part by beer and island drinks of all sorts. I had made frequent trips to Trinidad in the past, but I would usually go to the shops separately to collect. I'd listen to their gripes about spotty service or unfair pricing along the way, but I never had any issues or concerns for my safety during those chats. This time, however, there was one particular fellow who was outspoken and vociferous in his demands. He was in his late fifties and was normally a pleasant man to deal with, but this time was different. I suppose being in a room with all of his competitors raised his blood pressure past the point of reason. He was fighting with everyone over pricing, government intervention, and poaching of clients. He was shouting and hollering, evoking an instant and similar response from the others. It was getting contentious and uncomfortable— two things I never liked dealing with when collecting. When the atmosphere became too much, the oldest member of the group, the same man who had put his knife on the table, tried to bring order to the room.

"Quiet! Settle down! Let's get to the point." He was speaking loudly but not loudly enough to be heard over the others, who were now shouting at one another across the table. It was incomprehensible babble to me. There was zero chance I would be effective in calming the group. Since there were several leaders in the room, each wanted to flex his power.

"STOP! OR I WILL GIVE YOU *'TUNDER!'*" The elder's voice suddenly came to a crescendo as he slammed his hand down flat on the table.

Seizing the opportunity, one of the others grabbed the elder's knife and plunged it through the top of his hand and into the wooden tabletop. The elder's palm was stuck there as blood began to slowly ooze from his gaping wound like the beginning of an erupting volcano.

"Rebecca, take the bags and get out of here," I said in a whisper. She had shoved the assortment of paper bags and money into a larger plastic grocery bag to make it easier for her to carry into the ladies' room.

The fellow who swung the knife was swift and fierce looking. By his expertise, I calculated it wasn't his first scrape. He was still angry, which made me concerned about his next move. I wasn't sure if he would take another swing at the elder or someone else, and, frankly, I didn't want to stay around long enough to find out. Thankfully, he didn't act again, and we were able to get things under control. When everyone was calm, the elder man pried the knife from the table, then his hand, and wrapped it in a white button-down shirt someone gave him to use as a tourniquet. He spewed a few obscenities at the guy who attacked him, but no one was making a move to call the cops. It was business as usual down there, so when everyone was settled, we went on with our meeting. There were no apologies, but, oddly, the stabbing did have a calming effect.

At that point, I told everyone I would visit with them in their territories and give them the credence and respect they required one-on-one. Assembling like that was a disastrous clashing of egos. There was a lot of posturing and vying for attention and authority. I vowed this type of meeting would never happen again.

When I felt it was safe to leave, I stood up, knocked on the ladies' room door, and told Rebecca to come out.

"Get your stuff and head toward the door," I said. There was no reason for long good-byes or any pleasantries.

We had a considerable amount of TT as well as U.S. dollars with us, which made the plastic bags bulky and awkward to carry. In the past, there were trips where we collected as much as $200,000 that had to be divided up between briefcases and paper bags. I don't remember the exact amount of cash we collected that day, but it had to be up there in value based on its weight.

Normally Rebecca is like steel, but I will admit she was a little flustered from the drama that had unfolded.

"Holy shit! Are we going to be okay?" she asked in an unusually shaky voice.

"Yes. Let's allow things to calm down a bit before we reengage with any-one." I was doing my best to reassure her as we made our way to the green Datsun, with Leonard at the wheel, gun and all, and then onto the comfort of the hotel.

We were staying at the "upside-down" Hilton, as the locals called it. It's the only hotel in the world I know where the floor number gets higher as the elevator goes down. The hotel is built into the side of a cliff. The lobby is at the top of the cliff, and the penthouse suite is at the bottom. We frequently used the upside-down Hilton as our home base when we were conducting our business in Trinidad. It lent to our meetings a semblance of order and protection and managed to keep most of them from becoming too heated. And there were many times I expected the meetings to go that way. I certainly didn't foresee the outcome of the roundtable meeting earlier that day. If I had, I would never have put Rebecca in that room. In the end, nothing regrettable happened, but, as a father, I didn't want to ever risk the safety of my children again. There was no amount of money that would allow me to consciously do that. In fact, I took extreme precaution to avoid conflicts wherever I went with them.

When we traveled to other countries, there were always a handful of locals who knew we were there to collect lots of cash. That made us sitting ducks. Despite the inherent danger of being robbed, kidnapped, or worse— killed—I rarely felt threatened. In fact, most of the time, the people I dealt with were rather gentlemanly during our exchanges. Even so, there were times I had to take stock of the realities of my surroundings, especially when I was in Jamaica or Trinidad. Those were the only two countries where I hired a bodyguard for extra security—usually a police officer or firefighter, but always someone who could handle a weapon and who knew his way around—especially if we needed to make a quick or unexpected exit. They always knew why I was there and would shoot to kill if the circumstances called for it.

Later that night, I got to thinking about the elder man and his threat of "Tunder." I knew what he meant, but for me, the word conjured up the image of thunderous hooves racing around the dirt tracks I'd been around most of my life. Thoroughbred racing runs through me like the blood in my veins. It is the air in my lungs and the fuel that feeds me. There's nothing like being at a track as the sun rises on a crisp, cool morning and watching the horses work out. I especially like walking "hots." Hots are horses that need to be cooled down after they work out and before they are put back into the stall. There is a hush that surrounds the oval track. A quiet that muffles all sound but the horse's breath and the thump-thump of their hooves as they gallop past you at speeds that seem impossible to fathom from the ground on which you stand. It never gets old for me. I can't imagine any place on earth where I feel happier or more at home. I've been a hot walker, a groom, a jockey, a trainer, and an owner. I was the breeder of stakes horses and a racing official at two of the largest racing companies in the world: The New York Racing Association and what was once the Ontario Jockey Club. I played a part in changing the way people enjoyed the sport through the introduction of international simulcast racing. As a result of that unparalleled breakthrough in the sport of kings, international wagering on American Thoroughbred racing became a very lucrative business for me and the many others who followed my lead.

I looked at the bags of money in my hotel room that night and thought about the events of the day as well as all the other pivotal moments in my life that led me on the unforgettable journey I was on. I suppose there are many ways to die—and I've been exposed to more than most. Although it was close, this day would not be one of them.

CHAPTER ONE

Like a lot of people in the 1930s, my mother and father were victims of the Great Depression. Though we lived in Canada, the impact of the economic destruction that took place in America was rippling throughout the world. The depression originated in the United States, after the fall in stock prices that began around September 4, 1929, and became worldwide news with the stock market crash of October 29, 1929, known as Black Tuesday.

The Great Depression had devastating effects in countries rich and poor. Personal income, tax revenue, profits, and prices dropped, while international trade plummeted. Unemployment in the U.S. rose to 25 percent and in some countries climbed as high as 33 percent. After the United States, Canada was hit the hardest, with other countries around the world—especially those dependent on heavy industry—being impacted, too. Harshly affected by both the global economic downturn and the Dust Bowl, Canadian industrial production had fallen to 58 percent by 1932, the second lowest level in the world after the United States and well behind nations such as Great Britain.

Some economies started to recover by the mid-1930s, but, in many countries, the negative effects of the Great Depression lasted until the end of World War II. Canada's recovery, in particular, lagged far behind its neighbor to the south, especially in terms of development, but not so far as in the lack of job opportunities and industry. My family lived in the east end of Toronto, in a place called East York. Most of the families in our neighborhood

1

were Scottish and Irish, though there would be an influx of Italians that eventually settled there, too. All of us were struggling to make ends meet.

My father came from a very rough family life. His father was an alcoholic who died long before I was born in August of 1936. My grandmother remarried an English postman, who was at one time in his life a great and notable professional soccer player, though he never quite achieved the fame he deserved. He had one arm, having lost the other in an explosion during combat in the Boer War in South Africa.

My father's family was made up of committed racetrackers, including his two brothers, who were involved in the business all of their lives. His brother Wilfred was a successful Canadian jockey and a fifty-year racing official. Charles was also a longtime racing official, so naturally my father was lured to the track at a young age, too. He galloped horses and even rode as a jockey in a couple of races, but in time he grew too heavy and wasn't a good enough jockey to enjoy any real success. When he couldn't make it as a jockey or as a trainer, he did the next best thing—he galloped horses for the prominent American stable J. K. L. Ross. Although my dad tried to be a trainer, that wasn't his calling either. By the time he was twenty-two, he had a stable of horses that he was training at St. John's Park, in Jacksonville, Florida. St. John's Park was a lesser-known racetrack, so the horses there weren't big-money winners. This meant he didn't earn very much for his efforts. Due to the financial strain, he went to Cuba to train horses at Oriental Park. When he arrived, he was so broke that he resorted to retrieving coins from the tourists off of the Havana docks.

My great-grandfather, Charles Stevenson, worked on the Northwestern railway around the time George Stephenson (no relation) built the first train steam engine in 1814. By 1830, when the Liverpool-Manchester public railway opened, my great-grandfather had worked his way up to become the superintendent of the Northwestern railroad. While his position doesn't sound grand by today's standards, at the time, he was considered to be a high-ranking member of society who mingled with the British royal family. My mother's father came to Canada from Newcastle just as her mother, Mary, came from Cumberland in the high country near Manchester, England, in search of a better life.

I never understood the reasons my mother's family—the Ridgways—left England, but they did. The Ridgways were a rather industrious group. My maternal grandfather loved horse racing so much that he became an owner of many fine Thoroughbreds. And two of his sons became success-ful jockeys. John "Babs" and his older brother, Alex "Speck," Ridgway were both well known in Canadian and Californian racing circles. Alex was called Speck because he had a lot of freckles. Speck was extremely successful as a jockey, having ridden and won on a horse called Marine, son of the legend-ary Thoroughbred, Man o' War. My grandparents were extremely proud of Speck and his career, keeping all of his racing memorabilia on display at their home for everyone to admire.

The family called John "Babs" because he was the youngest son. He went to California as a young man, first galloping horses, then subsequently becoming a jockey. Babs also grew too heavy to continue as a jockey and sadly had to stop riding within a few years.

Unable to make a living in Cuba, my father returned to Toronto in the mid-1930s. His days of training horses were long behind him, but he still had a passion for being around racing. As a result, he gravitated toward working in the jockeys' room. As luck would have it, his first job was as a valet for the young, successful Speck Ridgway. The position of jockey valet is similar in many ways to a groom. They are there to aid and assist in every aspect of preparing both the horse and the jockey for a race. A valet cleans and prepares saddles and polishes boots. The term "valet" dates back to 1567, though its use in the medieval French-speaking English court is older. Its variant form "varlet" is cited as far back as 1456. It was used as another word for male servants who were personal attendants to their employers, responsi-ble for the care and upkeep of clothes and other personal belongings.

My father met my mother through his newfound friendship with Speck. My mother was a very beautiful woman who had always dreamt of becom-ing a dancer. Her dreams, as it turned out, were delayed because of their blossoming relationship.

At the height of his career, Speck was critically injured in a motorcycle accident in Toronto. A woman driving the wrong way on a road in Sunny-side, over in the west end of Toronto, hit him head-on. He was badly injured and rushed to a nearby hospital, where he died a few days later. I never had the chance to know my uncle because he passed away before I was born. I am told we looked a lot alike as kids. My grandmother never got over losing her son. She grieved for Speck until the day she died in 1955.

My parents married in 1935, which were tough times for most everyone. Their relationship was challenged from the start. Since they couldn't afford their own home, my uncle Percy, a carpenter by trade who was considered to be quite successful, offered them a place to live. It was a small home on First Avenue in Todmorden Mills, a settlement located in the Don River valley in Toronto, Ontario. Originally known as "Don Mills," it began as a lumberyard in the 1790s and grew into a small industrial complex and village before becoming part of East York in the twentieth century. The house was down the street from where my mother's aunt and uncle lived and from the home where I was born. I don't think my birth was expected, and, as a result, I became the cause of a lot of their early marital problems. Some people were pleased to have me around, but my father wasn't one of them. Even though I was young, I was fully aware that he didn't like me. But, at the time, I had no idea why.

I always thought, "You can't go wrong being born on First Avenue." I can still remember the light fixture that hung above my crib. It was very old-fashioned and had a shade hanging from the bottom. It looked like something my uncle might have bought at the local five-and-dime store.

Despite their financial woes, my mother somehow managed to look beautiful on a very small budget. She was good at making the best of what little she had and what little my father was able to provide for her. Even before I could talk, I always knew when my parents were headed out for the night because I could smell her perfume. The one night each year I loathed was New Year's Eve, because my father would always come home drunk and in a very bad mood. One year, I was sick with the flu and had thrown up all over my room. I'd made a terrible mess. When my parents returned, my father took one look at what I'd done and punished me. Even though I was just a small child. As I grew a little older, I subconsciously connected the smell of mom's perfume with my father's inevitable and incomprehensible punishments.

My parents didn't have any money to speak of, which was hard on my dad, who was a proud man. At the time, racing in Canada was a summer sport, so in the winter months, there was no way for him to make a decent living. To earn money, he went door-to-door selling pencils and eggs. While there was no obvious correlation between his products, they were the only two to which he had access in their dire situation. It was a humbling experience, one that proved to feed his ever-growing anger. Because we were unable to shop for groceries in the lean years, the only food we ate when I was young came from my grandparents' small farm on Cosburn Avenue.

Whether it was a chicken, a rabbit, or one of my grandfather's pigeons that he raised and raced, we at least had something to eat.

Although my father was naturally smart, he had no formal education and often felt like a failure. He was devastated by the Depression and the direction his life had taken him. Although he was a hard worker, he was a tough man to live with. His temper flared often and out of the blue. Sundays were especially bad in our household. My mom liked to cook breakfast for us on those mornings. Instead of the usual oatmeal, she cooked bacon and eggs as a treat. Out of anger and usually as a result of an argument over money, it wasn't unusual for my dad to take his plate and dump the leftover eggs over my mother's head. One time, he grabbed the toaster while it was still in use, snatching it from the wall, and threw it down the stairs, smashing it on the cement floor. When he realized it hadn't shattered, he got an ax from the garage and sliced the toaster in half. It was an act of rage I've never forgotten. Maybe his fury was the result of being a little hungover from Saturday night, or maybe it was his way of dealing with the mounting bills and problems he faced. Whatever the reason, I hated being at home on Sundays and relished the thought of someday leaving so I wouldn't have to live in fear of something worse happening. After the untimely death of our toaster, I began planning my departure for good.

Despite his erratic behavior, my father also had a jocular side to him that would periodically pull him out of his dark moods, especially when he was around people outside of our family. To them, he was a likeable and engaging man. He spoke with ease and comfort, something I never saw him do at home.

No one in my family was especially known for their communication skills. We were not what you'd call a "talky" family. It wasn't unusual to go an entire day without hearing much more than a "how are you?" I didn't know any different, so the occasional grunt or comment seemed normal to me. The only time anyone really spoke to me was when a meal was served that I refused to eat. Then, they would talk a blue streak. I hated tapioca pudding and always resented when my grandmother or mother made it. They insisted that I eat it until I learned to enjoy it even though they knew I didn't like it. In my mind, that would never happen. Looking back, I suppose their insistence was a reflection of all the lean years they had when food was scarce in their homes. Once they could provide food adequately, it was expected that I eat it. Reluctantly, I did. But I never liked it. Never.

Around the time I was three or four years old, my mother's parents came across a vacant plot of land next to their property. They offered to finance and subsidize the building of a home for my parents to live in so we could get out of the house on Cosburn Avenue. I suppose they didn't want their daughter living too far away from them with my father, the racetracker who couldn't rub two nickels together. My father tried to get a loan on his own but was turned down flat. I remember the day he came back from the bank—irate and cussing. Things got very tense between my parents, eventually causing my mother to have a nervous breakdown. Without realizing it, she had found herself in a marriage to a man who was extremely difficult and unable to provide for her. She had a child and was living in dire poverty. English people are very proud and don't like being reliant on someone else. Desperate and depressed, my mother moved in with her mother for a year to deal with her condition. I was allowed to see her, but only on a limited basis.

"Carry this up to your mother," my grandmother would say as she handed me a single fried egg on a plate. I dutifully went up the steep stairway that led to her bedroom to do this simple task. When I'd enter the room, my mother would break down crying. She was so distraught that I would turn around and run back down the stairs, still holding the plate in my trembling hands. I was desperate for affection and attention. I didn't want to let my grandmother down, but I also didn't know how to handle my mother's emotional response at the very sight of me. I couldn't understand why my presence would have this effect on her. Eventually, I learned to find affection from someone else other than my mother and father, mostly in spending time with my grandparents next door.

I spent more time with my grandmother than anyone else. She often babysat for me, which meant putting me on the front lawn of their house under their cherry tree with a stake and a rope attached to a harness around my chest so I could walk from side to side without her fearing that I would run away. I spent a lot of time with the two goats that grazed on the lush grass under that old cherry tree. As a baby, I only drank fresh goat milk because my grandmother believed it was better for me than cow's milk.

"It's TB free and doesn't carry the same germs," she declared with great authority. Surely it was also a sign of the times. They bottled the milk daily and put it in their icebox to keep it cool.

My grandmother was loving, but not especially warm. She and my grandfather were under great financial stress, too, which caused them to argue more and more as the Depression wore on.

My grandfather had many basic skills, and, because of that, he held many jobs over the years. He was an odd man but great to me when I was a little boy. My father didn't like him all that much because my grandfather was extremely authoritarian. He wasn't thrilled with his daughter being married to someone who couldn't support his own family. My grandfather worked as a chauffeur for a short time, then for the military as a night watchman, guarding the local Armory. He also raised pigeons that he raced to make extra money. Since he worked at the Armory most evenings, he would take his pigeons to work and liberate them from different distances. He trained them well and won a lot of races. Years ago, he won the young bird derby, a contest that began with the liberation of the pigeons by the King of Spain for their flight to Cheadle Hume in England. He had claimed a grand trophy to commemorate the victory. I'd tag along as often as he'd let me, riding in the rumble seat of his old Chevy with the pigeons in a box by my side.

As part of our training process, we drove to many towns in and around Ontario, where we'd liberate the pigeons and hurry home to prepare this old wooden box with a clock on the front. When each bird returned home, it was retrieved from the coop and its food was placed in a small compartment within the box. There, my grandfather had a mechanism that placed a pink rubber band around the bird's ankle. The band carried the time and date of each bird's arrival. The data were sent into a centrally located office, where the first ten winners were announced. The liberation of the birds was exhilarating, both for the old man and the young boy. It was a scene that generated ancient stories that were always recounted in the car on the way home. My grandfather talked of carrier pigeons that were used to convey military intelligence messages between England and France during the blitz in England. I listened to these fascinating stories for hours. I even wet my pants a few times in our haste to get back to the coop, where we'd wait or discover our first birds were already home. I was so excited, I didn't want to stop to use the bathroom. It was far better than the trivia forced upon me in a schoolroom. It was the only bond he and I ever knew.

By the early 1940s, Canada was deeply involved in World War II. Frustrated by the loss of his career as a jockey, Uncle Babs joined the United States Army so he could gain his American citizenship. He fought in World

War II with General Patton's 7th Army and was stationed in Africa for five years until he was critically wounded. I remember seeing his medals; however, I never knew if he had been shot or injured by some type of explosion.

Although there had been no bombings in our country, the government frequently prepared us for an attack. There were air raid wardens in every community who would dictate the nights when there would be intentional blackouts all around Toronto. The entire city went dark for several hours so the enemy couldn't see where to bomb. Britain was lost, and Churchill was on the radio nearly every night pleading with Hitler and Mussolini to leave Canada alone. He wasn't doing as well as he had hoped. When the city was dark, my grandmother, who was still caring for me while my mother was recuperating from her breakdown, used to take me by the hand and we'd go for walks together. Outside, we looked up at the bright twinkling stars in the sky while air raid sirens blared in the background. It was eerie and strangely beautiful at the same time, especially knowing that Babs was overseas somewhere fighting the Germans. The only time I recall seeing the stars shine bright over my house was during those blackouts. Otherwise, the city lights made the night sky appear dim.

Living in Toronto during the war took its toll on everyone. If you owned a car, gas was rationed, so it was hard to come by. You had to present gas ration stamps to the service station attendants to get fuel. Tires were impossible to find. And the economy suffered in every way.

Howe's was a family-run convenience store on the same street where we lived in East York; it was the pulse of the neighborhood. Here, the list of soldiers who were missing or killed in action was hung for all to see. Everyone in the neighborhood went there on a daily basis to see whether their son's name was on the list. My grandmother held her breath every time she ran her finger down the long list of names, hoping and praying her son Babs wouldn't be on it.

I had never met my Uncle Babs until he returned to Toronto after the war. I was around five years old when I first laid eyes on him. To me, he was a hero. But when he returned, he had a lot of problems dealing with what we would now refer to as posttraumatic stress, though there was no such name for his condition at the time. Uncle Babs had been shot many times, and though the Army gave him several Medals of Honor for his service, he didn't ever want to see them. They were painful reminders of the horror and agony he had endured during the war.

When he finally started to heal, Uncle Babs returned to California and to horse racing, but this time, training Thoroughbreds. A few years later, he started a feed company for the horse racing industry near Bay Meadows racetrack in San Francisco and turned it into a successful business he could focus on for many years to come. I didn't see much of Babs after he left. He died in 1964 of a heart attack.

By the time I was slated to start school, I had begun running away from home for days at a time. There were no school buses, so I had to walk about a mile and a half each way. In those days, parents dressed their kids and pushed them out the door expecting that they'd head right to school— no one led you there—and there were other kids to follow, so it was just expected that I'd go along with the plan. It didn't take me long to figure out that I could skip school. Instead of attending class, I spent my days collecting sticks to make little boats that I could float down the streets in the water-filled ditches. My imagination was always bigger than I, and I loved being outdoors.

By the time I was six, I had made a few good friends, including a boy named Pinky Ward. I think his given name was Leonard, but he didn't like it when I called him by his real name, so I didn't. Pinky was a little bigger than I and lived just up the street from us. He loved playing hooky and going to the Don Valley, a forest-like park near our neighborhood in the center of Toronto. We went into the chasm and valley, where we discovered that a train came through every day. When that train came rolling by, we ran along the side of it, grabbed onto one of the sidecars, and went for a hell of a ride. Pinky and I could stay out all day and night without anyone knowing where we had been or what we were doing.

We also spent time at a little fishing hole that was on a nearby farmer's property. We would take off all of our clothes and jump into the murky water. It was cold, but the joy of being in that pond was always worth the shock to my body. Afterward, Pinky and I would pull out a pipe and some tobacco I'd swiped from my dad and have a smoke. One day, three shots rang out. The bullets hit the water a few feet away from where we sat. We grabbed our clothes and ran as fast as we could for the railroad tracks. Unfortunately, we were in such a hurry that we left the pipe and tobacco behind. Up until then, every time I lit that pipe I'd think about how I would return it to my father's drawer without him ever knowing it had gone missing. Pinky and I never returned to that spot, for fear of being shot, and I never did retrieve that pipe. As strict as my father was, he wasn't a constant pipe smoker. He had a collection of pipes and didn't use them often enough to notice the one I had taken was missing. I anxiously awaited to be disciplined for what I had done, but somehow that day never came.

Throughout my early school days, my mother never met one of my teachers or ever set foot in my school. As long as we were home by the time the streetlights came on at night, our secrets were safe. It wasn't until I got into a fight with a bigger kid who had kneed me in the balls while we were playing soccer one day that my parents found out I hadn't been going to school. I'd gotten the strap from Mr. Shatz, the principal. Until that incident, I didn't know you could be beaten at home *and* at school. My father had given me the belt across my ass many times. It's how he disciplined me, so I expected it from him. I didn't see it coming from Mr. Shatz, though. Afterward, he sent a note home to my parents that divulged I had barely been showing up to school.

In an effort to find something constructive I could do in my spare time, my grandmother Ridgway arranged for me to take piano lessons. I'd heard many stories over the years about how my grandfather had been a drunken piano player, and she thought there might be some musical talent in my genes, too. I found out then that genes meant other things besides pants you wear. I hated learning the piano. In my mind, all practicing that instrument did was cut into my outside time. It made me crazy to sit with my teacher, an elderly woman who smelled of tuberose and hairspray, a combination I found only slightly less than revolting. She was slender and wore glasses. Although she was nice enough, I thought there was something wrong with her. Whenever she came out of the bathroom, it smelled like she was slowly rotting from the inside. There were not a lot of redeeming qualities about her except for her ability to teach classical music. She was strict and had a propensity to whack my hands with the yellow pencil she held, swinging it to the beat, keeping the rhythm like a metronome. If I hit the wrong note, she would come down hard on my hands. It doesn't seem like a thin pencil across the knuckles would hurt, but it did—a lot. By the time I performed in my first recital, however, I could play parts of Tchaikovsky's Concerto No. 1, though not well. She also taught me to appreciate symphony orchestras and the musical genius of Mozart and Chopin.

To get me out of my mother's hair, my father began taking me with him to the jockeys' room at a racetrack outside of Toronto called Thornecliff, where he still worked as a valet during the meets. I had never been to the track before and loved being on the inside of racing. The barn was wooden and painted white with green trim. It was boards over boards with a narrow entrance and a washroom. By today's standards, that jockeys' room was primitive. There were long wooden benches with bootjacks where my dad could screw the boots into place and shine them. When the jockeys came by at the start of the day, I began to get to know them. We'd visit while their boots were being polished. The Cuban jockeys couldn't speak English very well, so I would try to teach them a few words, and they, in turn, would teach me some very nasty words in Spanish and we'd laugh like hell as I repeatedly honed the dialect of the devil.

One afternoon, Pinky and I decided to ditch school and go to the races. I knew my way around the track and thought it would be easy for us to sneak in. We climbed over the big iron fence and found ourselves on the outside turn of the track near the three-quarter pole. We were standing on the fringe when there was a five-horse spill right in front of us. Jockeys and horses were down everywhere. It was a mess, yet terribly exciting to see.

By the time I was eight years old, I was sneaking into the track on a fairly regular basis. I knew how to get into the backstretch, an area that had a line of stables, each providing a home to the horses at the track. There were also dormitories where the workers lived, offices for the trainers to register horses for upcoming races, a big track kitchen, and sometimes a snack shack. I loved being there. Everyone I met knew I was supposed to be in school, but they didn't seem to mind.

One day I ran into a local trainer named Mike Long. He knew my dad, and I feared he would tell him what I was up to.

"Whatever you do, please don't say anything," I pleaded with him.

"What are you doing here, son?" Mike asked.

"I want to work here," I said without hesitation.

My matter-of-fact answer seemed to satisfy him. It wasn't long before he realized I was just the right size to lead his horse, Hogie. So he gave me a shot. I led Hogie around using a shank, thinking I had finally made it to where I wanted to be! Everyone else in the stables was laughing at me, thinking it was hilarious to watch this tiny boy take such a large horse for a walk. It was wonderful until Hogie stepped on my foot one morning. Although I screeched and hollered from the pain and my foot turned red and swollen, I was fortunate enough that he didn't break it.

For some, that experience would have been a reason to never be around horses again. But for me, it only fueled my desire to create a life around them. I knew right then and there that the track was where I wanted to be.

CHAPTER TWO

Throughout the early days of my childhood, there was little or no love, or any glue that made me want to stick around home. I couldn't think of a good reason to ever go back—that is, until my sister, Virginia "Ginny" Carol, was born on June 17, 1944, at Grace Hospital in Toronto. My parents had prepped me for her arrival when I began to notice my mother's tummy getting bigger.

Sometime toward the end of my mom's pregnancy, my parents and grandparents were throwing around possible names for the baby. They called this the "name game." I chimed in with the names Virginia and Carol because I knew a girl named Virginia and it sounded to me like a nice and exotic name at the time. Somehow, the name stuck, and I was blessed with the honor of naming my baby sister.

On the day my mother gave birth, no one told me she had gone into labor. She was just gone. I knew she didn't drive, so it was odd to me that she wasn't home.

Curious, I asked my grandmother where my mom was.

"She had her baby," she said, beaming with joy.

"Can I see it?" I asked.

"Not yet. They're coming home tomorrow."

There were countless baby bottles lined up in the kitchen and a stack of diapers, too. I was going to be a big brother. There was a certain responsibility that came with that title. I wasn't sure what it all meant, but I knew it would change my life forever.

When my mother brought Ginny home from the hospital, I was told she would have to lie down a lot and I couldn't be in the way. My grandmother explained that I had to behave myself and not be too rough with the baby. When my mother walked through the front door, she was glowing as she held tiny Ginny in her arms. I was immediately struck by the baby's straight, dark hair because mine was blonde and curly. This was puzzling to me. When I asked to hold her, my mother said no. She didn't trust me to sit still long enough to hold the baby without dropping her. My mom was probably right. I was a fidgety boy.

My wonderment turned into excitement about being a big brother. Although I was only eight, I wanted to do something to show my family that I was capable of being a big help, so I gathered together some pots and pans and cooked pork chops for everyone on the night they brought Ginny home. I'd never prepared a full meal before, but I have to admit, it was surprisingly good. Everyone was thrilled that I had made such an acceptable and edible dinner. If I hadn't, I am sure there would have been hell to pay.

Until Ginny was born, our home was always filled with tremendous stress and acts of severe discipline—that is, when they could catch me! For years, the favorite form of punishment in our home was a kick in the ass, and I was usually the one on the receiving end of it. My grandfather was especially good at hitting his mark as he called out his favorite expression, "I'll kick your ass 'til your nose bleeds!" And he did a time or two.

One day he was fixing a flat tire on his old Chevy. He had all of the nuts and bolts laid out on the ground next to the car. When he bent over to reach for the tire, I jabbed him in his ass with a sharp stick. I don't know why I did it. I was young, mischievous, and thought it was funny. My grandfather was so startled that he bumped his head hard on the fender of the car. He was incensed. I took off running, knowing he wasn't far behind. Sure enough, while I was in full stride, I felt the toe of his boot kick me hard in the butt. I went down hard. I stumbled head over heels as if I were doing a somersault.

"Ugh," was about all I could muster as his foot connected to my rear end.

I am sure it was funny to him, but to me, it was a fierce punishment. The fall knocked the wind out of me.

"I will kick you in the ass 'til your nose bleeds!" he said more intently than usual. I was impressionable, and it became something I recalled every time I thought about playing another practical joke on him.

Something about Ginny's presence lent an instant calm to our family. It was if God had sent an angel from heaven, and, from that point on, things got a little better. I am not saying we didn't have an odd Christmas where my family actually came together for a day of joy and family togetherness before. We did, but this was especially true after the birth of my sister. My father did what he could to provide for us, even bringing home a used electric train for me, which he put under the tree one year. Sometimes it worked; other times it didn't. Playing with that train was exciting for a short time, but I already knew my heart was someplace else—the racetrack.

I don't recall seeing a lot of affection between my parents. Dad would kiss mom hello and good-bye, but that was about it. And to be certain, neither directed any affection toward me. Not even when I needed it most. In those days, however, divorce wasn't really an option—at least not in my family. My parents stayed together, despite their unhappiness with each other and with themselves. Besides, there was nothing to split, so like many families, mine stayed together out of poverty. During the time, especially post-Depression, it seemed as though everyone was miserable; my family wasn't especially out of the norm. Somehow, misery served their marriage even if it didn't serve our family.

When I was around nine or ten, I was diagnosed with scarlet fever. There had been an epidemic of it in Toronto. A few months later, I contracted polio. Too sick and achy to be moved, two local doctors came to see me. Dr. Barnett, who was an older physician, and Dr. Sinclair made a house call, something that was pretty ordinary for the time.

"This is serious," they solemnly explained to my parents. "What can you afford if the disease progresses to the next step?" Of course, my parents couldn't afford anything, especially not the treatment the doctors were suggesting.

The doctors believed an iron lung might be necessary. I had no idea what they were talking about. But my grandmother explained to me that it was a ventilator consisting of an airtight metal tank that encloses the entire body except for the head, and that it forces the lungs to inhale and exhale through regulated changes in air pressure.

"You will likely never walk again," my mother said in a very cold, detached, and matter-of-fact way. I recall my grandmother sobbing while she told me all about the disease, but my mother barely shed a tear. My parents didn't like inconvenience of any kind. Getting sick became something that took up their days and nights. My mother never actually said I was in her way, but my father did, and I could feel it every time they entered the room.

I knew other kids in the neighborhood had died from polio. I spent at least three weeks in my darkened bedroom, where I lay in my bed, wishing the pain would just go away. My throat and head were on fire. My neck and back were almost immobile. I was losing muscle control in my arms and legs, which intensified the discussions between my parents and the doctors. The doctors kept saying that I would either die or the disease would subside. No one really knew which course to expect. I felt awful. They had to wrap my arms and legs in hot and cold towels several times a day to ease the pain, and they used old cloth diapers as compresses. I was so sore that I remember thinking it might be better to die than to live. It was a perilous time. There was no vaccine yet, and the disease was extremely contagious. Worried my sister might contract it from me, they removed her from our home.

I was very afraid. I kept picturing my puppy dying of distemper in the barn and thinking of the similarities. My grandfather said there was nothing we could do to help him. And now those who dared come into my room were using the same words about me. I was really on my own again, but this time I couldn't run away. I had no one to run to, and it was something that a kick in the ass wouldn't help. The racetrack seemed so elusive. All of that world didn't matter anymore.

Dr. Barnett came by the house daily, sometimes twice a day, to check on me. He wore a kerchief over his nose and mouth that he doused with alcohol to make sure he wasn't exposed. Exhaustion and weakness finally provided me with enough sleep and relief for several days in a row. It took weeks more of struggling before I finally rounded a corner and found myself on the mend.

My illness was a turning point. When I was fully recovered, I found myself questioning the reasons why my parents didn't like me. They may have loved me in their own way, but, as a young boy, it was clear I was a nuisance, an inconvenience, a bother. I knew my illness compounded those feelings.

The school thing never amounted to much for me. There was only one teacher I ever liked, Mrs. Marsh, who was tough but nice. The rest of my teachers throughout my on-again, off-again school years thought I had discipline issues. Mr. Hull, the football coach, was a Canadian Indian who was proud of his heritage and was also a pompous and rugged asshole. He had a show-no-mercy and take-no-prisoners attitude toward everyone and everything he encountered. I was in his agriculture class, and, because I was so small, he often singled me out. He sat me on a stool in the corner, making me feel like a fool. The only thing missing was a dunce cap. To him, I was an example of someone who would never make it in the real world. I was too small, too weak, and plain old useless. I resented him for his cruelty and for tagging me as a loser in front of my classmates. Whenever he'd turn his back, I'd make faces at him, stick out my tongue, and make gestures with my hands that would have gotten me beat if he could see what I was doing. All he cared about was football and winning. He had no time for anyone he viewed as hopeless. Although the other kids didn't see me the same way, I was hurt and angered by his treatment, which stuck in my head for years. Instead of caving, though, I used his put-downs as motivation. As a result, I became a tenacious teenager.

I'll show you, you son of bitch! I thought.

I may have been a bit of a misfit when it came to school or sports like football, but not when it came to horse racing.

The racetrack was a friendly place that welcomed me. It was where small people weren't frowned upon or discarded. I wanted to be there more than anywhere else and as often as possible. I loved connecting with the horses, the people, and the excitement. I wanted to be around jockeys, horses, and pretty much anything having to do with racing. There was only one problem: most tracks had a rule stating that you had to be sixteen to have a job. I was underage and constantly dodging security so they wouldn't throw me out.

Mr. Allen was the only security guard at Thorncliffe, the track closest to where I lived. He was a mean-looking old man who stood slightly over six feet tall. He was the guy who tossed out people who didn't belong. I'd been sneaking into the track since I was eight years old. Rules or not, I just "belonged."

When my father traveled to Stanford Park, near Niagara Falls, during the summer, I'd ride along and see if I could wrangle some work. He would board with people he knew, and I could only go if I found a place on my own to stay. I did—it was a tack room made from a horse stall at the end of the barn. I thought it was fun to sleep on dirt floors. The beds were really just mattresses sunk into the dirt. I don't know why they were set up that way, but they were. We'd heat up an old boiler outside the barn by lighting up some wood, then we'd use the water in it to bathe or cook. One summer, there was a horse in the stall next to me who would bang against the wall all night long. I took the wire and rope from the bails of straw and hay and used them as hooks. Then I created a makeshift ceiling from old laundry bags that I hung from the hooks. That way, the dust from the horses, hay, and straw couldn't reach us. Even old racing forms, which were plentiful at the track, were useful to place over the wire for cover, but not as good as the cleaning bags. We'd also tie our shoes to the hooks at night to keep the rats and mice from eating the laces.

Whenever my dad traveled to Stanford Park, his buddy Fred Newman tagged along. His nickname was "Midge" because of his size. Midge taught me how to ride my first stable pony when I was eleven or twelve years old.

My father also introduced me to great old trainers who hung around the track. Pat McMurchy was one of those guys.

"Teach him something," my father said to Pat.

"He's awfully small. You sure you want him to—" Pat said as he looked me up and down.

Before he could finish his sentence, my father jumped in and said, "Yeah. He's tough enough."

"I can do this, Mr. McMurchy," I pleaded. I was extremely determined to learn all I could about racing.

Mr. McMurchy gave me a shot at walking hots after they trained in the morning. At first, I got to walk the occasional docile horse. I was so short that I couldn't reach the irons very well, so I would steer them around. The more experience I got, the more horses I could handle. That's when another trainer by the name of Andy Bennie took me under his wing. Whenever we were at Old Woodbine or Long Branch track, he'd take me to his home on Lake Ontario to enjoy a hot, home-cooked meal prepared by his wife, who was a very glamorous woman. She tried to feed me all of the time because I looked like I needed a meal—or two. Andy was a good trainer, and someone who taught me a lot about horses from his experienced point of view.

One thing I learned early on about racing is that jockeys are always hungry and thirsty. Back then, they bought meal tickets so they wouldn't spend their money on other things like betting, liquor, or women. A favorite say-ing around the track was "Bet your money, but never bet your meal ticket." Although the saying "meal ticket" dates back to the mid-1800s—much fur-ther back than the days I was hearing it around the track—it always stuck with me.

The tracks I hung around didn't have snack bars, so unless the jockey had his own snacks, he was out of luck. I became the runner for the jocks' room and learned how to turn a profit by going back and forth to fetch hot dogs, hamburgers, and Cokes from the grandstand. Sometimes I'd have as many as ten hot dogs, sixteen bottles of Coke, and a handful of candy bars inside my rolled-up shirt. It was a balancing act that became a pretty lucrative business for a twelve-year-old boy. I'd sometimes make as much as twenty-five to thirty dollars a week running snacks.

Running meals for the jockeys not only paid well, but also afforded me the pleasure of just being around them. It wasn't long before I hatched another idea to make some extra money. As a young boy, my grandmother used to cut my hair. I always paid close attention to what she did and prac-ticed giving haircuts on my own. When my grandfather fell asleep in his big wingback chair, I'd make all the motions as if I were giving him a trim, but didn't dare actually use the scissors. I practiced long enough that I thought I could give a pretty good haircut to people at the track as a way to make some more money. Somehow I got my hands on a barber's kit, complete with scissors, a brush, and a comb. I knew most jockeys and backstretch work-ers never had time to leave for a decent cut during the day, so I became the local track barber. Jockeys are notoriously generous, especially when they're having a good day. Except for a few owners and trainers, racetrackers aren't especially glamorous. They didn't want to be coiffed and styled. They just wanted decent haircuts. It was easy money and a convenient service I offered daily from ten to noon. I charged twenty-five cents a haircut and made another forty dollars a week. Eventually, more and more people started to use my services until there were mornings when there was actually a line to see me. Guys were sitting around on upside-down buckets waiting for their turn. There were days when I had to turn people away or tell them to come back tomorrow because the races would be starting soon.

In the beginning, I may have made a few mistakes, but there was never a disgruntled customer. I pretty much followed the cut they already had, so my margin for error was low. I improved to the point where I was finally good enough to give my father a haircut.

"Why don't you try that shit on me?" was his way of asking for a trim.

I didn't question it. I simply looked at this exchange as a breakthrough moment. For the first time in my life, my dad actually trusted me.

I cut his hair for years after that.

CHAPTER THREE

Once I started making money at the racetrack, the financial stress on our family lightened a bit. My parents, grandparents, and I pooled our money to put a down payment on a large home outside of Toronto situated on three acres of land. Compared to our other homes, it was palatial. The gentleman we bought the house from was dying of cancer and agreed to carry the loan for us because we couldn't get one from the bank. I was confident in my ability to help pay for it because I was earning money now on a steady basis. At this point, no one was complaining about me missing school because they realized it wasn't my calling.

My father could do many things well, but he wasn't a very handy guy. I don't ever recall seeing him hold a screwdriver or swing a hammer. Mostly, he spent his time at the track, which meant someone had to deal with the maintenance that accompanies owning a large home. Big houses bring big problems, and the bulk of those became mine to solve. One afternoon, I was on our riding mower cutting the lawn, which was one of my responsibilities. Ginny was riding her small tricycle alongside the mower. I waved her off for fear she would come too close and get hurt, but she always liked to pretend we were racing. When my father came outside and saw the two of us riding neck and neck, he panicked. He was worried Ginny would fall in front of the mower and I would accidentally run her over. He was carrying a plate in his hand and hurled it right at my head like a Frisbee. I saw the plate coming, so I got off the lawnmower and tried to get out of its path. Unfortunately, it hit me hard, slicing the tendon along my right arm near the elbow. When it hit my arm, it broke and instantly cut through my skin. The tendon retracted toward my wrist into a ball. It was a bloody mess.

Despite our improved financial situation, my father's temper was still extreme and his fuse quite short. This wasn't the first time he threw a plate around, but it was the last time he would ever launch something at me. He was stressed and uptight again—I assumed it was because of the burden the new house placed on him. But I was able to escape during the summers, spending my time at the track and sending money home to help cover expenses. As I entered my teenage years, I could no longer tolerate his outbursts. My threshold for his temper had narrowed. When Uncle Speck died, my family inherited his three-gun collection, which was kept in the recreation room in the basement of our home. It was a constant reminder of his motorcycle accident and something we never talked about. I had shot the .22 rifle and pistol a number of times over the years and was quite comfortable using the gun for target practice or for occasionally hunting rabbits.

It was another Sunday morning, one I'll never forget, because my father was berating my mother, complaining she didn't do enough to contribute to the household. I heard him screaming at her clear across the house. When I went to see what all of the fuss was about, my dad pushed me hard to get out of his way. I stormed downstairs toward the gun case, got the .22, and loaded it. This particular rifle was an older model that could only hold one cartridge at a time, but I grabbed three rounds and was ready to pull the trigger if I had to. My father was in a rage as he came barreling down the basement stairs toward me. I raised the gun, cocked it, and pointed it right at him as he came through the door. I had to be careful not to miss; judging by the angry look on his face, missing would have presented an even greater problem. I had no doubt I was going to kill him. What I didn't know was whether he would care.

When he saw me holding the gun to my shoulder, he knew I wasn't bluffing.

He froze.

I was old enough to know the consequences of pulling the trigger, and I still didn't care. I had my own ideas about how I could argue my case if I had to. He knew I had ferocity and determination—a hell of a combination on this Sunday morning.

"If you come any closer, I am going to kill you," I said in a steady, calm voice.

I double-clicked it back and took aim. I definitely had his attention. I told him how I felt about him and his actions toward my mother, sister, and me. Unfortunately, holding a gun spoke to him louder than any of my words on that day. He stood silent for a moment, then turned and walked back up the stairs. I didn't hear a single sound from him as he disappeared from my sight.

Our relationship was never the same after that exchange. He knew we were past the point of reconciling our differences, and so did I. In my young mind, there was no other way out. How many more times could we stand at that excruciating crossroads and accept the same result?

From that day forward, he backed off and never confronted me in an aggressive way again. We never talked about what happened in the basement. There really wasn't anything to say. I wanted to believe my father got the message, but, secretly, I worried he might try to come after me again.

I went back to work at the track and occasionally even went to high school for events that involved friends. I kept a change of riding clothes in my locker and hitchhiked back and forth because there was no public transportation. Hitchhiking was no big deal back then. Besides, I was so small, no one was afraid of me. I looked like the male version of Goldilocks without the locks because my once curly hair was now relatively straight. I was always able to catch a ride from someone—except when my father came along in his car. He drove right past me, refusing to pick me up.

I spent as much time as I could at the track learning to ride and improving my horsemanship. I was good, but still not good enough. Besides, I was too young to compete. I was only thirteen years old.

When I finished at the track, I'd hitch a ride back to school. If it was early enough in the day, I'd go to a class. If not, I'd head home, pretending I'd been there all day long like I was supposed to be.

I started planning my exit strategy because everyone around school and at the track was convinced I was going to become a famous jockey someday. Frankly, up until this point, I had only walked hots and galloped and exercised the horses, mostly for a trainer named Andy Benny. I was aware that I had a natural ability, a skill that seemed to be part of my chemical and genetic makeup. I never had any doubt that I was going to become a jockey. The belief that I would be was there all along. It's funny when I think about how secure I was in those days. I never had a doubt about anything. That determination is ultimately what got me out of Toronto and out from under my father's heavy hand.

Kenny Clemes was an older jockey I'd befriended who rode for and introduced me to Morgan "Tex" Lewis, a trainer who worked for Jack and Joe Rogers, the owners of the stable. Tex stood about six-foot-two, looked to be in his midfifties, hailed from Pecos, Texas (something he was very proud of), and was a real rough son of a bitch. He was always chewing and spitting tobacco. And he didn't care where it landed or who he was with when he was doing it. A former professional cowpuncher, he always wore a dirty old cowboy hat and had a boisterous laugh and a bit of a pixie look for such a big man. He was a jovial guy who wasn't afraid of anything. The legend around the track was that Tex was on the last cattle drive from Abilene, Texas, before the invention of the modern cattle truck that is now used to move herds. To me, he was a larger-than-life character, and, in my young impressionable eyes, someone who was going places—places I wanted to go, too.

Tex came to Toronto to try his horses at the Old Woodbine and Long Branch local tracks. He raced at Hipódromo de las Américas, located in Mexico City, in the winter and in Toronto during the summer. What he didn't realize was that the condition book offered races mainly for Canadian-bred horses. Since he didn't have any, his horses had eligibility problems. Although there was an age gap between Kenny and me, he knew what I wanted to do and understood my capabilities. He was the person who taught me the most about horses. I thought I could handle working for a guy like Tex, so Kenny vouched for me. He said that I was a good kid who was industrious and that I wouldn't give Tex a lot of trouble. So Tex let me gallop a few horses for him during the summer meet. When I heard he was planning to head to Lexington, Kentucky, for the winter, I simply told him that I was going with him. There was very little dialogue between us about my decision. He just said, "Okay."

But one day Tex and I were discussing the dates for our departure, and the next day I awoke to find out he had left without me. Instead of getting discouraged, I rallied by making a few phone calls to figure out how I could get to Kentucky on my own. I talked to Kenny, who knew how to reach Tex. He promised to contact him and confirm the arrangements for me. Even though I was still a kid, I thought more like an adult. I had been on my own for a few summers already, spending time around other racetrackers, so I knew my way around. My biggest worry wasn't connecting with Tex, it was how I would get a ride to Union Station in downtown Toronto, where I could catch a train—the only feasible way for me to get to Lexington.

Determined to make my way, I put on my only suit. It was brown corduroy, and I wore it with beige argyle socks that came up to my knees. If I was going to Kentucky, I was going to look presentable. I threw a handful of underwear and socks into a bag along with the .22 caliber nine-shot pistol I retrieved from the cupboard downstairs, then I called the local cab company to come take me to the station. I had converted a bag of quarters from my haircut money into paper. In total, I had about thirty-seven dollars.

"We don't service your area," the dispatcher said. "It's too far away."

"What do you mean you don't service it? You're a cab company!" I was irate and in a hurry to catch my train. "Where do you pick up then?"

"Dawes's Road and Eglinton," he said. That was the border that defined freedom for me. It was only about two and a half miles away but I still had no way to get there. I pleaded with the dispatcher, telling him that I would pay an extra charge if he would send a car. I don't know how I did it, but I managed to talk him into it.

Thirty minutes later, a green-and-white Ford sedan pulled up to the house. There was no one there to say good-bye to, and, frankly, I was glad about that. Even though I loved my sister, I knew she would be okay. She was clearly a part of their family and I was the outcast. I got into the cab and looked forward as I headed off toward my future.

I had never been to Union Station before and had never officially taken a ride on a train. Sure, I had jumped on passing freighters in the Don Valley to get to the swimming hole, but I had never been an actual, ticketed passenger. As a result of my zealousness, I got to the station earlier than expected. I still had about two hours to kill before my departure, so I sat on a bench waiting and looking at the gigantic clock on the wall. I was eager and excited to move away from home and to finally get on with my life. While I was waiting for my train, a nice couple that looked like movie stars stopped by my bench and asked where I was going. People used to dress up to travel in those days, and they were very elegantly attired. They were taking the same train as I was, so I asked if I could tag along with them. I was very grateful they said yes. On the outside I was putting up a brave front, but, inside, I was a bit nervous and scared. I was a little too young to be on that train alone.

When the train rolled into Buffalo, I was unaware that customs and immigration folks would be asking for identification along with other papers I didn't have. Luckily, I had genuinely befriended the couple I'd met at the station. The wife mothered me, stroking my hair as I lay across the seat. I don't recall my mother ever being so nurturing. She and her husband took care of me like I was their own, and for the first time in my life, I felt like I met the kind of parents I always wanted. I was safe and secure enough to fall asleep next to them. Immigration must have assumed they were my folks because no one ever woke me to see my papers. I was sure glad I dressed up because I must have looked like I belonged. I can't tell you how many stops the train made between Buffalo and Lexington or how long it took to get there. I slept almost the entire trip until the couple got off someplace in Ohio. By the time we said good-bye, we were like old friends—or family. We hugged and kissed and said our final farewell moments before the train pulled away again. As they faded in the distance, I sat alone on the train, trying to gain some confidence. All I could hear was the eerie sound of the whistle. The rocking motion of the train as it picked up speed made me a little queasy and unexpectedly tired. I dozed off once again, until someone shook me awake. I was startled and wondered where I was at first. "We're pulling into Lexington, kid. Gather all your stuff," he told me.

It was early morning when I got off the train. It seemed as if the air were warmer. It wasn't a big station, and as I looked around I was relieved to see the familiar silhouette of a large man wearing a big hat. I wasn't sure he'd show up. At the time, I didn't have a lot of confidence in other people doing what they said they'd do—especially after he had already ditched me back in Toronto. It was Tex flanked by a man I'd never seen before. Tex heartily introduced me to Mr. Jack Rogers, one of the owners of the farm that he was working on in Versailles. They explained that one of their mules had gotten loose and was making a mess downtown, which was only a short distance from the farm. They had to catch him before heading back home. I thought that sounded really exciting because I'd never chased a mule before. They handed me a halter and a rolled-up coil of one-inch rope. They told me to hop in the back of their pickup truck. It was a well-used vehicle and older than the other trucks I had seen before. It had what looked like one-inch shiny knots sticking above the old wooden boards that had been worn out from serious use. Oats, hay, an old beer bottle, and several twisted pieces of bailing wire were strewn across the bed of the truck. I was still wearing my corduroy suit and was momentarily worried it might get ruined from the ride. But deep down, I really didn't care if it did. The important thing was I was finally in Lexington and looking to start a new life.

As we drove through town, Tex quickly spotted their mule. He jumped out of the truck before Mr. Jack got it stopped, snatched the halter and rope from me, then tried to herd the mule with his hands, waving and shouting an assortment of cuss words as he moved closer. Tex was real light on his feet for such a big guy. He swung the rope, threw it, and reined him in in a New York minute. That's when I knew without a doubt that his tales of being on those cattle drives in Kansas and Texas must have all been true. Tex reeled in that mule like he had just caught a feisty marlin. All of this had Mr. Jack laughing so hard he almost fell to the ground. When he regained his composure, he pulled the truck around, flipped the tailgate back down, handed me the excess rope, and said, "Okay, Sonny Boy. Hang on!"

They hopped back into the truck, slammed the doors shut, and drove away amidst the clatter of cylinders and a puff of stinky smoke. Sam the mule might have known where he was going, but I didn't have a clue. Those sons of bitches were sitting in the front of the truck going faster and faster, laughing their asses off until Sam could no longer keep up. I held the rope as tightly as I could. There was no way I was going to let go or turn him loose. This was my first day on the job. I had just arrived and wanted to impress Mr. Jack and prove to Tex that I knew what the hell I was doing.

Just when I thought I had things under control, we rolled up to a stop sign, and I noticed that Sam had caught his breath again. When the truck started moving once more, Sam dug in all four feet and was ready to bolt. His ears were pinned, his weight had shifted and was leaning back. I was no match for the eight-hundred-pound mule. With a lurch that felt like my arms were being pulled out of their sockets, I slid across the bed of the old pickup, over the shiny protruding knots like they had been greased, and dropped three feet onto the road. I could sense that the ass was torn off my britches as the entire backside of my pants flapped openly in the wind. My butt was hanging out while I was holding a rogue mule and sitting on the road. This wasn't what I had envisioned when I got off that train. I took one look at Sam and let him know it was either him or me. He didn't budge and neither did I. I guess we were both stubborn sons of bitches! By the time my new employers realized that we were no longer behind them in the truck, they turned around and sped back toward us. I was still holding that rope, and now there were two asses: mine, which felt like it was in flames, and the one attached to the rope I was still holding onto. Welcome to Versailles!

When we finally arrived at our destination, I was expecting it to be a fancy Thoroughbred farm with a nice barn, some cornfields, and endless pastures as described to me by so many. Instead, it was pretty run-down. Although it was named the Big Sink, because of the big round lake on the property that was about a half mile wide, no one ever called it that. It was more like the Big Dump.

The house that once stood on the property had burned down years earlier, so I was directed to put my things—and Sam—in the rickety old barn that was barely standing. When I walked Sam there, we were met by his better half, a female mule named Blue. Mules can't breed, I learned. They are the product of horses and donkeys mating, so there was no concern about Sam and Blue having a foal. They were more like best friends than lovers.

The barn had a small makeshift kitchen in the rafters with a single electric burner, a refrigerator that didn't work very well, and an old stove. Otherwise, there wasn't much else that defined the place as habitable for humans.

Joe and his brother, Jack, inherited the farm somewhere along the way but never lived there. Jack, the older brother, lived like a hermit as a boarder in a house in downtown Versailles. Joe and his wife resided in a beautiful old mansion not far from the farm where I was staying. The family had owned the home for generations, and it was a far cry from the quarters I was staying in. It didn't matter to me, though.

"This is where we sleep," Tex said, pointing to a turkey house. Clearly, it was no longer being used for raising turkeys.

I had slept in far worse quarters on racetracks than the eight-by-ten-foot space that would become my home. It was a tiny building with a wooden slope roof and no plumbing. The nearest toilet was seventy yards away in the barn. I could rinse the day's dirt off using cold water from a bucket; however, there was no tub or shower available to me unless I went into town, which became a Saturday night ritual. There were plenty of nights when I wouldn't go out to take a piss because I didn't want to deal with the cold. The floor slats had slight gaps, so you could see the ground in spots, which was about a foot beneath my feet. The turkey house was built on four pegs because domestic turkeys being raised for consumption are perishable and can't be kept too close to the ground. They are especially prone to pneumonia.

There were a couple of full-sized mattresses and some ratty sheets tossed across the old rusty chicken wire at the bottom of the pen, a single light bulb hanging from a cord, and a makeshift roof laid over the top. The pen sloped downward, so I had to choose which end of the mattress would be the top.

I wasn't too excited to be sharing the small quarters with Tex. I wasn't worried about him doing something like taking advantage of me, but I hated his lack of hygiene. He chewed tobacco all of the time, which he spit anywhere he pleased. He burped and farted without a care, and, as I would soon discover, snored worse than the mules we shared the barn with.

Tex walked me through the work duties and what was expected. I would be mucking stalls as well as tending to the cows and newborn foals. There were also several horses that were too old to be trained for racing or had never been broken that would require our attention. Our main purpose, though, was getting our Thoroughbreds ready for spring racing.

Joe and his wife showed up at the farm during my first week. His wife was a wonderful and proper lady who wore white gloves and pearls most every time I saw her. Jack had a paper from the state, technically making me a "tobacco farmer." I had to consent to this in order to gain exemption from the school system. I was the only white boy there with this distinction. Every other young boy working on the farm was black. I didn't realize that what they were doing was shady or that I should have been in school. He said my pay to work on the farm would be thirty dollars a month.

By this time, I had finally written my mother a few letters to let her know where I was and how I was doing. I told her that I was at a farm in Kentucky working for Tex Lewis and was doing just fine. The farm didn't have a telephone, so communicating by mail was the best way for me to keep in touch. My parents were angry that I left home the way that I did because they wanted me to finish school, but I believe they were as fed up with me as I was with them. They didn't know what to do with me, and by the time I left, I wasn't interested in anything they had to say. The more time I spent at the track, the surer I was that this was where I truly belonged.

Still concerned, my mother was able to convince Hugh Kenyon, my father's buddy who drove horse vans from Canada to Kentucky, to check on me the next time he came through Lexington. Of course, I knew Hugh would pass through and find everything was just fine.

Unbeknownst to me, Tex had drawn up a formal contract that indentured me to also be *his* laborer for three or four years, working exclusively for him and earning a paltry $150 a month. The Rogers brothers said they would give him my thirty dollars a month salary to put toward my monthly salary from Tex. Tex was supposed to pay the difference. Since I was still a minor, Tex had to get my parents to sign off on the agreement, which they did. I suppose they thought it was better to know I was committed to being in one job with someone they knew than wandering around always looking for work. The problem was that Tex never paid me more than the thirty bucks a month the Rogerses gave him—and sometimes, not even that!

Winter came fast that first year. It got cold by November but only snowed a couple of times. The turkey house didn't provide a lot of comfort on those frigid nights. Twice I remember going out and pissing on my hands to keep them warm. Tex stayed warm by drinking vast amounts of what he referred to as "jailhouse" coffee. It was the blackest coffee I'd ever seen and tasted worse than dirt. Tex liked to boil his coffee. He put the grounds in a pot, placed it on the burner, and brought it to a boil. When the coffee was done, the grounds would sink to the bottom of the pot. I don't believe I ever saw grounds in one of his empty mugs. I hated the sharp smell of the brew, but since I didn't have to drink it, I didn't give a shit that he did.

The farm was still an active tobacco farm with several families of share-croppers living there and working the fields. I soon became acquainted with the other help on the farm—T. Dunn and J. T. Smithers. J. T. was a mountain of a black man who looked like he could have been a linebacker for a professional football team. T. was a smaller man with refined features and a great vocabulary. I learned a lot from him. Everything he did around the farm was manual labor, so he was as strong as could be. In fact, I don't think there was an animal on that farm that could outpull J. T. in strength. J. T was a clean-living, deeply religious family man who lived his beliefs through his actions. I appreciated his passion for what he believed in. J. T and T. were both great guys and had wonderful families. Their word was their bond, something I hadn't experienced much of in my life up to that point. I never saw, let alone knew, many black people on the streets where I lived in Canada while growing up. Being around J. T. and T. and their families was always fun and reassuring. They had a depth of sincerity and purpose that was special, and I admired them.

We spent our days working the land of the five-hundred-acre farm, fixing the wire fencing that lined the perimeter and tending to the horses and cattle. The horses were stabled in a "tobacco barn," as it was called, that had

about a dozen stalls in it. The foals and their mamas were taken to a different barn until they were strong enough to be separated. I was the only rider.
We galloped the mature horses through the many pastures, most of which
had tobacco husks spread throughout them. Those were long, rough days
but worth the sweat and blood I poured into them. By February, it began to
warm up again, so, although the season was short, it was tolerable, especially
as spring racing in Canada quickly approached.

CHAPTER FOUR

There were some tough days on the farm in Lexington, but not nearly as tough as when we left Toronto to run a horse at Wheeling Downs. The location was a small half-mile racetrack in Wheeling, West Virginia, owned by the Elias brothers. Word on the street was that they were looking for an unknown fast horse to ship in and pay a big price for. Tex had made the clandestine deal before leaving Toronto. The gist of it was that the Elias Brothers' track would guarantee an 8-1 pari-mutuel on the winner, which meant the horse that won the race would pay big money. This was all over my head, but I knew enough to suspect that the track owners aren't supposed to guarantee mutuel odds, though somehow these brothers had the ability to do so. It made Tex happy just talking about the deal. Since they were as confident as the brothers were that they had the right horse to get the job done, Tex and Kenny were only concerned with the payoff.

At the time, Tex was training a horse called Devil's Grin. He was a very fast horse, a real "speedball" that easily stood out on the morning work tabs and was already a multiple winner going short. At Wheeling he would only have to run five-eighths of a mile, and with the short sharp turns of the "bull ring," as it was called, he looked like a sure thing. Kenny was going to come down from Canada to ride him, another key element in all this because he wouldn't be known in West Virginia. Tex was salivating at the chance. He knew Devil's Grin couldn't be topped out of the gate, and the banked, tight turns of the short track were in his favor.

At the time, I wasn't riding as a jockey, but I was getting good at breaking the wild horses on the farm. I loved every minute I spent in the saddle, even though I'd cry myself to sleep at night from the pain of getting so banged up from riding. Despite all the aches and bruises, I wouldn't have traded it for the world: I was learning to ride anything with hair! Besides, I couldn't officially ride as a jockey yet because I was only fifteen.

When we arrived at Wheeling Downs, there weren't enough stalls to stable our eleven horses, so we moved the stable fifty-two miles up the road to Waterford Park in East Liverpool, Ohio, just over the state border. Waterford Park sits on a rocky cliff at the top of the banks of the Ohio River. There's about a six-hundred-foot drop from the top of the bank to the water. It was a breathtaking sight to stand on the edge and look down.

It would take the Elias brothers several weeks to write the condition book (the list of anticipated races on any particular day) and put the race together. While they did their work, we did ours by training and running our horses at Waterford Park. About three weeks after we arrived, Tex and I were watching our four-year-old maiden filly named Small Play finish a well-beaten fifth in a late race of the day. I rubbed and galloped her daily and loved her very much. She was aggressive and worked well in the morning but didn't seem to run a lick in the afternoons. Her days were numbered because there are no races that allow a five-year-old maiden to run.

After the race and a long day of work, as night was drawing close, I met our rider at the edge of the track to unsaddle the horse and walk the filly back to the barn. With my head against her neck, I was talking softly to her and as much to myself. How could I make her understand that she had to do better or we would have to part ways? "Mommy" (the pet name I gave her) tried to break into a jog and nickered loudly while shaking her head from side to side. We were approaching the red-and-white quarter-pole marker on the track as we headed back to our barn when she changed her gait and attitude. I looked up in horror as several horses approached us, running wildly in a full gallop as if they had been spooked by something. I looked past Mommy's head and noticed grooms, hot walkers, and an assortment of other folks screaming at full volume. They ran wild-eyed away from the barn area, turning panicking horses loose and hollering at no one in particular.

And then I caught sight of it, bright and crackling. *Fire.*

As the flames licked at the buildings, I turned my gaze to the area where our barn *used to be*. The fire had already consumed it. Since the racetrack was located up high on a ridge, I knew the strong winds, dry conditions, and the hay and oats that filled the barn would only stoke the fire more. Time was running out. The orange and red flames raged higher than the thirty-foot lampposts placed all around the barn. Brown-and-white smoke billowed to what looked like hundreds of feet above.

There were no fire trucks on-site, and no sirens indicating help was near. One barn burned and quickly caught another on fire until all of the barns were engulfed in the out-of-control inferno. The tin roofs of the barns were collapsing as the bodies of nearly two hundred charred horses began to fall.

Horses can scream, I thought somewhere in my mind. I knew it was a stupid thought, especially in the panic of what was happening all around, but the thought was there nonetheless as I tried to reconcile with the surreal scene unfolding before me.

My eyes were watering—half from tears, half from smoke—and my heart was leaping out of my chest. As it got darker, it became even harder to see through the thick layers of black smoke. There was no way to know what was just one foot in front of me. Small Play was running circles around me at the end of the reins of the bridle, stopping my progress and whinnying desperately in a very high pitch.

Fire trucks had finally made their way up the dirt roads from the main pavement to the track and barn area. Unaware of the carnage, they were running over horses to get to the stables. The sirens only scared the horses that had gotten free more. Many ran and jumped off the cliff, free-falling six hundred feet into the Ohio River. Two of the big red trucks had damaged grills and bumpers. Much later I learned they had hit and killed a half dozen loose horses that made their way onto the highway. It was mayhem for what felt like an hour or more, until the few remaining horses could be herded to safety by driving a feed truck through the main racetrack fences, opening a refuge of sorts for them.

"You can't destroy that fence! It's a good fence!" someone shouted at me.

"Fuck the fence," I yelled back. It seemed like this type of language had become part of my regular vocabulary. But it made me sound tough, I thought, something that I needed badly to go with my four-foot frame and curly blonde hair.

"Drive through it. If you won't—I will!" I said. I was mad and cussing at everyone. My memory flashed back to my father at the end of the gun. It was rage! Seeing the seriousness on my face and the urgency of the situation, the driver chugged the truck through the metal fences in low gear, leaving ugly holes in the metal and dragging posts beneath it until there was a big enough of a gap to guide the horses through.

What the hell have I done? I thought in a flash of desperation. *Who am I?*

I couldn't handle Small Play any longer on foot and instinctively pulled the bridle off of her head while pointing her through the hole in the rail. She had jumped on my feet three times, and it felt like my toes were broken. She left me at full gait, accompanying a half dozen other terrified horses heading through the hole and into the centerfield at the same time. She was gone, and would I never see her again. I helped some other horses in an attempt to direct them into the centerfield. It was the only safe place to contain them.

It was getting darker by the minute, but the night sky glowed in the red-and-orange light of the fire that raged on. It was like the end of the world in my mind. The barn area stabled eight hundred horses or more, and pandemonium was everywhere. I stumbled toward what I thought was once our barn, brushing by dazed and mumbling stable hands clamoring about.

Where in hell is Tex? I wondered.

The last time I saw him had been in the paddock before the race.

As I came close to what I thought were the remnants of our barn, I could count seven waves in the tin that had fallen on top of charred horse carcasses. The heat was so intense that I couldn't get within forty feet of them. I knew there should have been one more besides Small Play, who had been with me. Maybe the eighth one made it, too. Could it be Devil's Grin, Tex's hope for a payoff? But the configuration of the tin suggested that Devil's Grin was in the second stall, where he lay in a fiery grave. I knew each of the horses' stall positions because I fed them all every morning. Devil's Grin was dead, and so were our chances to win the bet. I felt a peculiar empty feeling accompanied by shivers that made me nauseated. Most everything I loved and needed was beneath that smoldering tin. This thought added to the devastation, even though I didn't give a shit about the bet or the reason we were there. The fire had blown eastward onto many more barns, and the smoke was still heavy. I could smell meat from the dead horses cooking.

Before we left Toronto, Tex had hired a man he knew from Mexico named Clare More and his wife as a groom and a hot walker. *Where the hell were they?* I thought. *Are they dead, too?* It was early night now, as I picked up a shank that was obviously lost in the commotion. The leather, chain, and snap looked okay, so I rolled it up in my hand and decided to head back to the hole in the fences. The fire trucks looked like they were ahead of the spreading fire as best as I could see. There were still what appeared to be a hundred or so horses running wildly in a herd, aided by some portable police lighting that had been put in place. I moved past three guys and ducked under the two-by-fours that were blocking the hole on the inside rail.

"Where are you going?" one guy asked, like I was crazy for entering.

"I'm going to take a look," I said in a gruff tone.

"You'll get killed in there, kid. There are more than three hundred of the bastards running crazy, fighting and fucking and God knows what!"

I mulled over what he told me and rethought my plan. "Okay," I responded, changing my direction.

I slipped down an embankment and over a culvert and toward what I thought was a quieter group of horses off to the side. I could hear them nickering but couldn't see them well.

After what seemed like hours of walking around, I thought that I recognized one of our horses. I carefully moved closer, not anticipating what they might do. I didn't want to spook them and have to start all over again. My adrenaline felt like an electrical circuit pulsing from my head to my chest and into my arms. The excitement helped me overcome my fear.

And there he was—Right Move, a baby two-year-old that I had broken and nicknamed "Little Goof." He was between two others and looked at me with eyes as big as saucers. As I inched past the others on the outside, they took several steps, which put Little Goof's whole silhouette in front of me. He uttered a muffled nicker, which I took as a greeting. Slowly, I crept closer, grasping the uncoiled shank with the gold-colored snap and chain in my left hand. My right hand was extended in a gesture of friendship. I carefully snapped the shank on the ring of his halter and hoped to calm him with some reassuring sounds and my right hand. Little Goof was just a baby, barely two years old, but he had so much potential.

As I turned him, I noticed his entire back was burned down to his rump. The hair was gooey, mixed with blood and dirt. I tried to stabilize him after throwing the shank over the top of his neck and tying it to the right side of the halter. I had repositioned the chain from the ring through his mouth forming what would be portable reigns, and, even though I knew it would hurt like hell, I climbed on him. I threw myself up onto his back. It was a desperate situation and, in the moment, it was the only thing I could think of to save Little Goof and stay alive myself by perching above what could be deadly hooves. There were horses starting to run all around us. I could taste the dust and, in the darkness, feel it in my eyes. Mounting him created a frenzy all around us. At times, I was riding Little Goof at full gait inside a pack of fifty other horses. They were biting and kicking, struggling to find a place where they could feel safe. I steered Little Goof to the outside of the centerfield and finally got him settled down. I refused to let him go because he was one of the most valuable of the horses we had brought.

When I finally dismounted, we were both exhausted. We had gone most of the night, pacing around the centerfield and seeing glimpses of trucks and firemen dousing the flames that had destroyed nearly everything.

As the sun came up, I saw the absolute devastation. What was once a sanctuary for hundreds of beautiful horses was now the resting place for all too many quiet souls. The entire facility was nothing more than a tinderbox, a lot of which had burned to the ground. It was a disaster. The future had become our solemn past. We were able to save a few hundred or so horses in the centerfield, but the rest of the animals either ran away or died. I'd heard it was upward of two hundred or more. The veterinarians became the grim reapers, putting so many of them out of their misery. In the aftermath, the fire trucks were covered in horsehides and blood.

As I stood in the centerfield taking in the unfathomable sight, a man I didn't know came along and offered me a drink from a mickey of whiskey.

"What the hell are you doing here, kid?" he asked.

"I've been here all night," I said, exhausted. "This horse belongs to the barn I work for. I wasn't about to turn him loose."

"It's a miracle you're here. How did you make it through this mess?"

I didn't have an exact answer. The truth was, I wasn't sure. I just did. I survived.

"Here ya go kid—have a drink," he said, taking the lid off the short glass bottle and giving it to me.

I had never had a drink of alcohol before, but that early dawn felt like a good time to start.

"Holy shit" was all I could squeak out past my throat, which now felt like it was on fire, too.

By the time I found Tex, he was crouched near the back wheels of a horse van, sobbing. It looked like he had been there for hours. It was a sight I've never forgotten. The big, usually jovial cowpuncher from Pecos, Texas, had been brought to his knees. With his sweat-stained Stetson in hand, he looked like he'd been praying. But I couldn't ask him that. It wasn't a conversation that you took up with a guy like him.

Tex was a broken man. I never knew whether it was because of the dead horses or the opportunities denied. I don't think he was ever really the same after that horrible night.

None of us were.

I stood there with Right Move at the end of the shank as Tex cried and cried. I wanted to comfort him, but I didn't really know how. I didn't come from a soft and understanding background so I didn't know how to react to the situation.

"Take it easy, big boy. Try to pull yourself together," I said.

But he couldn't. No matter what I said, he couldn't stop crying.

Several hours later, Tex finally faced the inevitable. He called the Rogers brothers and told them the horrific news. It was a catastrophic loss—we had lost all but two horses out of nine. The Rogers brothers essentially told Tex that under the circumstances, they wanted to get out of the business.

People wandered around with note pads. I wasn't sure if they were newspaper reporters or insurance adjusters, but I knew they weren't racetrackers.

Clare More was alive. He'd gone to East Liverpool, Ohio, just across the river and got drunk. His wife was safe in a one-room flat. We were able to recover Small Play, who had been bred by an unknown horse, the vet said, amidst the frenzy. Right Move was treated and eventually placed on a van going south to Versailles. Despite the terrible injury, I thought there was a chance he could race again. I knew the physical wound would heal. The psychological effect on the horse was yet to be seen. As it would turn out, he never was the same and never saw the starting gate again.

The track kitchen had mostly made it, and we were treated to bacon and egg sandwiches, courtesy of Waterford Park. I ate four. There were so many horses left and no stalls. I had no clothes except for what I was wearing. They were all in the tack room that I had slept in each night located at the end of the barn. They were now casualties, too, including my barbering tools. I had tossed my riding boots in Tex's old Buick.

In an attempt to relocate the surviving horses and people who had no money and nowhere to go, the track found a variety of nearby temporary accommodations. Small Play and I were relegated to the Steubenville Fairground, which was an abandoned trotting track. It was located on the top of an Ohio mountain within twenty-five miles, about thirty minutes from Waterford Park.

Small Play and I rode in the back of an old horse van to Steubenville, along with roughly ten other horses and ten grooms and hot walkers who had also made it. Upon arrival at the fairgrounds, I bedded the filly down in an eight-by-eight stall and then hustled a bucket and a bail of local hay. After filling the bucket with water, I gave Small Play a kiss and told her I'd see her in the morning.

Many of the local farms and residences had heard about the fire and volunteered whatever accommodations and food they had. I got to stay with a very nice old couple just a mile away from the fairgrounds. Boy, did that bed in their attic ever feel good!

Other trainers connected to the horses and people who accompanied me to Steubenville showed up the next morning with a few saddles, bridles, and assorted hardware. I had walked there after tea and toast with the old farm couple and found I was the only exercise rider in the bunch. I spent the next week exercising about twenty to thirty horses for free and awaiting the next move.

Meanwhile, one question kept running through my mind: *Where the hell was Tex?*

No one knew the exact cause of the fire. It may have been electrical, they said, or a groom fell asleep with a cigarette. Of course, back in those days, we used wood-burning boilers to heat the water to wash the horses after training, and people smoked everywhere. In the end, there was no insurance money to pay for the losses.

Tex finally showed up at the fairgrounds after six days of being peculiarly absent. He was extremely quiet but seemed much better. Even so, he still wasn't able to make any rational decisions that day, so I took charge and told him we could talk and figure out our next move. I got no response. Normally, I rode in the back of the van with the horses while Tex drove the old 1936 Buick he had bought for ninety dollars. To me, it looked more like a hearse or something Al Capone would own than it did a car Tex should be driving.

When I told him that I needed some money, and that I was tired of washing the same clothes and drying them every night, he gave me twenty dollars. He said he talked again with Mr. Jack, and we were on our own until the end of November. However, we could return to the farm in Versailles, round up the derelict horses we could find, and try to start over. Tex was owed some money from Norm Heaton, a businessman in Toronto who owned most of Small Play, so we could get by on that. What Tex didn't tell me then was that he sold half of my contract to Heaton. He said we would take Small Play to Charles Town, West Virginia, and run her there. We put her on a truck with some others who had the same idea. I got to ride in the Buick this time, as there was no room in the back. So off we went to Charles Town, following the truck. We seemed to stop at every roadside saloon, where Tex would order a fishbowl of 3.2 percent beer, also known as "near beer." The alcohol content was so low, he spiked it with whiskey to get buzzed. Despite the fact that West Virginia was a dry state at the time, they did allow the sale of "nonintoxicating beer." The bartenders always seemed to be able to pass Tex a bootlegged shot of whiskey from behind the counter.

Part way to Charles Town, Tex said, "You drive." When we pulled over, he took a half-filled bag of oats out of the trunk and placed it partly under my ass and lower back so I could reach the clutch and brake pedals. I spent half of my time holding onto the steering wheel and standing up on the floor in order to see out the windshield. I'd sit on the oat bag whenever I had to shift or apply the brakes. It wasn't ideal, but it worked. With me handling the driving duties, Tex got to chew his Beech-Nut tobacco, which he spit all over the dashboard as I steered the old Buick through the winding roads of West Virginia. It wasn't a pretty sight, but we got there.

While Little Goof eventually recovered from his injuries, he never amounted to a great deal after that fateful night. On the other hand, it turned out Small Play had a good shot at running some races. Heaton and his wife, Marion, had taken a liking to me, especially once I started getting on their horse. He knew Tex wasn't making good on his contract payments to me and wanted to buy in on half of the deal. Tex was happy to take Norm's money, but he never passed any of it along my way.

By now I had come to understand Tex was a dreamer. He was better with a rope and a one-eared bridle in his hand than he was as a trainer. He was never going to be a big success because he always had ants in his pants. He was a hillbilly—a big ol' cowboy who looked like he just lost his horse. His big moneymaking scheme of running a horse at Wheeling Downs was a perfect example of how Tex liked to wander and take risks. He never planned well. He was and always would be a rough-and-ready drifter cowboy. And, as it turned out, the Rogers brothers didn't necessarily want to get out of the horse business so much as sever their ties with Tex. They were angry with him for taking all of their horses to Waterford Park on a whim of winning a guaranteed bet. Hell, everyone knows there's no such thing as a guarantee in horse racing.

But anyone who knew Tex understood he would get anxious and leave at the drop of a hat. And that's what we were about to do yet again as we packed up Small Play and drove to Charles Town.

Fall was quickly setting in, and the nights were getting cold by the time we made our way south. I had only one filly in tow, and Tex had limited resources to get us there in our gas-guzzling Buick. I could see the neon beer and wine signs of every local saloon we passed better than the road through the dense fog at night.

"Pull over there," Tex barked.

I dutifully pulled over, put the car in neutral, turned the key off, and hoped it would start again after he was done buying his booze.

On one stop, Tex went into a bar, and because I figured he might be a while, I followed close behind.

"Okay, Sonny Boy, let's sit over there," Tex said, pointing to the corner of the old musty bar.

"Put a double shot in a beer for me," he shouted out to the bartender.

The bartender slid what appeared to be a fishbowl of beer down the bar. I was a little surprised he could get any slippage from the surface because it felt sticky to the touch. The old man behind the bar looked like he belonged on a fishing boat more than he did in this place. His face was weathered and wrinkled and his teeth yellowed from cigarettes. He reached beneath the counter, grabbed a clear unmarked bottle of whiskey that was probably made in someone's basement, and poured two shots into Tex's beer.

"It's called a boilermaker," Tex said, spinning his glass without ever looking up.

Although Tex was always a drinker, he began drinking a lot more after the fire. He was terribly traumatized by that unforgettable summer night. I understood his pain, but I didn't understand his need to numb it with alcohol. Given my father's history, I didn't really have the patience or understanding for someone who used liquor as a crutch. I saw it as a weakness. And the longer I was around Tex, the more I began to understand he was really just a fragile man who could break at any given moment.

To make matters worse, Tex never stopped burping, farting, and chewing tobacco. He often sat in the passenger seat of the Buick, chewing and spitting all over the place. Sometimes he'd use a spare cup or bottle for his waste, but usually he'd just spit as he pleased and let the juice run down the dashboard near the gear shifter or window. I never understood why he didn't just roll down the window and spit outside. He knew it made me mad, but he didn't care. He'd laugh it off, thinking it was no big deal.

Charles Town was a cold and frozen waste of time—a total bust. We could barely train Small Play because the weather was always bad and the ground was frozen solid. If we tried to run her, she was at risk of fracturing a bone or chipping an ankle. If that happened, we'd be without a viable horse and therefore nothing left to try to earn some money.

Winter was fast approaching. I had lost most of my clothes in the fire and hadn't been able to save enough money to buy anything new other than a pair of Levi's and a shirt, because Tex still wasn't paying me more than thirty dollars a month against my contract. He was so far in arrears that he would never catch up. As a result, I was constantly cold and found myself mad at Tex most of the time, especially putting up with the endless nights of boilermakers, spitting, burping, and farting. At the end of October, Tex talked Mr. Joe into letting us return to the farm earlier than planned. I must admit that was one of the best decisions I'd ever seen him make.

So, it was back to Versailles.

I drove most of the way, listening to more stories about cattle drives, cow punching, and the lore of the Wild West. One night as we neared Lexington, I couldn't manage to shut Tex up. He'd already had a half dozen boilermakers and was well into a cowboy story that had him in the midst of a raucous laugh with a mouthful of Beech-Nut. It was then, out of the corner of my eye, I caught a glimpse of a cop car doing a screeching U-turn behind us.

"Holy shit!" I hollered, standing behind the wheel.

Tex wouldn't stop his story or his laughter, and I had this cop roaring full tilt up my ass.

"Tex! Tex!" I shouted as I swung the steering wheel hard to the right, sending the old Buick up on the inside of a tractor-trailer that was in front of us. Still, Tex was carrying on.

"Shut the fuck up!" I hollered again.

I had never been that pissed at Tex before, but it seemed to me like I had to get his attention—and fast. I was fifteen years old but I looked twelve, had no credentials, not even a birth certificate and no legal documentation allowing me to enter into the United States. Finally, Tex sat bolt upright after I snapped at him. I gave him a brief rundown of my concerns while maneuvering between the truck and the sidewalk on the right. Fortunately, the semi was tardy enough for me to get in front of him, hiding us from the cop as he made a right turn. A block in front of us, I could see the glow of a large neon beer and wine sign, so I made a hard right and stopped the old Buick between a group of cars alongside the bar. *Whew*, I sighed as the cop car drove past us, all lit up and with its siren still screaming.

Tex, in a proud moment of alcoholic courage, laughed heartily and said, "Sonny Boy, you're never going to make it if you let shit like that hold you back!"

I had no problem getting him out of the car and into the bar. After that scare, I thought to myself, *Maybe that juice'll work on me, but I have no intentions of ever becoming like Tex.* At that moment, the turkey house sounded awfully good, and I couldn't wait to get off of the road and enjoy all that it offered again.

CHAPTER FIVE

It was nice to visit with J. T. Smithers and T. Dunn again when they arrived at our makeshift barn kitchen. They wanted "a firsthand" account regarding the fire and became emotional when hearing about the dead horses they had watched over and assisted.

"Those horses were like family," Smithers said. "They didn't deserve that."

Mr. Joe arrived and, after managing a brief welcome without a smile, began to question Smithers and Dunn as to where they last saw the cast-off horses and where they might be located on the farm. He was talking about horses that had been bred on the farm. Due to leg and other severe problems, they had been passed over for training but were still kept in residency in the bushy, unused lands on the farm. I listened intently to plans to round them up, as those horses, or what was left of them, would be the only future I had.

"It ain't goin' to be easy," Dunn said, a painful scowl forming a hundred or more deep-brown wrinkles on a normally very positive face.

Smithers, with his hat in hand, was scratching his balding gray pate. "Them's growed-up horses, and all they're lacking is horns to be devils," he said. "We seen some carcasses back there a few times, so don't count on many bein' left. And those that are, gotta be more than five years old."

I looked at Tex to see any signs of encouragement or even possibility. There weren't any. The usual pixie smile was gone as the big guy sat staring at the ground. It was too early for a boilermaker. Or was it? The strange meeting adjourned as Mr. Joe raced off in his new truck but not without a final comment from Smithers.

"We need a lot o' rope," he said, "about five or six rope halters, some hoods and rope hobbles. An' we best go back there about dawn before da bugs comes to life."

I watched Tex's eyes brighten and his mouth form a grin when J. T. mentioned the rope. He knew he was our main man when it came to rope.

I thought, *This is like hunting deer with no gun.*

Tex decided we would "start out right," as he put it, and go into town for a bath. It had been too long, and we both smelled like billy goats. As we pulled up to the Colonial Hotel in Versailles, a man Tex knew named Mr. Freeman was standing by the front door. The structure resembled Civil War architecture with crisscrossed painted board over stucco. Mr. Freeman also looked like he'd been in the Civil War—a General Custer with a suit on. His gray-and-white blended mustache and goatee were accented by a derby-type trilby perched askew on his head. I was mildly shocked when he brushed aside part of his suit to reach for his chew and exposed a shiny six-shooter in a holster. The gun sure belied Mr. Freeman's dapper stance. As the two of them engaged in an aggressive four-handed shake, Tex explained Mr. Freeman was the hotel manager and introduced us. We entered the hotel and paid the dollar to the little old clerk behind the reservations desk. After getting an enormous key, Tex and I went up to room 10, where we were met by an attendant with well-worn towels, one bar of soap, and a couple of washcloths.

The water for the tub was heated by lighting a fire under a bucket and then pouring the hot water into the tub. You were allowed two pours, which had to be done manually. We took turns, so I waited over on an old wooden chair, sometimes for hours, until Tex was done.

The trip soon became part of our routine. By the time we got to the Colonial each week, we were both filthy from working with the horses and only washing our face and hands with cold water in the barn. This was the only real bath each of us had all week, something I really looked forward to every Saturday. When we were spic-and-span clean, we'd go out to eat. We always went for the fish sandwiches in the pool hall not far from the hotel. They were cheap and filling. The fried fish was served wrapped in brown wax paper, which was always saturated by grease and seasonings. Sometimes, I'd lick the excess salt straight from the paper because it tasted so good.

When we were done eating, Tex would say, "I'll be back, Sonny Boy," and adjourn to the local whorehouse. I sat alone in the Buick, waiting for Tex to finish, listening to the small transistor radio I had and playing my harmonica. That was my usual Saturday night entertainment when it wasn't too cold.

The horses loose on the farm weren't worth much to anyone, unless someone could wrangle them up. And when it came to that, there was no man better for the job than Tex.

Early Sunday, we choked down a cup of Tex's jailhouse coffee and a slice of cornbread he had made. I started drinking his coffee out of desperation when we ran out of milk and there was nothing else to drink except whiskey. Given the choice, I swigged the coffee and hid the awful taste with the cornbread he made in a rusty old tin pan. Every time he called it "Kentucky Weddin' cake," I couldn't help but bust out laughing. If the cornbread was more than a day or two old, it was drier than a wooden god.

The plan was pretty simple and had been laid out two days before. J. T. Smithers had located a coil of one-inch rope, half of a dozen homemade rope hobbles, several rope halters, four homemade hoods with holes for ears but none for eyes, a hammer, and what looked like an old kitchen knife. I wondered what the hell the hammer was for, but I didn't ask. Tex never liked a lot of questions, especially when he had a determined look on his face. It was just starting to turn daylight when three of us got into the Buick, and T. Dunn followed in the old pickup that I was familiar with from the train station episode. We continued down the dirt road on the perimeter of the farm until we reached a fairly thick stand of trees, a stream, and plenty of scattered underbrush.

How in the hell are we going to find them? I thought.

Just then, T. Dunn dropped to his hands and knees on the bank of the stream. "These look pretty fresh," he said quietly as we all crouched to verify the discovery of hoof prints.

Dunn signaled for us to wait and set off through a thicket that parted enough to be a trail from the water. His silhouette and patch of uncombed hair at the back of his head made him look like an Indian as he vanished into the brush. We waited for what seemed like an hour and spoke very little, as there wasn't much to say anyway.

"I seen three," Dunn said as he emerged upright from the same path that he left on. "Follow me."

It was getting a little lighter now, and following hoof prints in the soft ground was easier. In about a quarter mile, we huddled at Dunn's direction. Tex already had the rope, and I had the hoods and the halters. Smithers had thrown the hobbles, knife, and hammer into an oat bag. Tex was already rigging the rope into a lasso.

"Okay, J. T. will go with Tex straight ahead," Dunn told us. "David, you walk over to the left about thirty paces and then turn right. I will head right and then cut left so they won't know which way to run."

As I made the right turn, the images were vague; two very close together and one by itself. Then they spotted me, and the two started walking to my right. The one by himself broke into a trot to catch up. Then I caught sight of T. nearly straight across from me. My stomach was churning the coffee and cornbread into what felt like a ball of nails. I wanted to shout but knew better. It seemed like the patches of thicket were slowing our prey to a walk. And Dunn's plan was directing them down the middle between us. There obviously was a leader, a stout light bay about sixteen hands with a large, white blaze from his nose up past his eyes and a dark bay three-quarters of a length back, much lighter in conformation and a touch smaller. When they both saw T. Dunn and me, they broke into a slow trot. As they passed between us, Tex lunged from behind three large bushes directly in front of them. The rope twirled twice and fell onto the neck of the lead horse quicker than you could say what was happening, as Tex attempted to reel him in. Up he went on his hind legs, letting out a defiant series of snorts, his front legs thrashing. As big as he was, Tex was having trouble and losing ground to the big ferocious bay. Up he went again, when Smithers emerged from behind. With Tex at full gait, he hurled himself into the rib cage of the vertical bay horse, knocking him off of his hind legs and into a small tree. Tex, in what appeared to be a coordinated strategy, charged to the downed horse, shortening the rope as he went. He wrapped four quick turns around his front legs just above the ankles, knotting what appeared to be a bowline connected to the remaining rope. Realizing that I had the hoods, I discarded all but one and fearfully stuck my arm out close enough for Smithers's reach while he straddled the horse's neck. T. Dunn had picked up Smithers's oat bag and dumped its contents on the ground, quickly retrieving one set of hobbles. Tex pulled the lasso from the thick part of his neck to just behind his ears.

Every time the bay fought it, the rope tightened around him, bringing him to the point of desperation and drawing a line of blood from his neck where the hide was barked off, meaning the pressure was so great, the rope cut deep into his hide. It seemed like fifteen minutes passed before he quit! Dunn placed the hobbles higher than the rope wrap on the horse's front legs. Tex picked the kitchen knife off the ground and sawed what appeared to be about six feet off of the remaining coil of rope still connected to the legs. I could hardly believe what I was seeing! Smithers then sat on the bay's hocks and held his cannon bones as still as he could, while Tex did a wrap of rope tight enough to connect another set of hobbles. A rope halter was fixed in place.

Well, we caught him but what the hell are we going to do with him now? I thought.

Interestingly enough, the small, darker bay horse that was part of the catch didn't wander off too far and continued to circle us as if not wanting to leave his downed leader.

"That's it for now," Tex barked. "We'll bring the tractor down here this afternoon, tie him onto the hitch, get him on his feet, and slowly bring him back up to the tobacco barn."

I was glad I wasn't going to be part of that. Little did we know then that the big bay's name was Speak Free. He was a five-year-old horse by Four Freedoms, whom we'd become well acquainted with by the time we shipped him northward to Canada in the spring. We might have broken him that day, but he wouldn't have stayed "broke" until my ass and head hit the ground so many times that one of the two had to finally take root!

We spent three more days using the same plan within a half-mile circumference of where we captured the first two horses. It wasn't tobacco-growing time, so the beds had been burned to eliminate the weed seed using wood scraps, and the planting wasn't expected to start again until well into the spring. This freed up T. Dunn and J. T. to complete the "horse-snatchin' team," as Dunn called it. The three days netted us five more horses, including a monstrous gray cold-blood that was running with the Thoroughbreds and appeared to be much more accustomed to people. I voted to leave the big gray gelding alone in the thicket, as did Dunn and Smithers, but Tex had had enough rope in his hands over the last week to restore an image of himself from his old Wild West days in his head. The site of all seventeen hands of "Silver," as he was soon to be crowned, held a certain allure. He was big enough to haul all two hundred and twenty pounds and Tex's big ass around and would prove to be more than a symbolic pedestal for the old cowboy to mount. Tex knew he earned his keep by catching wild horses that could jump higher and run faster than I could ride on some days!

With Smithers proclaiming, "There weren't nothing left out there but dead carcasses," we abandoned our search. Mr. Joe, a Yale grad, as told by many in town, consulted the records in the big old desk in the mansion and officially stated that the catch pretty much matched his records over the years. Meaning there were six Thoroughbreds not counting the cold-bloods.

The big problem did not unravel until about a month later when the two Rogers brothers matched their records and concluded that the six Thoroughbreds were theirs. They had two seven-year-olds, a six-year-old, and two five-year-olds, but only the latter two had certificates and were registered with the Jockey Club in New York. Our newfound herd was in jeopardy. None of them had tattoos, so the looming, major question was whether the Jockey Club would respond positively to Mr. Joe's letter requesting registration on the four without papers. It was during this time that I learned the importance of officiating and what it took to race horses at the big tracks.

Tex didn't have a clue about what was involved and appeared optimistic as he boldly stated his experiences in Mexico City, where, he said, "All they give a shit about is what color they are!"

Mr. Joe said, "It ain't that way here at the big tracks, but maybe it's different in Canada," disclosing the limit of his knowledge by the statement.

What about names? I thought. Only one of them had one. But I wasn't about to enter the argument or limit the optimism that Tex held before him.

"It's November now, and it's going to take a lot of time to break 'em and train 'em," Tex said. "We don't have a starting gate on the farm. We've got to make him look like a racehorse. Waiting for some sort of registration foal papers ain't smart!"

I remember visiting the "heavenly seven," as I called our captives, in the tobacco barn during their first taste of civilization.

There wasn't a stick of straw longer than a cigarette butt, I thought as I peeked through the wooden slats on a bitterly cold morning.

They'd been running around in circles in their ten-by-twelve stalls, and every time they snorted, large plumes of frozen breath exhaled in centripetal configurations about a foot long.

Was that breath or smoke? I wondered. "These bastards are breathing fire!" Their eyes appeared like saucers.

"I have to feed 'em on the ground," T. Dunn hollered. "If I snap the metal feed bins in there, they'd be wearin' 'em in no time."

"Yeah, yeah," I replied an octave higher than usual and with much trepidation from the mental pictures my mind was painting.

That day we went into town to purchase the second-hand bridles, saddles, girths, and assorted equipment needed to replace what we lost in the fire. Tex had a pissing match with Mr. Joe regarding who would own and pay for the stuff.

Mr. Joe won the debate, but we went along anyway.

We stopped by the feed mill on our way because Tex wanted to check how much I weighed. I got on the pallet used to weigh bales of hay, straw, and grain.

"Seventy-two pounds," said the old man in the office. That was fully dressed, boots and all.

The big gray cold-blood proved the easiest of all to deal with because he'd been broke to death and well-used for other work. Tex threw the old Western saddle on him and pulled the one-eared bridle over his head. J. T. stood in front while Tex mounted Silver. It was a nonevent, as Tex cantered off across the tobacco stocks and did figure eights on him for about twenty minutes. He neck reigned a little slow at first but improved as Tex dug a spur in his right side. The Rogers brothers said they never knew where he came from, but T. Dunn said somebody had dropped him off at the farm to pay part of a tobacco bill incurred from the auction in Lexington. It didn't matter a damn. The cowboy was grinning ear to ear! The next thing to do was to trim his feet along with the rest and we were good to go.

However, training was delayed several days as we encountered serious problems: first with controlling the five horses we got out of the thicket, then exchanging rope halters for leather ones and getting the chain end of a shank through their mouths. After two days of working tirelessly, J. T. and T. had them stabilized well enough to shear off the long hair up and down the heart line and to the back of their ears. The manes were too thick and would take too long to pull, so the shears did the trick enough to see what was under there. The tails would have to wait until they were more manageable, as their ass-ends were in the air as much as their shoulders. They were plain dangerous to be around. The next day, canvas surcingles were tightened around their girths and left on for several hours. That presented a side show you could have sold tickets to. They would rear up, fall over backwards, throw themselves at the walls, and buck and kick to the point of exhaustion. It didn't help my confidence much, as I would be the last piece of equipment applied.

We were just on our way from running about twenty cows out of the ten acres adjacent to the tobacco barn where the horses were stabled. I was hoping that we could have found a smaller paddock, but there just wasn't anything suitable. When these bastards got loose in a large field, it took us all day to catch them. If we could contain them in a smaller area, it would make things a lot easier to herd them up.

While J. T. and T. spent most of their mornings working with the horses, Tex and I made a huge oval starting in a corner where the two exterior fences met. We spread tobacco stalks and horseshit from a buckboard wagon drawn by Sam and Blue. Except for loading, it was a fun exercise that took us several days to complete.

"It ain't pretty," Tex said, "but it'll give you something to aim at, my boy."

We brought Small Play and Right Move, now recovered from his burn injuries suffered during the fire, from the cow barn to the training barn. It was beginning to look like a stable—in numbers anyway. Mr. Jack had written letters to the Jockey Club in New York offering approximate foaling dates, color, pedigree, and year of birth for each of the horses from the thicket. He included why they had been left so long without sending the information. He and Mr. Joe thought they had enough information to apply for registration, and gradually we connected the data to each animal. They did have names, but they had never been submitted. Some of them had been pasture bred, and the studs had either died or gone somewhere else, I guess.

The team assembled several times. Smithers had gotten a bridle on three of them and had guided them around each stall with some degree of discipline. We all discussed the "what ifs" and how we were going to exit the stall in each case. Tex would man the door. T. Dunn would lead them with a shank over the bridle. J. T. would stand in the middle of the stall to give me a leg up. It *sounded* good! Tomorrow would bring it all to reality.

It was a cool, crisp Kentucky morning. Tex and I were up and out of the turkey house by 5 a.m. He had the coffee grounds boiling furiously, and I was into my first slice of corn bread from the rusty old tin pan We both were antsy as hell. He had an unusually serious look on his face that replaced the pixie smile. I had saddle soaped my riding boots the night before, along with the old, used bridle with the new lighter-colored chin strap. It had looked to be the most durable, although the rubber coating on the reigns was well worn and gave the age of the equipment away. I had opened the keeper that holds the stirrup straps onto the saddle, soaped it well, and left it in the barn with the leather girth and saddle pad, ready for our first day of training. I removed the stirrups, as I knew we wouldn't need them for the first day with the wild horses. In fact, we wouldn't use them at all until the horses became used to me being on their backs and riding them.

We hurried out of the kitchen and drove the old Buick to the tobacco barn that was now serving as the training barn. T. and J. T. were already busy pulling the feed tubs out from under the big, gray cold-bloods—Small Play and Right Move.

Lucky for us, Right Move had healed up nicely after his back was burned in the fire. I did a final check on the equipment, which was on the ground in front of the first stall, with the exception of the shanks. We all agreed to start with the wild horses that would be ridden in the stalls. We'd leave the other broke horses until last. They were the ones going to the big "shit ring" we had made in the pasture. We thought employing this strategy might keep the wild horses from getting too stirred up by the comings and goings of the other horses, as they were ridden past their stalls.

Tex and I watched as J. T. and T. put the bridle on the first bay, strapped the saddle on, and tightened the girth. Dunn had a hold of the reigns with one hand and an ear with the other. They were ready for me. I had on an Irish tweed cap, a light jacket, and a pair of khaki pants that I had purchased recently from the dry goods store in town. (It was many years later that helmets and safety vests became part of the game.) In the first attempt, J. T. gave me a leg up on the unnamed bay that we guessed was a seven-year-old. I laid across his back with J. T. holding one of my legs. The skittish bastard reared up slightly and lunged forward, pinning T. to the wall. I hit my head against that same wall with full force. J. T. still had my leg but moved forward with the Thoroughbred, pinning him against the board wall with all his weight. T. managed to escape under the bay's front legs. We were making such a racket, but I am sure things sounded much worse to Tex, who was still loyally manning the steel door lock. My head hurt, and the pea cap (a knit wool cap with a brim) slid down slightly over my eyes. J. T. pulled me back by my leg and, in one full motion, threw me across the stall. T., who was upright by now, regained command of the reigns, bent the horse's neck and head into his, and turned left to retard the forward motion of the horse. The bay was wringing wet, snorting what appeared to be smoke rings and rolling his eye at us with fierce determination.

"I am as useless as a sack o' shit just going along for the ride," I proclaimed to the rest of the team. "I've got to have more control in order to help."

T. Dunn was a fairly stout fellow but was little match for the thousand-pound seven-year-old who was pasture-fit and herd-savvy. After all, this was a wild animal. We regrouped and discussed a new strategy that we employed without much further talking. Tex handed a halter and shank to Dunn, who strapped it over the bridle, leaving the reigns free for me to apply pressure to the bit and bridle. Tex handed the two stirrups and webbing attached, and J. T. and I fitted them into the keepers on the saddle, while T. placed the chain end of the shank through the halter, biting on the horse's ear, a crude but common practice back then. J. T. eased me up high enough to get my right leg over the saddle. I managed a fairly short half-cross with the reins. T. was making strange sounds in an attempt to talk with the horse's ear in his mouth. I had rigged the stirrups rather long to have a deep purchase with which to stay aboard. Although I had never ridden wild horses out of a shoot in competition, my mind sent a message that this was close to what it was like being there. The bay was leaning back on all fours, which signaled a lunge to me. J. T. remained in the center of the stall, not far off of the left leg, when T. spit his ear out.

The signal was correct. All hell broke loose, but it was different this time. T. had me helping, and we synchronized two "flying" left turns while remaining somewhat in command. The jumping and rearing subsided after the second leap, while loud farts accompanied several "bucks." The stalls in the tobacco barn had no ceiling, so I was free from the worry of how high we went, but the hulk of J. T. looked a lot smaller from that altitude. I had remained glued to the son of a bitch but winced several times as my right foot, calf, and knee came in contact with the sides of the stall. After approximately thirty minutes, the dark bay yielded, soaking wet and with nostrils expanded into near perfect circles. I relished the give in him and could tell the worst in this one was over. We only had five of the wild ones left and two to train on our new shit ring in the pasture.

We were wrong about not stirring the others up. While I was oblivious to the sounds during the tumult, Tex said the commotion was somewhere akin to a roundup or a whorehouse fight. I hadn't ever heard either, but I knew he had, so I benefitted from his secondhand account.

We purposely took about thirty minutes between our sessions with the new horses because T., J. T., and I needed to catch our breath and wash the sweat and froth off in a bucket of cold water. We also discussed tweaking some of our strategy. Tex was enjoying it all, as he envisioned the making of his new stable.

The reactions from each of the other horses were similar, but J. T. and T. were tough, loyal, and knowledgeable. Above all, they were patient with the animals. In due course, they brought my feelings from respect and affection to genuine love and admiration. I had not experienced that before.

We'd finally gotten to where we had just one of the renegades left. We knew his age and name, as they matched the only foal registration that Mr. Joe found in the big desk at the mansion. He was the first one that we had captured in the thicket days before. He was a lighter bay and had a big wide blaze running down his face. He must have remembered us, or at least remembered J. T., who had knocked him over backwards and into a tree in the early morning of our first encounter. Once cleaned up, you could tell he had a solid four corners and a slight Arab design to his head. His chest and shoulders were big, and he had an ass end that resembled a wall by the roundly muscled triangle from his fibula to rump and gaskin. He looked special to me, and what was special was his absolute disdain for being kept out of the wild. It was quite clear that he hated people.

It was shortly after foaling that he was kicked by another mare and given up for dead.

"I gave this one some nurse mare milk for ten days until he could stand on his own again. It was milk from another mare used to help feed a baby when its mother can't. After that, the mare rejected her baby. When he could finally eat some grass, we took him down to the thicket and turned him loose with the other orphans and cripples. That was the last I seen him . . . didn't know he had a name. Mr. Joe said he was bred good by a horse called Four Freedoms or something, but we couldn't take any more time out of our tobacco crop to tend to him. That was the last time I seen him. He sure growed up!" T said.

Growed up he had, I thought as we watched his big ass go by the spaces in the boards of the stall. He was stirred up plenty and would be the last of the wild ones for the day.

J. T. was the first to enter Speak Free's stall. The horse was standing upright on his hind legs, with his ears pinned and a wide bracket of teeth showing. He looked more like a grizzly bear than a horse.

J. T. called out for help.

As the horse landed on all four feet, J. T. rushed him and managed to snap a shank through the halter and over his nose, using his weight to hold the horse's front quarters on the ground. T. scooted to the horse's right side and quickly placed a twitch on the soft part of his nose. Luckily, that did the trick! Now I was manning the stall door and Tex was in the stall with a bridle in one hand and a saddle cradled in the other. The three big men pushed the horse to the corner. They navigated the handle of the twitch through the headstall of the bridle and onto the horse's head. Tex and J. T., on opposite sides, quickly strapped on the saddle and tightened its girth to extreme proportions. All heads then turned in my direction. I left the opened door to Tex and inched toward the left side of the big bay. His head pushed forward in subservience to the twitch, and he appeared disabled—for now. I gathered the reigns in my left hand with a finger full of mane. The stirrups were pulled down to full length for maximum purchase as quickly as I hit the saddle.

In a flash, as the horse felt my presence, I could feel him gather his strength. Up he went on two hind legs. Feeling T.'s pressure on the shank in his mouth, he fought back, completing the backward motion into the heavy board wall in the back of the stall. I was thrown higher and bounced off of the wall approximately six feet above where my mount was attempting to gain footing. All J. T. could grab was the upper part of my arm, including a piece of my jacket, which became detached as I cleared the horse's body in a flailing motion. I landed by the open door, where Tex conveniently dragged me the rest of the way out of the stall. Adrenaline must have masked the pain because I quickly jumped back to my feet. T. shortened the shank on the five-year-old horse with hopes of managing him as he regained his footing. The saddle was crooked, leaning off to one side, and had J. T.'s attention. As he reached to correct it, Speak Free lunged directly at T., knocking him down against the wall. J. T., the much bigger man, grabbed the shank and part of the halter that covered the bridle. He yanked the horse violently away from the fallen T.

Assessing the scene, Tex hollered, "If we stop now we'll never break that bastard!"

With that, he pushed me through the opening toward the group. Tex retrieved the twitch from the next stall and pushed it toward J. T. There was no time for T. and me to brush ourselves off. We had pretty much worn through the deep straw bedding and dug holes in the dirt floor. Equipment in place and a determined brace against the big horse, J. T. hoisted me up into the saddle.

"Keep turning him left, T.," I blurted out, gathering the reins, my feet firmly planted in the irons.

J. T. joined us on the right side parallel to Dunn in a series of left turns. He bucked and kicked for about ten minutes, but the two big men provided an anchor on his head.

"Let's turn him and go right," I instructed, tightening the bit in his mouth. We all agreed not to stop, although we were fatigued. We gave him about an hour of combined turns. He didn't like it, but he must have felt outnumbered and chose not to fight.

In the last ten minutes, T. unwound the twitch while I patted up and down his neck with shaky trepidation. We had made progress, but T. and I were limping badly.

"Let's pack it in for today," Tex bellowed disappointedly. "We'll get to the others tomorrow."

Those were the kindest words that I ever heard come out of Tex's mouth, I thought as I was washing the girth and bridle and readying for the next morning. I ached all over, and my right leg was beginning to feel fat around the knee joint as the swelling began. Mr. Jack showed up as we were about to leave and asked J. T. to go down to the south field and fetch the two two-year-old fillies to the training barn to be broken and ridden with the rest. Sometime later, we would find out the big chestnut was called Fine Spun, and the bay, equally big, was to be known as Fine Buff. They had been left turned out since they were weaned. The herd was getting bigger, and Tex was grinning wider and longer.

T. brought three more tobacco people to the farm to muck stalls, and to feed and water the horses. The farm wasn't new to them, as they had previously stripped tobacco and processed it for auction in the little lean-to building attached to the middle of the barn. This was a big help, except when they brought their little kids who would climb high up over the stalls to where the tobacco was hung and they'd giggle, causing the horses below to prop and wheel.

The first day of training was the beginning of a long and difficult time in my young life. The weather was cold and reminded me of Canada. We slept in our clothes when the temperatures dipped, as the blankets we had were secondhand and well used, containing little stuffing.

There was no turning back, I thought as I pondered what the rest of the winter would bring. My head, ass, and legs really hurt as I got out of the old Buick at the turkey house. Tex had anticipated the long part and had been cooking a ham hock simmering in water and frijoles beans in the upstairs kitchen of the partially burned-out barn.

I looked forward to eating as I dunked my crumbling corn bread into the bowl of hot frijoles and managed to pick out several chunks of ham that were hidden amongst the red pepper shells in the thick bubbly mix. Tex had poured himself a coffee cup full of whiskey before he started his beans. He talked about all the good times we were going to have and which of the horses he thought would be the best. He regaled as if there were other people besides me listening to the diatribe against unnamed foes "whose asses were going to be kicked." With arms waving between long slurps from the cup, we sounded like a formidable team.

"It's been a great day!" he stated loudly.

For who? I thought as I rose from the table and found my way in the dim light from the hanging bulb over our heads to the wire clothesline I had rigged from a door jam and a beam that was big enough to hold two days' wash from the sink. I slowly removed my shirt and washed up with a rub rag that we used as a washcloth. I had heated some water in a cooking pot and gingerly applied it. My left arm was purple from the elbow to the shoulder where J. T. had retrieved me several times from the hairy mix of dirt and horsehide.

Better than the alternative, I thought as I began to rethink briefly what we had done.

I picked out what I hoped would be a warmer replacement shirt, put my torn jacket back on, and headed for the turkey house. It was eight o'clock and getting very dark. My right riding boot was difficult to remove, as my leg had swollen from the knee down. I heard Tex bump his head on the little door and cuss as I woke up briefly, then fell quickly back to sleep.

The next morning was cold and rainy as we met at the barn. J. T. and T. had spent the preceding hour with large hand clippers, twitch, and shank. They had knocked the hair off three of the horses that would do heavier training out of the stalls and around the interior of the barn. T. advised that they be tranquilized several days before in order to allow the blacksmith to do their feet. *These guys are really self-starters*, I thought—so reliable.

The day began and ended as a day of caution and method. The wild-assed horses from the thicket took the longest and acted like they'd forgotten everything we did the previous day. But we were ready for them. We applied our teamwork and tools and commenced to show significant improvement toward the end of each individual session. The two two-year-olds were amateurs and pieces of cake compared to the other six. Small Play and Right Move jogged outside of the stalls and gave me the first relief on horseback. This went on day after day. We advanced the difficult ones to where we could train them out of the stalls but within the barn. Ten days later Tex announced we would train outside with all but the pair of two-year-olds.

It was a Saturday morning just after sunrise. I didn't anticipate the day from hell we were about to endure. I had my suspicions about what might unfold, but I certainly didn't know for sure.

Tex was mounted on Silver, the big gray cold-blood gelding. The plan was for Tex to lead and accompany me to our makeshift, tobacco-littered manure ring that was approximately a half-mile in circumference. Tex said he had measured it with the old Buick, though details were not expected. We used straw and horseshit mixed with the tobacco stalks to define our surface over the half-frozen grass.

I started the morning with the two seasoned horses that had trained on racetracks before. They were sharp and excited and offered no unusual characteristics once I had a half-cross and eased them into a canter. Silver was acting fine, and Tex had been managing him well. Because our training track was located a hundred yards from the barn on an eighty-acre tobacco field, I recommended that we leave the halters loosely over the bridles on each of the wild-assed horses. Our team agreed. Because Tex was anxious to train Speak Free, the only one with a name and papers, he went first. I walked and jogged him twice around on the inside of the barn. He threw his head and bucked several times but was otherwise generally manageable.

Then, the big barn door was opened, revealing an ominous gray sky and cool intermittent rain. The four-year-old pricked his ears at the prospect of going outside. It had been a while. Tex was mounted with a coil of rope and ready to accompany me as I rode Speak Free. I nudged him lightly in the rib cage, getting him through the door and into the open. After he walked and jogged for about thirty yards from the barn, I could feel him gather himself by the tenseness of his muscles. He reared up and lunged high into the air toward Tex and the pony. I made it through the first phase of his demonstration, managing to stay aboard and somewhat in control. Tex inched the pony toward us. Speak Free recoiled and lunged at the middle of the big gray horse, knocking Tex to the ground and straddling the pony. Steering the big bay became increasingly difficult. He lunged again, loosening us from the pony and heading off at full gait in a series of furious bucks. I stayed with him for about an eighth of a mile until he suddenly propped and ducked, like he turned inside out in a fierce reversal of direction. I not only didn't make the turn, I careened off to one side in an ascending trajectory until the sudden jerk snapped me in the same direction as the fleeing bay.

I was hung up—the most paralyzing realization any jockey can have! I stayed dangling and twisting during a series of cow kicks at full gait, one of which was planted in the cheek of my ass—anywhere else would have resulted in more serious consequences. The force must have jerked the right stirrup webbing free from the rusted "keeper," a small trigger-like apparatus that holds the stirrup straps in place on the saddle. Fortunately, the centrifugal force at such a high speed spun me into the half frozen ground after three rotations. I managed to sit upright, sensing the soft cold rain on my face. I was dazed and needed all fours in my struggle to stand but didn't manage it on the first attempt. Back in a sitting position, I saw T. and J. T. assisting Tex onto the buckboard with Sam and Blue attached. As I slowly came to my senses, they were heading for me. I hadn't known of their decision to park the mules and buckboard conveniently close to the training barn in anticipation of needing a rescue team. *I must have missed the meeting about that*, I thought in muddled introspection. In the midst of my pain, my mind suddenly started to race. I found myself thinking about how smart these two men are and what a team we were becoming.

"Are you all right, little man?" J. T. hollered as he clucked the mules to speed up. I didn't answer because I didn't know yet. Tex was sitting on the buckboard, legs dangling. He was obviously okay. The guys carefully helped me to my feet and onto the seat beside him. I was having trouble sitting on the hard planks, as the left cheek of my ass burned, reminding me of what had just occurred. I lay down in retreat from the pain, cupping my head in my left hand and arm. But I still hurt all over and could feel where the buckboard was jarred from the unevenness of the frozen ground below us.

"Where's the horse?" I yelled.

"The gray pony ran back into the barn, and the racehorse is down by the Big Sink. It looks like the saddle is half-off on his right side. Other than that, he looks like he's ready for you, Davie," J. T. shouted. The statement was punctuated by repeated laughter from both men.

Speak Free was too far away to be walking after him, so Tex and I got in the Buick with a coil of rope and J. T. and T. on the buckboard. Off we went in an attempt to capture the wayward horse. The softness of the front seat's old worn-out upholstery was forgiving on my body following the morning's escapade.

"I ain't going to be too speedy when we get to this horse," I told Tex. He nodded without a word, and then, after a brief pause, said, "We got seven more of these bastards to train today. Maybe we should keep 'em jogging inside."

"Yup," I said, knowing something had to be done with them.

Speak Free had his back to the Big Sink as Tex positioned the car. He angled the vehicle toward the water and was careful not to park too close, as that might make the horse feel cornered. J. T. and T. had donned two well-worn slickers they pulled from the back of the wagon as the rain intensified. Tex left the seat of the Buick after reaching for the coil of rope. I could see the anger on his face. T. placed the mules and wagon in a *V* formation with the Buick, creating a funnel effect. With the water in the back, there was nowhere for the horse to go except straight ahead between them. I positioned myself in a place that helped close up the hole. Tex and the other two walked slowly toward him. The horse raised his tail in confidence as he jogged straight ahead on the soft ground, as if to signal that he was going to run over them. Tex didn't wait to negotiate. With two twirls of the rope, he found the mark with his lasso.

Maybe all of those bullshit stories are true, I thought, still wincing from my pain. This old guy is good!

The other two joined Tex in the tug-of-war with the horse, and, much to my surprise, he stood and waited as they made their way hand over hand up the rope to his head. J. T. slipped the chain end of the shank through the horse's mouth and snapped it back on the halter. It was a long way back to the barn. Tex motioned for me to come closer as T. repositioned the saddle, tightened the girth, and threw me up onto Speak Free's back. My legs felt like red hot rods stuck through pieces of cement. Both of my knees were swollen. But this time J. T. had a death grip on the shank, and I had a fairly short cross of the reins even though my legs felt like spare parts I couldn't use.

How I got through the rest of the day was something I have never understood. Fortunately, the other five wild horses were easier to break than we had anticipated. J. T. went the first two turns with me before I rode them myself for twenty minutes each. He could see how pale my face was, and he sensed my fatigue from the earlier part of the day. One of the seven-year-olds threw his head and hit me in the face. My nose bled until I could get off and wash it in a bucket of cold water. Thankfully, the two-year-olds went around the stalls without any glitches.

Although it wasn't Saturday night, Tex left for the pool hall after I declined his invitation. He said he needed some whiskey and offered to bring me back a fish sandwich. After I nodded and shut the door to the turkey house, I waited for the sound of the old Buick to fade as it headed down the lane before I started crying. I wasn't going to let Tex see me like that.

The fish sandwich lay uneaten as I stirred in the morning darkness. It had been a stressful night. I put my boots on, picked up the paper bag, and proceeded across the road and up the stairs to the barn kitchen. The air was cold but dry. I hadn't eaten since the afternoon before and contemplated the taste of the two boiled eggs, corn bread, and black coffee that were cooking on the stove. I found a heavy sweater, socks, and a small bottle of vitamins. There was also a note from Mr. Joe's wife. I felt grateful for the compassion expressed in the short message as well as for the contents of the package. Her note expressed concerns about my health and was complimentary to me. It was the first time I'd ever heard such kind words from a woman who could have been my mother. She had no children and looked at me with the longing of something lost. She brought the kind of warmth that could only come from a woman. I completed my daily cold-water wash, knocked the dirt and sticks from my hair, and reached to grab clean underwear and a shirt from the bailing wire clothesline.

Tex showed up in a rush, ate half of a bowl of old bean stew, and declared that we were off! I was not in a hurry to get to the barn, but I remained resolute. The crying hadn't helped. It showed weakness and brought something to the surface from deep within me. I couldn't understand my feelings, and I didn't try to. I wasn't going to cry again, I pledged, though that vow would be broken in the coming nights.

Over the weeks and months, the tasks grew easier, though they were still spotted with numerous crash landings, bites, and nosebleeds that accompanied severe pitches, flailing heads, and equipment failure. I was riding smarter and stronger and was in much greater control. The horses began to enjoy their daily schooling, and now we could turn them out each night after training. They were happier horses, I thought.

CHAPTER SIX

Tex was a real six-foot-two beauty in his long johns and woolly socks, crawling bald-headed out of the turkey house first each morning. I wondered whether the women at the whorehouse in town, where he went every Saturday evening, would like a pinup photo of him for their wall. He defended them loyally and told me the girls you could get for four dollars in Versailles were the same as those who charged ten at the LaFayette hotel in Lexington. Vanity meant something for the big cowboy, and telling me made it real, I guess.

One late afternoon after training, I shot a possum on a fence with the little .22 caliber, nine-shot pistol I kept in my bag. Thinking it would make for some good eats later that night, T.'s wife met me on my way back to the turkey house and offered to cook it up for dinner. Whenever she cooked, it felt like I was in a real home. She could throw together a hearty meal out of the most basic and unusual ingredients and make it taste like what I imagined gourmet fare tasted like. It was always a welcome break from eating our usual "cowboy food" in the barn kitchen. Tex was pretty good at making ham hock stew with frijoles beans, but Mrs. Dunn's grub was better. When Tex made a fresh batch, though, it lasted us for days. I don't know why, but it always tasted best on the second or third day, especially when I poured in extra hot sauce. Every once in a while, as an added treat, Tex would buy a six-pack and pour beer in it, too, which gave the stew a richer flavor.

I spent some wonderful evenings and dinners with both the Dunn and Smithers families, including time playing with their dogs and kids. The kids liked to sit and listen to me play the mouth organ. To be honest, there were many nights I thought of the Dunn and Smithers families as true godsends, because I craved a sense of belonging to a family, even if they weren't my own.

There are snapshots I hold in my mind of times in which certain people showed me unexpected affection during those early years in Kentucky. I think they must have felt sorry for me—as if they knew I needed a little extra help. I never asked for it, and, at the time, I didn't think I was being transparent in my need for it, but sometimes people just understand the things we need even if we aren't aware of it ourselves.

The Rogerses never had any children, and, after being around the farm for some time, they had really taken a liking to me, especially Mr. and Mrs. Joe Rogers. Jack Rogers's wife had died long before we arrived, and he had become something of a recluse ever since her passing. Whenever I saw him, he was usually dressed in dingy clothing. By looking at him, you'd never guess the man had even two nickels to rub together. I don't know what he was like before his wife died, but it appeared he didn't much care about anything now.

Mrs. Joe Rogers was an elegant woman who was always dressed impeccably, like something out of a movie. I asked Mr. Joe if there was something wrong with her hands and arms because she always had long gloves on. He told me that was the way women dressed in the South. I didn't press it, but I didn't see anybody else in town who dressed like that. She occasionally invited Tex and me to their mansion for dinner, so we dressed up the best we could, though neither of us had the proper clothing for the occasion. I was always happy to have a home-cooked meal served on silver trays. There was something special about being invited to the mansion. Tex would be on his very best behavior, but he'd grumble afterward about missing his chew and whiskey.

One afternoon, Mrs. Rogers made a special trip to the farm just to visit me. When her husband heard about it, he was utterly stunned. He said she had never been to the barn before that visit. Mrs. Rogers was always telling me I was too thin, that I needed to eat more. I guess that was why she invited me to dinner from time to time. She may have been right, because I was fifteen years old and weighed just seventy-three pounds. I accepted the vitamins, thanked her for her concern, and chucked them in my bag.

Christmas came and went, and I had brief moments thinking of the family I had left in Toronto. I wondered how big my sister Ginny had become. I thought about Christmas in Canada with all of the music and decorations. There was some of it in Versailles. The pool hall had a Christmas special menu, and we had brief reminders of Christmas when we came in on Saturday evening. There was a tree and some decorations there, but there were no cards or gifts. Until I saw those holiday decorations, I had forgotten what day it was. For a brief moment, I wondered what my family was doing and thought about how they were. Time passed quickly, though, and we basically worked on through the holiday, so it became just another day.

Over the next several months, the older horses were taking shape, and it got to the point where we could clip them and groom them without a fight. I let them fast gallop on the straightaways of the makeshift track, and their eagerness increased. They wanted to go faster. We had come about as far as we could with what we had.

We had nothing like a practice gate on the farm and no racetrack with fences or rails to run between. The starting gate is a noisy contraption. It clangs, bangs, rocks, and can be startling when the door slams behind you. Horses act up and can sometimes flip backwards or rear up. All sorts of accidents can happen in an instant. It's like standing in the middle of two passing subway trains going in opposite directions. Everything happens so fast, and your feelings of chaos and excitement collide.

We had fields and could steer them, but it wasn't the same experience for the horse or the jockey. They had to progress to the next step. We'd have to figure something out to get them used to the starting gates if we stood any real shot of making racehorses out of them before we shipped them all the way to Canada, which was the plan. After many inquiries, our only option was the Red Mile in Lexington. It was a standardbred track with a dirt surface, and they would rent stalls by the day. Mr. Jack made the arrangements for stalls and available dates. There was no trot meet going on yet so we had time to work.

The Rogers brothers bitched and moaned about the cost of vanning us in to Lexington, but it had to be done. Still, no names or confirmation on registration papers came back from the Jockey Club in New York. Several of the horses had been pasture bred, which created another hurdle. Times bred and foaled and other details were scant, and the answers were slow in coming.

Against all odds, by March 1953, we had done the impossible. We had finally trained those wild horses and made something out of them. The Rogers brothers drove out to the farm and were stunned by the miraculous feat we had pulled off. They were actually prideful and amazed at what we had done. When they walked through the barn, they barely recognized the horses they hadn't seen for years. I really felt good about their comments. It made the pain and suffering seem worth it, and it taught me a lot.

The six-horse bobtail van pulled up to the barn to take two of the horses with us to the Red Mile for training and some gate work. Tex chose which two horses would go. The decision to take only a couple at a time made sense. They had never been that close to a truck before, let alone *in* one. We planned to make three separate trips. The ramp on the bobtailed van was put down. I was to direct the loading and lead the horse with the three big men, including the van driver who was assisting us.

What followed was a scene Barnum & Bailey would have paid a lot to stage—and even more if Clyde Beatty conducted the show! After receiving a slap on the ass with a shank, the first horse jumped from the ground to the floor of the van without even touching the ramp. The men raised the ramp quickly, leaving me in charge of the six-year-old in the close quarters of the truck. He lunged forward and into the partition; I snatched the shank in a down-and-backward motion. His ass and hocks hit the side of the stall as he backed up. He kicked so hard that he split the boards and dented the inside of the truck's metal body. I immediately snapped the two chains of the guideposts that were on either side of his head to his halter, but he wouldn't stop kicking! I hollered for the others to drop the ramp and help me put the breast bar in place to keep him from lunging against the chains. They raced to comply while I ducked out of the truck to retrieve a hay net that I had prepared from the barn.

"Not yet!" Smithers barked. "There's not enough room."

He was right. I placed the shank through the halter and mouth of the second horse to be placed in the truck. It was Speak Free. Tex was anxious to train him for a lot of reasons. He jogged out of the stall, pulling me along with him to the foot of the ramp. This bastard was breathing fire again in the cold morning air. Speak Free could see the head of the other horse in the van and hear its digging and kicking against the old board floors. If I got that far I was going to have to turn the second horse to the right and back him into the stall, facing the six-year-old that was already inside with the breast bar in front of him. I figured Speak Free recognized our team from previous encounters and knew of our tenacity. The three men got behind the horse again, and J. T. and T. locked arms just above his hocks. I was glad they didn't hit him. This bastard didn't like people anyway. Speak Free reared up as high as he could and threw his head against the pressure of the shank that I was holding. Then he flipped completely upside down, and as he did, his thrashing head caught the leg of the van driver, sending him to the ground in a dusty heap. I slackened the shank and moved quickly toward the horse to keep from letting go.

The driver rolled around in pain, holding his left leg. "I think it's broke!" he screamed. Fortunately, it wasn't.

Speak Free righted himself and quickly bounded to his feet. J. T. raced toward me, retrieved the shank I was holding, and secured the horse by turning him in circles. T. rushed into the barn to get an old hood from the tack trunk on the floor of the feed room. By bearing down on the shank, J. T. forced the horse's head low enough for T. to slip the hood in place. Then, J. T. handed the shank back to me. Tex was tending to the downed driver for fear he would retreat and leave us stranded. As a result of the somersault, we were a dozen feet from the truck now. This time, I had a blind horse to contend with. J. T. and T. locked arms again and leaned into the horse's ass. Somehow they managed to shove him toward the ramp. Speak Free was resisting, but at least he was facing in the right direction. I took baby steps onto the ramp. Tex joined the back pair's efforts to get him to move, until he finally scrambled up into the truck. I kept pace, turned him quickly, and was met by J. T., who, with a shoulder to the horse's chest, gave a mighty shove sending the animal back between the partitions. I reached for the chains on the guideposts and snapped them into place on the halter. We had done it! T. joined J. T. in placing the heavy iron breast bar in the locks, and I tied two hay nets in front of the horses. The driver was limping badly as we put the saddle, bridle, a bucket, brush, and sponge in the small boot of the truck.

"Do you want me to drive?" Tex offered.

"No," grunted the van driver as he pulled himself up and into the cab. "We're already two hours late, and I don't get paid extra for clusterfucks."

We were sweating through our shirts in the forty-degree air. After I got into the back with the horses, the ramp was raised and locked into place. I turned a water bucket upside down to sit. I didn't have a very good feeling about the ride to Lexington. Between the horses' sharp snorts of disapproval and their loud chomping on snatches of hay, they dug in their hooves and continued to kick about. The unevenness of the ride kept them braced and occupied for most of the time. I couldn't see outside because the windows were so small and placed up high, so I scanned the interior for an exit strategy instead. Although I didn't find one, I felt better when I realized Speak Free still had his hood on.

In about thirty minutes, the truck slowed to a stop, and the ramp banged to the ground. I undid the hay nets and threw them to one side. We were in a barn area with a lot of funny little carts leaning up against their sides.

"Them's sulkies," the driver blurted out.

Sulkies are two-wheeled carts that trotters and pacers use during standardbred racing. It was nothing like anything we'd ever used in the Thoroughbred business.

Tex approached Speak Free, fidgeted with the breast bar to release it, secured the shank, and led the horse hesitantly down the ramp. The driver grimaced in pain as he too climbed the steep ramp. He undid the breast bar in front of the other horse. I had placed the extra shank through the halter and through his mouth before snapping it in place on the other side. The driver moved out of the way, and I commenced to lead the six-year-old from his stall, pausing at the top of the ramp for a moment. The next thing I knew, a thousand pounds of fur were flying right past me, sending me up into the air on the end of the shank. I let go and realized the bastard had jumped and crashed headfirst into Tex and Speak Free. When I landed headfirst on the ground, I caught sight of the flying horse broadsiding Tex and Speak Free, releasing the latter from his hood and hold. Tex was just sitting on the ground coughing convulsively as the two horses bolted wildly toward a shitpit. Amid his violent choking, Tex vomited, and out came an awful brown mess. It took me a minute to realize that he had swallowed his mouthful of Beech-Nut chew!

"Jesus Christ, Sonny Boy! Why in the hell did you turn him loose?" he hollered in a loud accusing tone.

"Because I can't fucking fly," I retorted in a loud angry voice.

People began gathering around and pointing to where they thought the horses went. The driver slowly descended the ramp, nursing his leg in the process.

"Get your shit out of the van. I ain't taking you back!" he yelled.

By then, Tex was on his feet, chest stuck out in an imposing stance. "What the hell are you talking about?" he shot back.

"You've tore the shit out of my track, nearly killed me, and spit tobacco all over the cab!" the driver shouted. "This is a horse van, not a fuckin' circus!"

"Now looky here, you asshole," Tex bellowed with clenched fists.

I stepped in and grabbed his arm. "Come on Tex, let's find the horses," I said. I had never seen him so mad, and I could picture us all in jail if it got any worse. Luckily, he let it go.

The two horses were captured and placed in stalls allotted by the Red Mile folks. We examined them and found no injuries or ill effects. It was too late to train them that day, as there were stipulated times that ended at noon. So we contacted a different van company to make arrangements to take the horses back to the farm the following morning after training. We also convinced a guy stabled next to us to feed and water the two horses at the end of the day. I volunteered to stay behind with the horses, but Tex insisted we return to the farm and train the rest.

We inquired and found a van going to Versailles and rode it back with saddle and bridle in hand. I was exhausted but frankly more tired of the random and rugged contingencies we had to deal with from day to day.

It took a week longer to execute the training plan, but at least, with the exception of the loading and vanning, things went unusually well. We abandoned the starting gate work, as it was only operating two days a week, and the lineup because the volume of horses made it prohibitive, even though it was really the main reason we came to the track.

Time passed slowly, but the horses were manageable, and the training we were able to accomplish in the dramatically shortened training time we had left went well. The weather was improving, so I rode down after training to swim all but the two-year-olds in the cold water of the Big Sink. It was fun for me, and it provided a badly needed bath for the horses. By the time I finished breaking and training them, I could ride anything under pretty much any circumstances. We were ready. It was late March and time to pack up and head north to Canada.

Knowing we were getting out of Versailles left me with one overwhelming thought: *I'm finally going to see civilization again!*

Deep down, the idea of seeing my mom and dad didn't sound too bad, either.

To celebrate our impending departure, Tex took me aside and asked, "Sonny Boy, what do you want to do tonight?" He was acting like a real big shot and grinning like a jackass eating briars.

"Let's go to the pool hall and have a fish sandwich. You can do your thing with the ladies at the Colonial, and I can come back and get you when you're done," I said.

Tex thought that was a swell idea.

I wanted to go to bed at a decent hour because I knew we were going to get an early start the next day. I drove back to the hotel to pick up Tex as planned and sat in the parking lot like always. I waited and waited, but still there was no sign of Tex. I'd periodically start the engine so the heat could keep me warm, but I didn't leave it running for too long, as I wanted to preserve fuel. We had a long trip ahead of us, and I didn't want to waste gas idling outside the Colonial. I was dead tired, and I wanted to go to sleep. I was growing impatient with every passing second. Finally, I couldn't stand it anymore.

I stormed into the hotel and banged on the door where I thought Tex was, but no one answered. So I walked around to the front of the building and headed down a long hallway, where I spotted Tex holding a bottle of whiskey and wearing nothing but his long underwear—the kind with the trap door in the back.

"What the hell are you doing, Tex?" I asked.

"Oh, who let you in?" he slurred, sounding more like a bear who just woke up after his winter slumber. "I'm a comin', Sonny Boy. I'll be out in a minute."

"I am not waiting. I am going to leave you here if you don't come out now," I insisted.

Tex was done screwing, but he was having a party of some sort. He was having a hell of a good time while making me wait outside in the cold.

One of the "ladies of the night" peeked through a cracked door and whispered, "I'll get him out of here for ya. Don't you worry, son."

I looked at her without saying a word. I could smell her cheap French perfume from ten feet away. I didn't particularly care for the fragrance.

I stormed back to the car, still seething mad. We had a stable of horses ready to trailer before leaving for Canada the next day. I really needed to get some shut-eye. I didn't want to sit in that cold car one minute longer, especially with the fifty-hour ride I had in the back of the van earlier.

Yet I sat.

And waited.

And waited.

Seeing Tex in the whorehouse that night was like watching a massive out-of-control bull in a china shop. I wondered how he ever got laid chewing tobacco the way he did. I couldn't imagine anyone wanting to be intimate with him.

And then I remembered asking Tex once why he liked drinking whiskey right out of the bottle instead of a glass. He said he didn't want it to get contaminated. He wouldn't drink it out of an empty peanut butter jar for the same reason. I guess he liked his whiskey pure and his women dirty.

Finally, after what felt like another hour, Tex opened the passenger door and slid his drunken, limp body into the car.

"Sonny Boy, everything is going to be great. You can't worry so much at your age. By God, son. You're fifteen years old. Be happy!"

I didn't know what to say.

"You don't understand, boy. These are the same girls that are at the Lafayette Hotel for twenty dollars, and they're ten dollars here at the Colonial . . ."

He was mumbling more than talking sense at this point, but I knew what he was trying to say. He thought he was making a great business decision, paying half the price for the same women. Each time he brought it up, though, he changed the price.

I saw a few of the women out of the corner of my eye when I was inside the hotel. They were all warhorses. They looked like my aunts, and, believe me, there wasn't one part of me that wanted to lay any of those old broads. I was still a maiden and willing to wait it out if those women were my only options.

I put the car in first gear and punched the gas. We weren't even out of the hotel parking lot before Tex was passed out and snoring.

CHAPTER SEVEN

By the time we got up to Toronto, I was so fit, I squeaked. I felt sharp and strong—like I could fly. I was full of fresh, young enthusiasm and ready to ride my first race as a professional jockey. After putting in my time as a groom, hot walker, and exercise boy, I was finally going to get my shot at it. Hell, I earned the honor from the ground up.

In the mid-1950s there were three or four racecourses around Toronto that were each owned by different people or organizations. Each track had six-, seven-, and ten-day meetings that shifted from one to another like a stage play shifts theaters. The first meet we went to was at Woodbine, located at Woodbine Avenue and Lake Ontario, about ten miles away from where my parents lived, so I didn't see them when I first returned to Toronto. Besides, I was too focused on the opportunity I had to ride these sons of bitches to make those arrangements just yet. I knew I could race successfully, and soon a lot of other people would see I could, too.

The Ontario Jockey Club, led by directors E. P. Taylor, George C. Hendrie, and J. E. Frowde Seagram, ran Woodbine. The company was established to improve the overall quality of horse racing in Ontario. The racing commission was the governing body in charge of all the rules. You might say my fate was in their hands. To be approved, the starter also had to okay you out of the gate. There is a process they go through to make sure you are capable and not a danger to yourself or to those around you. Luckily, a lot of people at the track remembered me from the days when I used to run sandwiches and food to the jockey room. I wasn't a stranger to anyone at this particular track. I had established myself as a budding, talented rider long before I ever left for Kentucky.

Unfortunately, there was no room for us when we got to Toronto. Stalls were at a premium at Woodbine, so we were stabled at Long Branch race-course, which was about twelve miles away. We had a lot to do upon arrival. None of the "wild-assed horses" had been in or around a starting gate, and getting them used to it wasn't going to be easy. Tex had to hire a couple of grooms, because I couldn't do it all. Of course, he wasn't very happy about that. Word was spreading fast about the bunch of horses we had brought with us. Tex asked two other exercise riders to come by and ride in the mornings so we could school the horses in company. Tex had purchased two more used saddles and bridles, and I was really looking forward to the help. But the two grooms who worked for us were terrified of the horses and didn't do a very good job. They eventually quit and were replaced by two more.

The first morning the two riders showed up, we had three horses tacked up and ready to go. It became a circus. They were to ride the two six-year-olds, and I was on Speak Free. They never made it to the racetrack. Their two horses pitched and lunged, and the riders eventually bailed. I continued onto the track and completed my round. When I returned to the barn, Tex was holding one of the loose horses, and the other was in a stall. I rode them all that morning and for the next several weeks. We couldn't hire anyone else. The word was out! The stories multiplied.

They said, "Some crazy bastards shipped in with five-, six-, and seven-year-old wild horses."

We were known as brand X, and no one would come near us. The racing officials were getting leery of the entire mess. Tex was called to the steward's office to explain the circumstances over and over again.

"They're pickin' on us," he told me. "They don't understand."

Because of the fact my father and uncles were all racing officials, I was familiar with everyone working there. Doug Haig was the starter. In other words, he was the official in charge of schooling and approving horses and jockeys out of the starter gate. It is an important job. I had known Doug since I was a little kid. He was a friend, and now I needed his support badly. I spent a lot of time explaining our plight to him. After many hours of schooling sessions and many difficult episodes, Doug eventually approved the horses and me as their jockey. But the matter was not resolved in the usual manner. These horses could never be totally integrated into the system and would always need "special" assistance, meaning that they would be required to be "tong and tailed" whenever they used the starting gate. Tongs are very much like large hinged nutcrackers that are placed on the horse's ear while he's in the gate. Tailing means a man or several men have to hold the horse's tail upward to help keep him from flipping backward or sitting down in the contraption. Doug and his crew worked tirelessly with the horses and me to arrive at this solution. It was the safest measure under the conditions. It was a masterful act on his part, and I was very grateful.

It didn't take long for other trainers to begin asking me to ride their horses during morning training. It wasn't instant, and it didn't come easy. But once it started, it never stopped.

Tex and I decided I would ride Small Play, the filly we recovered after the fire at Waterford Park. She knew me well, and I had groomed her, fed her, and galloped her every morning. We were like close friends. Sometimes she'd buck and play with me when I was on her. But it was always done with affection. Despite what she had been through in the past, Small Play had always worked well with me. Now it was time to see if we could transfer that union to the afternoon races.

On the day before my first race, I was so excited. After finishing work for Tex that morning, I galloped two outside horses and received four dollars in cash. I asked jockey Kenny Clemes for a ride in his car on the way to Woodbine. Kenny had always been my mentor. He taught me so much of what it would be like to race. He dropped me off at a small store that carried kids clothes. I wanted to look nice for the jockeys' room. I bought a new pair of pants and a checkered shirt, size six, and hitchhiked back to Long Branch racetrack, where I was staying in a tack room at Tex's end of the barn. Kenny had made arrangements for me to borrow secondhand riding pants, boots, a jock strap, and a ten-pound saddle when I arrived at Woodbine the next day. I didn't have to worry about a whip, because they wouldn't let ten-pound apprentices use one, even though I had carried one in the mornings a hundred times before for workouts.

I proceeded to the track kitchen with two of our grooms, Fred Bixler and a man named Tuckey. I don't know if he had a real name. Fred had been a sailor on the *Wasp*, a navy aircraft carrier that I think he said sank in the war. He talked about it all the time. We had meal tickets that we bought on payday, which the staff would punch every time we ate at the kitchen, which was most of the time. The favorite expression was, "You can't drink your meal ticket." We all had heard at one time or another that meal tickets saved lives because they kept the stable help on the premises and out of the beer halls. I spent most of the afternoon pulling Small Play's mane and tail and trimming the hair out of her eyes and under her chin; that way she would look like a stakes horse when I rode her, even though she was running in a claiming race. I also cleaned the bridle until it shone. I had learned to be a really good groom in my few years with Tex.

I knew the racetrack community well and could call most of its members by their first names. After all, I had walked hots, galloped, collected lunch, and cut hair for many of them just a few years earlier. It was my home, and I felt like everyone was rooting for me. I can't say that I grew up there, because I hadn't really grown up yet, but I did spend my formative years there.

Tex said I couldn't drive the old Buick, because the town was too big and I'd get caught, even though I had already put thousands of miles on it while Tex slept.

That night, I closed the tack room door after topping off the horses' water buckets and filling the wood-burning boiler for the their baths the next morning after training. Somebody stepping off a van that was returning from the races at Woodbine handed me an overnight sheet listing all of the next day's entries and races. Unlike the turkey house in Kentucky, the tack room had a naked light bulb at the end of an extension cord. I stood under it looking for the horse's name and mine. Once I found it, I climbed into the cot, covered myself with a heavy blanket, and fell sound asleep staring at it. It was one of the most exciting few minutes of my life.

I was finally a jockey.

Five a.m. came quickly. I banged on the stall door at the end of the barn where the two grooms slept.

"Let's go," I said, in a nice but hurried voice.

I started unsnapping the big metal feed tubs from their hanging positions across from each horse's stall. Tuckey staggered out about twenty feet in front of the barn and lit the kindling under the boiler. Fred joined me carrying each tub to the feed room, where he remained to ladle ten quarts of oats, a fistful of salt, and half a beaker of flaxseed into each of the colts' and geldings' tubs. The fillies got eight quarts each.

"Don't forget to put the muzzle on Small Play when she's done," I hollered at Fred. We had to take her off of all feed and water before she raced.

It was called "drawing," which helped prevent horses from bleeding through the nostrils when they competed.

Tex arrived just before six o'clock and handed me a set of black-and-red silks with a big *L* on the front.

"Take these with you when you head to the jock's room," he ordered.

I immediately hung the silks with my new clothes in the tack room so I didn't forget them.

"I'll have to leave an hour earlier," I advised Tex. "The track doctor's got to inspect me or something before I can ride, and I got to get a skullcap from somewhere."

The skullcap was a corrugated headpiece that you wore under the silk riding cap for protection. (It offered about as much protection as cardboard, I would find out later.) Tex announced that he hired two freelance hot walkers to help out.

Morning training and chores went off without a hitch. Small Play didn't train that morning because she was racing, so I got done earlier than usual.

I grabbed the racing silks and headed off to catch a horse van to the jock's room. Most young guys would feel some sort of nervousness and anticipation when entering a new environment. I had a distinct edge, though, as I had been frequenting jockey's rooms for a number of years before I left for Kentucky.

The jock's room consisted of a couple of offices to house the weigh scales, rows of wooden lockers, and large wooden tables used to clean and polish boots, saddles, and assorted equipment. The other office room housed the racing silks, which hung from elevated racks. There were a half dozen cots where jockeys could sleep or rest before racing. The competition is a whole lot different when you're in the jock's room as a rider. You might think it is going to bring you closer to the other riders, but it doesn't. I suppose it's like any other competition where you have to wear your game face. For the first time in my life, I was no longer in the jock's room to make friends. I was there to win races.

As I entered, I started to feel a little uneasy, but not because I was concerned about the race. I was as close to Small Play as a boy could be to an animal. And she knew me, too. We'd gone through a horrible fire together. I'd fed and groomed her and been on her in morning training hundreds of times. I was familiar with the starter, Doug Haig, and his crew working with the wild ass horses, and I'd been on the Woodbine racetrack since I started to learn how to gallop.

The uneasy feeling came more because I was finally acknowledging how close to home I really was. I hadn't talked to or seen my father or mother in over two years. What would they be like? Would my father still harbor hate for me dating back to the day I confronted him with the gun? My life was very different from what it was when I left home.

To hell with it, I thought.

One thing was certain: I wasn't going to take any shit from my father.

I knew I would run into him because he worked at the track. There would surely be a confrontation. Or would there? I had no idea how he would react. He had no reason to be nice. Neither did I. As I was mulling these thoughts over, I rounded the turn off the parking lot and entered the scale room on the ground floor. The main body of work was always done upstairs. I headed through the glass door, and there they were, the two brothers: my father and my uncle. Both had ridden races years ago, so they understood what I was about to do. They got up from their chairs, stuck their hands out, and gave me a sincere handshake.

"Hello," I said. "Good to see you both."

"Welcome back, Joe," my father responded, using a nickname that he called me ever since I could remember. I was relieved that he chose "Joe" over "Asshole" or "Little Asshole," which were two of his favorite expressions he used while I was growing up. At least "Joe" was softer and a little more palatable.

They both smiled, and I surprisingly sensed some pride from my father. He instructed me to sign the apprentice jockey license that he had laid on the desk.

"Go upstairs, turn the silks in, and find Midge Newman. He's your valet and expecting you," he said.

I bounded up the stairs two at a time and thought, *Did that really just happen?* I was eager to get past that initial meeting and the starkness of that confrontation. I had only pictured seeing my father one-on-one. I was very grateful and relieved my uncle was there to cushion the blow. It was different from what I thought it would be and much better than I expected or could have hoped.

Midge Newman was happy to see me. We fussed with the saddle. He set the stirrup webbings a little longer than I wanted, but I knew that I could adjust them in the paddock. The doctor came and went and asked about some bruises on my back and arm, but overall it was a half-assed medical check. The old doc was a bettor, and he was anxious to get away from this green kid and talk to the other, more seasoned riders who could try and give him a winner. The next step was to check my weight with the saddle and equipment (you don't weigh out with the skullcap and whip). I had tried on several skullcaps and found only one that was comfortable. The borrowed boots and pants already fit, so I was all set.

Several riders I knew really teased me by asking if I would run out and get them some Cokes and roast beef sandwiches. I laughed with them and thought about how far I had come in only a few short years.

I was in an early race, and it came quick. I weighed out, received a few pats on the ass for good luck, and entered the saddling paddock. Norm and Marion Heaton stepped forward as I approached the saddling stalls. I received a kiss from Marion and a handshake from Norm. They were the proud owners of a horse that had done no good at their expense. They were good sports, though, and were anxious to know if I would make a difference today.

Tex was chewing on a big cigar, even though he seldom ever lit one. He was about as dressed up as he could be with an old suit jacket over a stained plaid shirt. Small Play's coat just shined. She looked so good, I thought.

The paddock had attracted a good group of well-wishers. I felt important, as Tex responded to the paddock judge's command of "Riders Up." There hadn't been much instruction from Tex as to how to ride the race. It's difficult to give instructions on how to ride a five-year-old maiden.

I was impressed with the ritual of the post parade. It was a pretty sight, well-controlled and well-timed with the horses arriving at the starting gate at post time, which was observed closely by the stewards from the information on the centerfield tote board.

As we approached the starting gate, most of the maidens got into a nervous prance. Some were sweating on a rather cool and overcast spring day. I don't think horses or people alike ever feel truly comfortable in this padded metal contraption. It rocks and clangs as the doors slam shut and the inmates squat, kick, and sometimes charge the bars on the V-shaped front doors. Riders holler, "no chance boss," sporadically from within the cage. The assistant starters crouch, bridle in hand, on the left side of each mount. One rears up, and the ceremony of clamor starts. There isn't much that's nice about it. Eyes straight ahead, a half-cross of the reins against a finger full of mane in the left hand, with the right stick hand free. Small Play was always a little difficult to get into the gate. She was hesitant because she was a bitchy, headstrong mare. Those few seconds before the announcer calls the start of a race are extremely intense. A Thoroughbred race going short can be one of the highest forms of organized chaos. In a short race, the emphasis on the start is more acute than in a long race.

In a split second, an ear-piercing bell will explode atop the gate, and the front doors will open with a loud clang. Little men on thousand-pound beasts will accelerate from a standstill to a full panicked gait in only two jumps. It's a perilous, frenzied start that happens nine times a day at the track. No athlete in any other sport in the world confronts this dizzying and desperate beginning to a contest!

It's a complete, combustible excitement that makes you feel as if you're a bullet being shot out of a 9mm handgun.

I left the gate moderately urging my horse to keep up with the field, but I was totally unprepared for what was taking place around me. Things were happening at an incredible speed. It was not like the fast works of our morning training. It was insanely noisy. Horses were in desperately close quarters. Their exhalations were like a chorus of low octave roars, while the stinging acceleration of their bodies hummed backup. The blurred forms all around us seemed to be guided toward the inside rail, but I could see we were a long way from the turn. Jockeys were snatching the horses' bobbing heads to keep them from funneling into the danger of closing holes.

I had a moderate hold of the reins in mild restraint. We were being outrun, and by now we were on the outside of four horses. I felt Small Play's lead change with a jarring vibration all through her bones as we entered the turn. I am a passenger, I thought—not a pilot! What I was experiencing had absolutely no connection to watching a race from the grandstand. From my crouched position on the outside, I took a rough count of six horses in front of us as we flashed by the black-and-white pole at the point of the turn. I hadn't helped this mare one damned bit yet. A cold shiver of frustration ran up my spine as we sped by the quarter pole. In what seemed an instinctive gesture, I changed the position of my hands and took a fresh cross higher on her neck as I hollered, "Get on with it, Mommy!" My body suddenly conformed to the mare's stride with energetic forward motion. A synchronized trill of clucking and chirping emanated from my mouth. I had no whip, so my arms began to pump the air beneath them in a coordinated fashion. First, one ear came back and then the other flattened as the mare's gait lengthened in a determined mass of exertion.

We passed by one horse and then another.

What a feeling! I concluded mentally.

But it was too late. Even though we caught two more horses in less than a sixteenth of a mile, we finished a closing fourth as we sped under the wire.

While I had the instinct to be a good rider, my lack of experience cost Small Play her opportunity to win the race. After acknowledging that truth, I secretly vowed never to let inexperience get in the way of winning again. I was happy, though, to get through the race and make a good showing. At least I had one try under my belt. There was also some consolation in knowing what to expect the next time around. No matter how much time I spent on horses after that day, I never experienced the same electricity while training them as I did when I was riding with them in a competition— reading them based on what the other horses are doing and anticipating their response. You simply can't get that sensation or develop that instinct in training. It comes with every moment you spend in a race.

When you are in a competition, you get a feeling of how much horse you have under you and whether he or she has a chance. And, if they do, you have to have an arsenal of strategies in place based on his or her competency and fitness to increase those chances. While I had good instincts, I didn't yet have a strategy. I knew the basics, but I didn't have enough experience to master the nuances and intricacies that separate great jockeys from the rest of the athletes.

When I cantered back, The Heatons and Tex were at the unsaddling area in front of the grandstand, adjacent to the scale house where jockeys weigh in after a race. They were elated. Small Play had never run that well before, and, for a fourth-place finish, the group would get a check. They were so excited that I decided not to disclose what they couldn't see from the grandstand: that the level of my inexperience may have cost them a bigger check. I was happy for Small Play. I loved her, and I think she loved me, so why put a damper on her accomplishment—even if it was in a cheap claiming race. I walked back to the jock's room through a crowd of well-wishers and smiling faces. This was a kind of theater I hadn't expected. It was part of the essence of the sport, and in an instant I realized that I had become a small part of that essence too!

I showered, dressed, and walked to the barn area, where the happy group greeted me again. Tex had ordered me to hurry so I could finish cooling out the mare, which I did.

All great athletes understand victory comes from the neck up. While natural ability and supreme physical fitness will get you a long way, strategy, calculation, common sense, and mindset dictate your outcome. If you don't have those, you won't win very often.

Several days later, Tex entered the first of the Rogers brothers' group in a race. The horse was a seventeen-hand, three-year-old, first-time starter named Finespun, a chestnut filly with enormous ears. The conditions weren't ideal, and it was raining heavily. The track was sloppy, and, unless you were at the head of the pack, it was going to be nearly impossible to see. There was consternation over whether it was even safe to compete in such conditions. I begged and pleaded with Tex. We were both green, so we weren't expected to do well, let alone win. Under those circumstances, it didn't seem as if participating was going to hurt us. Tex finally relented, agreeing that there was no threat to our chances, because Finespun had no real chances.

The orders in the paddock were minimal, as she was a maiden and had no prior racing experience. I was the only jockey who had ever ridden her. Tex doubted she could win—not to mention coming in the money. There was no background to judge her on. He told me to do the best I could as he threw me up.

"Have a good trip, Sonny Boy," Tex said.

The post parade was cut short due to the weather. It was starting to rain again, and the track was already sloppy. It was a rare occurrence to let a bug boy, an apprentice, run in a race like this. It was only my second ride. Luckily, I was granted permission to carry a whip. I thought it would enhance her performance and therefore increase my chances of winning. If you hit some horses in the ass hard enough, they'll run like hell. I knew this big filly could run, so I wanted every edge I could get.

They loaded her into the gate fine. She broke a little tardy, but I urged her up and outside of two horses going into the turn.

I am cookin' an lookin', I thought with a hand full of horse.

As we left the quarter pole at the head of the stretch, I steered her out in what I thought would be the shallower passage, clucked to her once, and put away the leader with just a hand ride. It was hard to describe what it was like to be on the lead going under the wire.

I just won, I thought, feeling my heart pound in jubilation. Finespun and I had come a long way from Versailles, Kentucky, and we weren't maidens anymore!

I was covered in slop, but I felt totally ecstatic. And, unlike my first race, this time I contributed to the win because I went in with a strategy.

Any ceremony there would have been was "tamped" by the weather, but I was requested to go up to the steward's stand, where stewards Bill Risewick and Wilbur Weber congratulated me.

Tex had shown up late for the picture in the winner's circle. His eyes displayed total astonishment from under his soiled Stetson.

"Tell me about it, Sonny Boy," he said. "I didn't see most of it. Hurry back to the barn so we can talk."

When I walked into the jock's room and up the stairs, four jockeys cornered me. They immediately grabbed me in a hammerlock and pulled down my mud-soaked britches, while a fifth painted my balls and dick with bright-red boot dye. It was a ritual that followed a maiden victory, my smiling father explained. While maiden victories are still celebrated today, I believe jockeys mostly endure a bucket of water over their heads. No matter how you celebrate, it's still a great feeling for the jockey to earn that first win.

Kenny Clemes, the jockey who originally introduced me to Tex and was my main mentor in the early stages of my riding career, was very happy and prideful in his tone.

"Helluva ride, kid!" he said as he gave me a one-armed hug.

Everyone in the place was slapping me on the back and giving me the adulation of a champ.

Winning my first race signaled many things, including special attention from owners, trainers, and the entire backstretch. My mother even suddenly became interested in where I was living and my general well-being. Naturally, my father took home the daily scuttlebutt from the racetrack. My two uncles, Wilf and Charlie Stevenson, were impressed, especially since Wilf, clerk of the scales, had been the one to weigh me in and out for my first victory.

Weight is important to horsemen and horseplayers, and rulebooks, which to the best of my knowledge haven't changed much if at all since I was racing, allowed special concession throughout North America. For instance, an apprentice jockey may claim the following weight allowances in all overnight races except stakes and handicaps:

1. Ten-pound allowance beginning with the first mount and continuing until the apprentice has ridden five winners.

2. A seven-pound allowance until the apprentice has ridden an additional thirty-five winners.

3. If an apprentice has ridden a total of forty winners prior to the end of a period of one year from the date of riding his/her fifth winner, he/she shall have an allowance of five pounds until one year from the date of the fifth winning mount.

4. If, after one year from the date of the fifth winning mount, the apprentice jockey has not ridden forty winners, the applicable weight allowances shall continue for one more year from the date of the fifth winning mount, or until the fortieth winner, whichever comes first. In no event shall a weight allowance be claimed for more than two years from the date of the fifth winning mount, unless an extension has been granted pursuant to subsection (e) of this Section.

5. A contracted apprentice may claim an allowance of three pounds for an additional one year when riding horses owned or trained by the original contract employer.

Tex showed up at Long Branch in the early morning hours as usual, but this time he was frantic, the unlit cigar making circular motions while he attempted to speak.

"Read this," he slurred in the dim light of morning.

I took the letter into the tack room where I slept and turned on the extension cord with the naked light at the end.

"I got five months of training in these bastards, and now those hardboots don't want to pay me," he chanted over my shoulder as I was trying to read.

The letter contained a ruling by the registrar and the stewards of the Jockey Club. The summation stated that two unnamed seven-year-olds and two unnamed six-year-olds could not be registered. Two five-year-olds, Speak Free and The Rake, were accepted. It appeared, according to the description, that The Rake must be the big lanky horse that is showing some run in the mornings.

"At least we have two of the best ones," I told Tex.

But he continued to be dismayed. Joe Rogers had scribbled all over the letter and indicated he wouldn't be paying for the ones that were turned down.

I understood Tex's frustrations, but his attitude was beginning to grate on me. It wasn't only how he reacted to this news, but how he was reacting to my growing success as well.

Because I had literally grown up in the backstretch, I became an integral part of the colony that inhabited it. I knew everyone there and shared their successes and failures. In turn, they wished for my success. It became almost religious. Now that I was beginning to win races and could ride every rogue and problem horse, morning or afternoon, my main challenge became how to manage my success, however small it was at this point.

My other problem was how to manage Tex. He wouldn't advise me of when and what races he was considering. He disliked the fact I was constantly being sought out in the mornings to exercise or diagnose the trouble with a horse trained by someone else. He insisted I go immediately to the barn to cool out the horses after racing. Perhaps his actions were justified in some way, but nobody else was under those constraints. I just had to find a way to solve the problem. And fast.

I needed an agent!

Jockeys employ agents all the time to solicit mounts for daily programs and to follow the careers of horses intently. They make selections that avoid conflicts between owners and trainers. The good ones are more adept as managers than agents. Though there's very little difference between the two roles, a jockey's agent takes precedence in the rulebooks. It was my father who introduced me to Bob Maxwell, a mild-mannered veteran with good people skills. We had a lengthy discussion that involved my current situation and where I wanted to go in the future. He agreed that he could be helpful, and we made a deal that would last four sensational years.

I was like a child prodigy—a tiny but powerful force that was quickly becoming unstoppable. Owners and trainers alike were clamoring for my services. Tex was the one receiving many of their offers because of the contract he still held for me as a laborer. Of course, Norm Heaton, who had bought half of my contract from a very cash-strapped Tex after the horrible fire in Ohio, was contributing to pay half of my salary too. Norm's young wife, Marion, loved me like a mother loves a son. She didn't have any children of her own, so just like Mrs. Joe Rogers, she kept a loving and watchful eye on me. But that still wasn't enough.

My contract didn't give Tex a piece of my earnings. The only benefit Tex had was the ability to either hold or sell my contract and to have a preference on my services. But the contract did prohibit me from riding against one of Tex's other horses in a race. And it also gave him authority to have me walk his horse after the race even if I rode the race. Despite my clear potential as a jockey, Tex had no intention of letting me out of that agreement or relieving me of my obligation as his stable boy. So in a way, he was holding me back from becoming a better rider merely because he couldn't provide me with better horses. That dichotomy really pissed me off. Whenever I was offered other mounts, I basically had to turn them down unless Tex agreed to it. At this point, Tex had never won so many races in his life. With the exception of Right Move, the two-year-old that was injured in the fire, and the horses with no papers, the rest of the horses I was riding for him were multiple winners.

There are some trainers who do nothing but train and trade horses by claiming races. Because of her recent win, Small Play was claimed in her next start. Basically, Tex had entered her in a $1,500 claiming race; I rode her; and naturally she won. After the group claimed her, they immediately approached me about riding her again—this time for them. I didn't hesitate to say yes. I loved that mare and didn't want to stop riding her. Besides, I knew I could win again on her, and winning races was why I became a jockey. Tex didn't like that very much, because I won four or five straight races on Small Play after that.

"Why didn't you do that for me, Sonny Boy?" he asked in a bristling tone.

The truth is, Tex didn't think much of Small Play, or he wouldn't have run her in so cheap a race in the first place. Her value quickly appreciated upwards of $5,000 as she rose up in the ranks. Tex had clearly left money on the table with his decision.

I told the new owners that I thought Small Play was a decent horse, but I also knew all about the odd quirks they bought into as well. They needed to stretch her out and go long, because she didn't like to go short. If they gave her that, she would win again. And by winning, her status would be elevated even more.

Through feel and instinct I attained the knack of diagnosing or identifying injuries long before a vet could even see them. For example, horses lug in or out during a race and react to heat in a joint as a result of jarring the limb. Jarring causes heat and pressure to build in the joints. These little nuances are the things that a good, experienced, and educated jockey learns when spending time on and around their horses. Not many jockeys begin their racing careers as grooms, but, if they did, they'd have a distinct advantage over those who do not. I had years of experience as a groom before my first mount. Aside from my horsemanship, I was bright and had a good mind and liked my job. I was also fearless and experimental. The more races I rode, the more diagnostic I became. Trainers received information from me that saved and salvaged many horses in a short period of time. I savored much pride in that, and it brought me many good friends. It also improved my confidence to have people recognize that I was good at it.

Among the other owners I helped were the Mezens, who hailed from Western Canada. Harold was a real likeable cowboy, but his wife, Mamie, was an Indian woman with a severe temper. I think they had been part of a Wild West show and had made enough money doing that to buy a farm where they put together a stable of horses a few years before I met them. They had two adopted sons, Les and Jake Nemet.

"Davey, I'm in a real pickle," Harold said one morning. Apparently, he and Mamie had hocked their farm and were about to go broke. Mamie had been drinking heavily and punched Harold, nearly breaking his jaw. Everything they had was at stake.

"Come get on this horse I got," he urged me. "He's runnin' bad, and I don't know what to do."

The horse was named Beach Party. He was a big, stout, flashy chestnut with a white blaze from above his eyes to his nostrils. The boys tacked him up after Harold showed me an old past performance and the latest chart from the *Daily Racing Form*. It appeared he was on his way down from a decent allowance level. I observed it wasn't because of his health, as Jimmy walked him out of the barn. You could almost see your face in the glisten of the coat on his ass.

"Do what you want with him," Harold said, throwing me up. "He's pretty fit 'cause he just run."

I couldn't tell much as we walked to the gap on the outside rail and onto the track. I jogged Beach Party a good eighth of a mile before I let him break into a gallop. I kept a long half-cross in the reigns down his neck, fairly close to his withers just in front of the saddle. To me, the experience was like reading gauges on the dashboard of a car. I couldn't explain it in the same terms then, but I was extrapolating the kinetic energy generating up through the front half of the horse's skeleton to his withers with each motion. To me, it was always detectable. It was always there and exaggerated as the gait increased. The jarring condition would change as conditions in the foot and lower extremities reacted to the banking of the surfaces they were on.

I clucked to Beach Party as he entered a full gallop. He began to lay on the bit into the left side, known as "lugging in." He changed leads several times in an attempt to take the weight off of the left or inside leg. I pulled to the outside, eased him up, and let him walk to the gap where Harold and Les were waiting. I dismounted, and the boys pulled the tack off of the big horse.

"Hold him right there," I ordered, well into my analysis.

I stooped and ran my hands down both legs from just above the knee joint to the coronet band (top of the hoof). There were no visible signs of a popped splint on either cannon bone. (That's when a small swelling occurs on the upper inside of the long tube-shaped bone in the lower leg of a horse.) The ankles felt cold. The suspensory ligaments connecting the tendon sheath to the back of the ankle were tight and also cold. I went back up to the left knee, applied light pressure with my right thumb, and stopped. There definitely was heat in the front of the joint.

"Get me a little cold water and a sponge in a bucket," I told Jake.

After he did, I soaked both knees generously with the sponge. Then, I dangled both hands into the bucket to reduce the heat in my thumbs. I felt the knee again. The heat felt more pronounced.

"There's our problem Harold," I stated confidently.

"Shit," he mumbled.

I then checked the right knee using the same application. It was cold.

The verdict was to call the vet, tap the knee (remove the synovial fluid), and inject synthetic fluid into the joint. At the time, this was a very common procedure, especially to get another race or two out of a horse before laying them up. Today, this procedure has been banned in American racing. Harold was able to enter the horse for the same claiming level he last ran in for four or five days, and I rode him.

So, in five days, we were celebrating a win at 35-1 that yielded a substantial payoff. The purse was small, but Harold and Mamie wagered a hundred dollars in small bills that measured the distance between poverty and success for them.

The winner's circle was boisterous and out of control. I was threatened by near suffocation between Mamie's gigantic bosoms. The most dangerous part of the trip! The horse was fine.

Harold caught me halfway back to the jock's room and thanked me again profusely.

"What's next?" I asked.

"Tell me," he exclaimed.

"Raise him up twenty-five hundred, and run him right back," I said without hesitation.

Harold did as I advised, and five days later we duplicated the plan. Beach Party won with ease, and the raise in claiming price yielded an even higher pari-mutuel return. This time, the Mezens bet three hundred, and the farm was out of hock. Beach Party earned a two-month layoff, and I was left with the memory of just how the expression "betting the farm" originated. I was so happy for them, I wept silently in the seclusion of my tack room and fell sound asleep.

Pari-mutuel wagering, more commonly referred to as "betting," is the blood of horse racing. Governments worldwide separated horse racing from other sports and gambling on the basis that pari-mutuel is a cerebral skill and not a game of chance. In so doing, horse racing has survived as one of the oldest and longest living sports. It benefits all people as a form of entertainment. And as a handicapping sport, it also benefits the minions of laborers who support it—the horse owners, breeders, trainers, and jockeys. Because of small purses, wagering was a common source of occasional revenue for many people.

CHAPTER EIGHT

1953

"That's *my* David. . . ," my grandmother said with great pride every time she saw my picture in the paper after winning a big race.

"I always knew he would make it big," she'd say, beaming from ear to ear.

To her, my success as a young jockey was like the second coming of Speck Ridgway. I quickly became a celebrity around Toronto, especially among the neighborhood friends and cronies who knew our family over the years.

By this time, my father was well aware of many details surrounding my burgeoning career. He knew how much money I was making because he had a position at the tracks—and because people in racing like to talk. In those days, jockeys got their winnings in brown envelopes at the end of the week. My envelopes were beginning to get very big. This is about the time my parents decided I should move back home. They told me they'd look after my earnings so I didn't have to worry about anything but winning races.

I thought about their offer long and hard. But there was no way I would ever move back home and go through their bullshit again. If I returned, it would have to be under my terms. They agreed, as long as I paid "rent."

My father was pleased as punch with the way my career was going. He was rooting for me at every race and relished every win. I was doing all of the things he never did, and he got to live vicariously through those victories. Although our relationship remained contentious, we did find some common ground at the track—especially in the winner's circle.

I wasn't able to enjoy my success as much as my parents did. My mother insisted on opening a joint bank account.

"What if you get killed, and we can't get the money?" she asked.

I knew she meant well, so I consented. Of course, she was happy about that.

I remember seeing one of my first bank statements and thinking, "That's a lot of money!"

I was soon introduced to income tax and had to start paying attention to my finances. I was always more focused on riding than the money I was earning. I was never in the sport for the prize so much as the pride.

I bought a car for myself—a 1952 Ford Meteor, the first car I ever owned—and a car for my parents, too. I even got them a washer and dryer for their house and other appliances to make life a little nicer and easier. I paid the mortgage, made improvements, and footed the bill for everything along the way. I didn't begrudge them, because money was never a turn-on for me. I never thought about it as anything other than a by-product of success. In some ways, I felt obligated, like I should do those things because I was their son and I was able to.

Besides, what was I going to do with all of that money?

I couldn't go out at night because I was racing. The one luxury I did indulge in was shopping for nice clothes; though I would still limit myself to the boys' department at Eaton's or Simpson's. I shopped there until I was in my twenties.

Eating and drinking was pretty much out of the question anyway, because I couldn't afford to put on any extra weight. So food became my enemy. My typical breakfast consisted of a single slice of cinnamon toast in the morning, a boiled egg or two for lunch, and maybe a little more bread later in the day. That's about all I ate on any given day. The more I rode, the stronger I got, and the more developed I became. Everything I did was exercise. When you are wrestling and riding thousand-pound horses every day, it bulks you up. So I was starting to get very muscular, which meant I was putting on unwanted weight. While this might have been appealing for most sixteen-year-old boys, for a budding young jockey, it became a nemesis I had to combat in ways that weren't very pleasant. I restricted my diet and ate as little as I possibly could to survive. There were plenty of days I didn't eat at all. I even got to the point where I started using diuretics to drop excess weight. I didn't start to purge until I absolutely felt the need to out of desperation. From my perspective, muscles were a problem. I needed to remain lean and mean if I wanted to be a force of reckoning on the track. And believe me: being a winner is all I could think about day and night.

The more I won, the bigger the social circle got. Suddenly, we were invited to a lot of parties around town. My mother loved to dress up, and now she was able to do that. She was living the life she always dreamt of when I was a boy. To see my mother and father act like they were in love, when I never thought they could be, was incredible, because I never saw that connection growing up. I didn't have to be Dr. Freud to understand something was missing for a very long time. But now, well, they seemed happy. I was providing for my parents in a way they never could have lived on their own. Perhaps that financial freedom gave them some sense of peace. It was clear they would never have to worry about scraping to make ends meet again. If my success had something to do with them finally finding some happiness, then it would have made all of my hard work, sweat, pain, and angst worth it just to see those two smile. While our relationship was never what I'd call close, we certainly found common ground to come together as a family again when I returned home.

While my career as a jockey was catching fire, I could tell that Tex was getting restless. Right around the time things were really starting to take off for me, Tex was itching to ship out, because none of the races were suiting the horses we had. Tex was a notorious drifter. It didn't matter to him one bit that I was the leading apprentice jockey at most of the meetings. In fact, I think it really got under his skin. Even though I was under contract to him and Norm, Tex wasn't making as much money as I was from the races I was in, and he resented my success. To make matters worse, once I started riding as a jockey and winning, the relationship shifted. In his mind, I was no longer an effective barn worker—someone who could ride him all over town, someone he could order to sleep on the ground, or someone he could just boss around. I had money, and he didn't. Tex no longer called all the shots. The only control he had over me was his ability to say when and where we raced. Since I was only a year into my three-year contract, he could still decide when it was time to ship out. As a result, I had to go whenever he got the itch to leave, regardless of how I felt about it.

At the height of my success in Toronto and roughly one hundred wins during my first year as a jockey, Tex came to me and said, "Pack your bags, Sonny Boy. It's time to go."

Shocked by his announcement and unready to leave, I reminded Tex that I had to get immigration papers before I could exit Canada. I didn't have a passport. The last time I went, I didn't have any documentation, and I knew I wouldn't be able to slip through a second time, especially if I intended to continue being a professional rider.

"That's got nothing to do with me. It's not my problem; it's your problem. Figure it out. I'm leaving, and if I'm leaving, you're leaving." He was cold and detached when he spoke.

I knew Tex could have prevented me from riding if he wanted to, so I reluctantly agreed to go without papers. He wanted to head to Thistle Downs, a racecourse in Maple Heights, Ohio, outside of Cleveland. In those days, it was an okay track. It wasn't big, and it wasn't little. Somehow, he picked it out of a hat, convincing himself it would be good for "us."

"We can get a better price on these horses there. They've got a 5-1 mutual. . . ," he started, with the same bullshit I'd heard so many times before. I don't know where he came up with this line of crap, but he used it over and over like it was a broken soundtrack that never stopped repeating.

I had grown in a different direction. I was riding well, I loved the competition, and I was in demand.

Without the proper documents, I wasn't able to take my car, which made Tex happy but me miserable. It relegated me to the back of Bill Wright's old bobtail truck while he hauled our horses down to Ohio. Bill was a drinking buddy of Tex's who could hardly see because he was always hunched over. We loaded up the old boiler in the truck along with four horses and me. Once again, I found myself riding in the back of a filthy van with cracks in the wooden slats beneath my ass. All I I could think at the time was, *Here we go again.*

The truck couldn't drive more than 40 miles per hour, which made the trip linger on for what felt like an eternity. The ride down to Cleveland was an aimless, long, dirty, disastrous stretch that took a full day and night to make. It was topped off by an unexpected flat tire, which only added insult to my ego's injury.

I had gone from being a winning rookie jockey back to being a stable boy overnight. Somehow, thanks to Tex and his need to be on the move, I was right back where I started. It was maddening to be in this position. I was getting more pissed off with every cold and bumpy mile we clocked.

And just when I thought things couldn't get any worse, Bill unexpectedly jerked the wheel of the truck hard to the right, causing the lid of the old wood-burning boiler to slide across the truck and hit one of the fillies in the leg. I was sitting on a turned-over feed tub with a shank on her halter. She immediately flipped over backward and was completely upside down. There was no way to let Bill or Tex, who was following us from behind in his Buick, know what had happened or to tell them to stop the truck. All I could do was try and calm the filly and keep her down until I could get some sense into her. The more restless she got, the more agitated and stirred up the other horses were getting. The truck was rocking back and forth. Straw, hay, lids, rakes, and brooms were flying, and I could hardly see. There was so much commotion coming from the truck that Bill finally stopped it, thinking there was problem with a tire.

Bang!

Clang!

I was locked in the back with four horses going nuts.

When Bill unlatched the truck door, he found me wrestling with them all, trying to keep them safe while fighting for my own life.

It was a hell of a mess to see—scary and hysterical and something I hope to never experience ever again.

The filly suffered some cuts and lacerations, but luckily, they weren't serious. I couldn't take her out of the truck on the highway, so I talked to her, put some oats in a bucket, and got her calmed down before we hit the road again.

When we finally got to Thistle Downs, I got temporary approval to ride without any official documentation. None of the racing officials at the track knew me except for a fellow named Billy Christmas, who had lost some horses in the Waterford Park fire. But it's not like Billy gave a shit about me. There were no Canadian charts in American racing forms, so there were no real connections or even a way to know who I was or where I came from. As far as the American officials were concerned, I didn't exist. Despite that, I showed up with a stable and had a license. I could prove I was a jockey prior to arriving, so somehow the officials allowed me to race.

I buddied up with a fellow rider named Billy Hartack, an apprentice from Pennsylvania who was having a hell of a season. He was such a good rider that I couldn't figure out why he was at Thistle Downs, but I was glad

he was because we got to know each other. He went on to become the leading rider in America in 1953, winning the most races that year.

A couple of days after we arrived, I quickly found an agent who offered
to help me get mounts in exchange for 10 percent of my earnings, plus a little extra on top of that if I did well. I may have paid a little more than the
standard rate, but I was eager to get mounts. To accomplish that, I needed
someone who knew the horsemen and racing officials, so I was willing to be
generous. I wasn't sure how long Tex was planning to stay at Thistle Downs,
but I knew I wanted to make a name for myself, so I went all out, galloping
as many horses as I could, in addition to Tex's, while I was there. I went from
barn to barn visiting and trying to explain how good I was.

It took me about a week and a half of riding like hell before I was riding
high again. I wasn't beating Hartack, but I was gaining on him—and fast.
People began noticing that I was winning on long shots, paying big prices,
that I had a good seat and hands and was very athletic. Everyone liked little
Davey again, and I loved the way that made me feel.

In the mornings after training hours when I wasn't riding, I set up my
barbershop business again, too. I used a tack box or a feed tub upside down
for seating and carried my tools in a small cloth bag.

There were so many familiar grooms, hot walkers, trainers, and the odd
owner coming around saying, "You know my head; can you just give me a
quick trim?"

I thought to myself, *Why not?*

Even if I said I couldn't do it or I was busy, guys would always wait until
I was free. So I figured, what the hell?

Thistle Downs turned out to be a much better experience than I had
expected. I was back in the saddle and riding well, winning eighteen or so
races in less than two weeks at the track on very ordinary horses. I was the
poor man's hope, and the feeling was mutual because no one else wanted to
ride the horses I was on anyway.

It felt great to be back in the States, though, doing what I loved. Now
that I was a little over a year into my riding career, I had slightly more than
one hundred wins under my belt. Today that wouldn't be considered much
of a feat because jockeys ride more horses, have pony escorts going to the
starting gate, and don't get on as many in the mornings. Plus there are more
races, so, generally speaking, it's easier to do. But in the early '50s the herd
was smaller and the rate of incidents with horses that weren't disciplined was

overwhelming, so it was hard to get that many mounts and wins in such a short period of time.

About four weeks into the season, Tex came over to the barn one morning. He stood in front of me with his big cigar off to the side of his mouth, chewing on it like it was a gooey chocolate bar, with brown tobacco juice running down his chin.

"These races . . . they're not suiting me. We gotta go. . . ."

"Son of a Bitch! I am getting bigger and older by the day, Tex. I am doing well. Why are we leaving again?" I wasn't taking his shit quite as well as I used to. This time, I didn't want to leave without a fight.

"We got to go."

"Where? *Where* are we going now?

"New Orleans. But we are going to stop at the Rogers brothers' farm first," he announced.

"No we aren't." I was dead set against ever going back to that farm.

"Yes we are, Sonny Boy. I want to see if there might be one more rogue horse we can pick up and break—"

"Tex, I am telling you, I am not doing that anymore! I am not going back there and busting my ass." And I meant it.

Every word.

Of course, Tex got his way like he always did.

We stopped at the Rogers brothers' farm, dropped off all of the horses that were theirs, kept Small Play (Tex had claimed her back in Toronto), and picked up one other horse before we'd make our way south to New Orleans. The horse we picked up at the Rogers farm had hair so long, he looked like he was living in a tent. He surely had never seen a brush or a curry comb. At the rear side of the pastern on each limb of a horse are two small sesamoid bones that provide anchor points for the two branches of the suspensory ligament. As elements of the pastern joint, the sesamoids are under stress each time the horse takes a step. Small Play had a sesamoid injury which would stop her from racing for several months. Before Tex and I shoved off, I had a chance to confront Mr. Joe Rogers about the stakes money still owed to me from the races I'd won in Canada during the summer meets.

"Sonny, you ought to be thankful for all of the good horses you had to ride from us. There's really nothing else owed."

I was shocked by his response because I was expecting a fistful of money. According to the rules of the game, they owed me the money. But as I would quickly learn, these boys had their own rules—*Kentucky* rules, hardboot rules . . . whatever you want to call it—it was a lesson I didn't need to learn twice. Things weren't looking very bright as we left Kentucky. Needless to say, Tex and I were barely on speaking terms as we pulled out of Versailles.

As I suspected, New Orleans was the worst decision Tex had made in a long time. It was so rainy and cold that there was ice in the buckets for much of the winter. The base of the track was so saturated that horses were punching holes in it. The conditions were dangerous. There were times when the bottom came out of the racetrack, which made riding downright treacherous. I only rode one winner out of a lot of bad mounts during that entire meeting. Bill Reseguet did me a favor and put me on Peas Puddin' Hot. I won the race but had no great desire to get back on the track anytime soon.

One day at the track I had the chance to meet the jazz great Louis Prima, who offered me the chance to ride for his stable while I was in New Orleans. But with bad horses, the weather, and the competition, I couldn't seem to get it together. The riders there had perennially done well on the track in these conditions. They were Louisiana-based and had connections with forty or fifty horse stables. The top riders, P.J. Bailey, Red Keene, Bobby Baird, and Jimmy Nickles, were well positioned early. It was difficult to overcome their advantages. Besides, as much as I liked Louis and his wife, Keely Smith, their horses just weren't that good. As much as I loved hearing Louis talk about Sinatra and Gleason, I had to tell them in a polite way that I wasn't the right rider for them.

At least I had rented a very fancy apartment for us on Esplanade Avenue, which is on the ritzy side of the city. Thankfully, we were no longer sleeping on floors or in dumps. Unfortunately, Tex didn't belong in a nice place like the one we were living in. He was still chewing tobacco and spitting it up against the nice wallpaper all night from his bed. He made a terrible mess. When he wasn't sleeping, snoring, burping, and farting the night away, he was drinking heavily to pass the days.

In my mind, we weren't moving up in the world. I thought Tex needed to change his habits and be more respectful. But he didn't agree. He didn't care what other people thought about him. He didn't want to answer to anyone, especially me. The more successful I got, the more mature I became. With that, though, came more self-respect and dignity. My tolerance for his disgusting behavior and hygiene was shot. I could no longer tolerate the gross things I once did, especially at my own expense.

"You belong outside. You don't belong inside. You're an animal!" I screamed. I had hit my limit. His behavior was embarrassing. We had made a deposit with my money I knew we'd never get back, and we had no foreseeable future as far as I could tell.

"I'm done," I said.

"You can't be done!" Tex shot back, still thinking he was in control.

"Well, I am. I am going to do something else with someone else. I don't have any future with you. I can't hustle rides. You're miserable. I'm angry. There are riders out there doing well, and you don't want that for me. I am not staying here like this because it's not a holiday and I'm wasting my time!"

I wanted out of my contract.

And I had finally figured out how I could break it.

It turned out that Tex and Norm Heaton hadn't lived up to the terms of the agreement we had signed. The Rogers brothers only paid me thirty dollars a month on the farm against the total amount of the hundred-dollars-a-month agreement. There was no 10 percent stakes money on the races I had won for them. Traditionally and contractually, I should have been paid a sum and 10 percent on the win for every horse I rode, but they never paid me for any of that. Once I started riding, I was making so much money that, even though they were still obligated to pay me, I suppose they thought I didn't need the money. And I didn't. But by law of the agreement, that didn't let them off the hook from their financial obligation. To be fair, I wouldn't have asked for the monthly stipend at the time because I was getting enough money from racing to more than cover my expenses and then some. It would have been embarrassing to ask anyone for it. I never paid much attention to the terms of the agreement until someone asked me if Tex and Norm had lived up to their end and honored their obligations when I was looking for ways to get out. That's when I started to figure out my exit strategy. I wasn't under contract to the Rogers brothers, but they treated the agreement like it was theirs, knowing full well that they had no ownership in my contract.

I thought back on my conversation with Mr. Joe at the farm before we left for New Orleans and his refusal to pay me. His arrogant and condescending answer didn't sit well with me. In fact, it was the confirmation I needed to solidify my decision to leave Tex for good. He confused my kindness for weakness. I didn't say anything to Mr. Joe that day. I kept quiet about my feelings, waiting until the time was right. I knew the day would come with Tex when he and I would come to blows and I'd be able to walk away with my dignity. I didn't know exactly when that would happen, but I knew things would boil over sometime that winter. It was an undignified and intolerable existence!

The environment around a racetrack is a lot like the circus or rodeo. It's a very coarse environment. You don't run around screaming about calling lawyers or filing lawsuits. If you did, they'd basically tell you to go fuck yourself. Besides, by the time I told Tex I was leaving, he didn't have a decent horse for me to ride anyway, so where was the glue to keep me stuck to him? He never shared a plan that made me believe things might improve. There was no effort on his part to make things better. He didn't have an ounce of ambition. If anything, his jealousy was killing my career. At the age of sixteen, I couldn't afford to let someone do that to me. I was still learning about the ins and outs of the horse business. Sure, I could ride like the devil, but as far as finances were concerned, I wasn't prepared for the real world yet. What I did know was the agreement that kept me tied to Tex and Norm was nothing more than a ramshackle arrangement. It was all about horses. They didn't have me indentured as a jockey; they had me tied up as a farm worker. I suppose the semantics didn't really matter.

New Orleans put a gun to our heads like a desperate game of Russian roulette. I was so desperate, anxious, and full of ambition, I was willing to pay my way out of my agreement with Tex and Norm if it came down to it. There was lots of money in the bank, and I had plenty in reserve. I suppose I had more money than brains at the time, but then again, I was worried about my future, not about my past. I felt like a horse that was never being let out of the starting gate.

When the reality of our situation finally set in, Tex's only response was "How could you do this to me?"

He was genuinely forlorn about what was happening.

As the desperation grew, I called my father in Canada and explained what I thought my position was. He volunteered to speak with Bill Risewick, supervisor of racing for the Ontario Racing Commission, where the contract originated.

A few days later, my father called me back and gave me Mr. Risewick's advice. From his perspective, the contract *had been broken*, and they were the governing body. It was not a United States matter.

Subsequently, Tex and I went back and forth, talking about the next steps, doing a dance as if we were negotiating who got the crystal and who got the family dog in a divorce.

"What are you offering, Sonny Boy?"

"I'll give you $1,000 as a contribution toward your future." I said. I really didn't know how else to frame it.

Tex lowered his head and muttered in a quiet and somewhat defeated voice from his huge and bowed frame, "I'll take it."

Much to my surprise, he relented with very little fight. Whether he actually saw it the way I did or not, or whether he was just as frustrated as me with his own life and career, I will never really know why he gave in so fast.

My relationship with Tex was finally over.

We didn't have a teary good-bye. In fact, we didn't even shake hands.

Why would we?

I was his meal ticket, and now I was leaving. With only the $1,000 I had just handed him, Tex had nothing else to his name other than his old '36 Buick and a loaded six-shooter in the wooden trunk. I didn't know how or where he would get his next dollar, and, frankly, I didn't care. I was relieved to be rid of him.

As for me, I was done spinning my wheels. There was a lot of fuel left in my tank. I needed to get back in the saddle and get some wins. I signed with a new agent named George Sewing, who was leaving for Oaklawn Park in Hot Springs, Arkansas, in a few days. The track there was a popular winter track that attracted a lot of quality horses and riders from the Kentucky Derby. I'd never been there before, so it was completely new territory and just what I needed.

With my contract in my back pocket, a brand new Pontiac Chieftain that I had bought, my newfound freedom, and exciting enterprises in front of me, I was ready to take chances and start anew.

CHAPTER NINE

On one of my first mornings at Oaklawn Park, I met a trainer named Tater Watley. He worked for a man named Olin Sledge. Olin had a stable of horses, Thoroughbreds, quarter horses, and exercise riders who all wore uniforms with the Phillips 66 gas and oil logo on it. They hailed from Duncan, Oklahoma, and all talked with a perfect drawl. They were the most perfectly well-presented bunch of riders and team I had ever seen.

Unlike Tex, Tater was a refined cowboy with a lovely wife and a bright young son. I didn't know what Olin's tie was to Phillips 66, but I could tell he was a very wealthy oil guy—he sure was flamboyant. In all of my years spent around tracks, I had never seen so much money invested in horses as was spent at Oaklawn. I thought I had died and gone to heaven.

As I soon found out, there's always a lot of money wagered on the races west of the Mississippi, which means there's a lot to be gained for the winner. The most famous matched races in America often pit quarter horses against Thoroughbreds to see which is the fastest. This has been a hotly debated topic among horsemen, especially amongst the cattlemen and cowboys in the West, for as long as anyone can remember. The difference between quarter horses and Thoroughbreds is that quarter horses are cold-bloods that are trained to run from four hundred to eight hundred yards maximum, while Thoroughbreds are strictly pedigreed. Of course, many a cowboy would argue with me on this point, but as a jockey I'm partial to the spirit and durability of the Thoroughbred.

One of the most legendary races to test all the theories on this subject took place in August 1947 when Barbara B, a hardworking unregistered quarter horse owned by Roy Gill, who'd only raced on the "bush" tracks throughout the Southwest, met Fair Truckle, a four-year-old Thoroughbred owned by Charles S. Howard, the auto magnate who also owned Sea Biscuit, for a quarter-mile battle of the breeds at Hollywood Park in California.

The little mare, ridden by Tony Licata, jumped into the lead, but at the halfway mark Fair Truckle, ridden by seasoned jockey Johnny Longden, made his move to overtake that cow pony. Barbara B wasn't going down without a fight; she put on a little more sprint and took the lead by two-and-a-half lengths all the way to the finish—her fastest time ever clocked around the track. Legend has it there was more than $50,000 at stake on either side that day. After the race, the payoff took place in a room under the bleachers so Gill could count Howard's money to make sure it was all there. I grew to know both Tony and Johnny very well over the years.

I got to talking with Tater and Olin that morning, and I guess you could say we clicked, because they asked me to ride "first call" for their stable. I'd never heard that term before. They were offering me a retainer of $500 a week, which obligated me to ride their horses before anyone else's. I took a look at their stock, got on a few of the horses, and knew it was a sweetheart of a deal for both of us, so I agreed on the spot. Being connected to a high-class operation like theirs was a dream come true. Besides, Oaklawn is a relatively short meeting, lasting only a couple of months, so this arrangement saved me from walking the barn area trying to pick up independent mounts all over the place day in and day out.

I started riding for Tater and Olin when I was around sixteen or seventeen years old, and we instantly had a lot of success. We were winning two to three races every day. They had some outstanding horses, better than any I had ever ridden, which made my job as a jockey sheer bliss. It was a marriage made in heaven. The cash flow was terrific, too. Not only was I banking a lot of money, but they were including me in the wagering. The only owner I knew who did this was Eric Craddock, a Bay Street financier from Toronto who owned many horses. Butch Taylor, the stable manager, always placed a one-hundred-dollar wagering ticket in my boot in the paddock each time I rode as an incentive. Seeing a hundred-dollar bet on me before a race was a genuine encouragement to win. It sent a clear message that said, "I believe in you." This wasn't a common practice.

I found out early in my career as a jockey that wagering was a serious endeavor. Like golf, it created a different business dynamic that placed a fine point on each event. It took the experience from a "joy ride" to a plethora of "business decisions" in my young mind. You didn't just ride your horse; you were riding every horse in the race. Strategy was bolder, more capricious, and more threatening in 1953, where, in Canada, we had no films. Strategy became more refined as I entered the U.S. but was still essential to gain every edge. It was not a game for little boys in short pants, and my pants grew longer with each event and business venture.

The "I believe in you"s were important to me because I didn't get a lot of those as a kid. Every time I got any type of support or an "'Atta boy," it energized me. For the first time in my career as a jockey, I was working in an atmosphere with no jealousies or aggravation. It was a positive feeling of camaraderie right from the start. These two gentlemen were happy to have me ride for their stable, and I was thrilled for every mount they gave me. In addition to letting me ride six days a week, Tater Wateley and Olin Sledge gave me the opportunity to ride the quarter horses on Sundays, when there were no recognized meetings. I got to learn another dimension of racing, which helped me become a better rider. Tater had shipped in his quarter horses because they had a starting gate at the track, and he wanted to prep them to race in two divisions. When a Thoroughbred leaves the starting gate, a jockey looks to rate his horses, reserving their speed and ability. When a quarter horse leaves the gate—it's balls to the wall. Believe me, spending time in the gate with a feisty quarter horse being tailed and tonged will make the most seasoned jock a better rider. I was grateful for the experience and appreciative that they let me have the time in the saddle.

Things were going swell. I didn't think life could get any better. My agent, George Sewing, was happy because he was getting residuals from my winnings. We were staying in the same place with another rider named Ralph, who had come with us from New Orleans. Ralph and George liked going out and celebrating quite a bit, but I didn't like to partake. This was the one thing that brought back memories of being around Tex, especially when they begged to borrow my car. I never liked it when other people drove my car. It was a fancy new car, and I especially didn't trust those two with it.

One night I finally said, "Fuck it. I'll come with you." That way I would get them wherever they needed to go, and I would be able to drive.

I thought they wanted to go out and cruise. George and Ralph had other plans.

"We are going out to get laid," they said.

I had been on a couple of dates, but, given the environment I had been living in before I got to Arkansas, I was never in one place long enough to have a girlfriend. There were plenty of women who hung around outside the jock's room in Canada. I used to look at the array of gals sitting on the bench waiting for the older jockeys to finish racing while waiting their turn for a "ride," but I never once considered taking a shot of my own. I was just a fresh-faced kid who didn't think I had a chance in situations I didn't know a lot about.

"How does this work?" I asked George.

I felt dumb as a post, especially when George and Ralph roared with laughter at my naïveté.

"Do I get to have sex without having to ask for it?"

I wasn't being coy. I just didn't know what to say to the girls or what to do. I had never really gone to school or attended a dance. I didn't want to offend them. All of the times I'd taken Tex to get laid, I never thought about getting laid myself because those women were so unappealing to me. They looked like my grandmother! This was the first time I was going for my own enjoyment. I was an awkward little squirt who was stuck somewhere between being a man and a boy. I was uneasy, unsure, and insecure when I got off a horse.

Do I ask her to lunch?

Should I ask her to the track?

Maybe I should ask her to dance?

These were the thoughts running through my head as I pointed my Chieftain toward the little brothel up the road also known as the Prospect Hotel. By the time we reached the parking lot, my fear and anxiety turned to excitement and anticipation. I nearly ejaculated before we got through the front door.

I felt funny.

I was flustered, nervous, and very eager to get on with things.

George could tell I was restless and told me to settle down. I was chomping at the bit. Within a few minutes, an older woman walked us toward a private room where we were met by a lady who looked like she was running the joint. She was quite pleasant and smelled a little like cigarettes and roses.

"Is this your son?" she said to George.

"No, he's not my son."

I felt embarrassed if not slightly humiliated. Maybe this was a bad idea. *I should get out of here*, I thought to myself.

Just as I was about to turn and tell George I was leaving, I saw the most incredible sight.

"Gentleman, make your selection from these ladies. . . ," the madame said as she swung her arm wide revealing a bevy of beauties.

I stood motionless.

The angels in front of my eyes were more heavenly than any women I had ever seen.

"Who goes first?" I asked. "I am ready. . . ."

And I was. A cute little dirty blonde with long hair had caught my eye. She was shorter than the rest of the girls, which was perfect for me. She looked older, but not too old.

"Can I have her?" I pointed, asking the Madame as politely as I could.

No drinks.

No small talk required.

I didn't know what to expect.

I was a wreck, and I was quickly falling in love.

She told me to follow her.

I dutifully obliged.

She sat on her bed and I pulled up a chair.

I didn't know what to do.

Should I kiss her?

I was trying to be polite.

"Do you want to sit here?" she said as she placed her hand on the bed next to her hip.

I slowly got up and walked over to her. She knew just what to do. She sensed I was nervous and that I didn't know how to proceed. She was kind, gentle, understanding, and made me feel special. She slipped out of her clothes, and in no time mine were strewn all over the place. I climbed into bed—and she let me go at it.

Her skin was soft—like velvet. She wore perfume in places I never knew women could. I never paid much attention to how a woman smelled before, but now I would never forget. Her hair felt silky, luxurious, and different in my hands than the mane of the Thoroughbreds I held in control.

It was exhilarating and better than I imagined.

"Don't go so fast," she whispered in my ear. "You're like a little rabbit. Slow, easy. You didn't give me a chance. . . ," she said.

I didn't know sex was about her. I thought it was all about me. She was being sincere and trying to teach me to be a better lover—like we had a relationship.

"Think of the woman," she said.

I never forgot that.

I was so emotional afterwards—more than I had ever been in my life. I thought she would be my friend forever.

When we were through, I still wanted to kiss her over and over. I couldn't keep my hands off of her. She kept patting me on the head, treating me like a little boy, which bothered me a bit because I was doing a manly thing.

It was a big day for me—a major breakthrough. I never stayed up late and never felt things like I did that night.

I thought I knew all about life, but I didn't.

This encounter changed my view of the world, especially with my mother and father. I didn't understand what affection and closeness meant. I'd heard sex was something you stay away from because it wasn't good or meaningful if the circumstances aren't right. In that moment, I had no idea why anyone would say such a thing.

I did my best to get dressed without looking like a fool. I had my shorts on backwards, and I could only find one sock. I had to get myself together. My knees were shaking, and I was a mess. It was dramatic and unforgettable. I felt like I wanted to sing but didn't. I had discovered a dimension of my body and mind I never knew I had!

When I went out to the lobby, nobody was there. I looked around for George and Ralph, but they were nowhere to be found.

What's taking them so long? I thought.

It had been thirty-five minutes since I had met the girl of my dreams.

I paid for everyone's girls and waited for the fellas.

Thirty minutes later, Ralph came out grinning. "Hey Champ!"

And then George came out. "How was that, little buddy? Did you enjoy yourself?"

"Fabulous!" was the only word I could utter.

It was over, but I was still feeling shy. Ralph just giggled.

"C'mon Dave. Let's go get something to eat," George said, slapping me on the back.

"I'm not going anywhere," I said.

"What do you mean?"

"I am going to stay here," I said.

"You can't stay here, Dave."

"You are joking, right?" Ralph asked.

"I'm not joking. I am going to stay here. You guys go back to the boarding house, go get something to eat, do whatever you want, but I am going to stay here and think this over."

"Davey . . . you can't do that. You have to go." George's tone had turned serious.

"George, you work for me. I don't work for you. I like it here. It's a wonderful place and the people are so nice. I can't leave this."

"You're fucking crazy. You've got to get out of here. You can't stay!" George was one octave shy of shouting.

"It's a hotel, ain't it? I don't give a shit what you think. I am staying!"

The fellas shook their heads, turned, and walked out the door.

I turned, knocked on the madame's door, and asked if I could rent a room.

We worked out a rate that didn't include any "extras," and then she handed me a set of keys. Screwing was an additional charge—one I was all too happy to pay. As soon as I got to my room, I tried two or three other women who came close to my "first," but I was in love, so no one could really match how I felt about her.

I was so happy living at the Prospect Hotel. I was winning races during the day and got laid every night. I got educational time from every woman I was with, most of whom wanted to lecture me on the finer points of lovemaking while laughing and teasing me. And while the operation wasn't legal, no one seemed to care what was happening behind closed doors. I got to meet the chief of police, some politicians, and lots of other notables who frequented the Prospect on a regular basis. When I wasn't enjoying the company of women, I played the old piano in the parlor for guests and the girls who weren't otherwise occupied.

I really didn't think life could get any better.

This had to be the highest point anyone's life could possibly reach, I thought almost every day.

It certainly was the greatest time of my life!

The girls treated me like their kid brother. I loved it, too, especially when they all came to the track dressed to the nines to watch me race and cheer me on. They would come to the paddock and I would give them betting tips. The other jocks would drive me crazy, hooting and hollering at the girls as they walked by. I tipped my hat a bit, trying to be gentlemanly, giving the ladies the respect I felt they deserved. Besides, when I was in the saddle, I was in combat mode, which earned me more respect from them, too. There was no downside to my situation.

The more I got to know the girls, the harder it became for me to think of them as whores, hookers, call girls, or any other name that described them in a disrespectful manner. I couldn't stand hearing anyone talk about them in those terms, let alone refer to the hotel as a whorehouse. They became friends. I grew defensive on their behalf. A few had children, came from broken homes, endured difficult situations, or were just trying to make ends meet. All of them were good human beings. Nobody drank or did illicit drugs. Almost all of them were trying to better their lives by studying for another job or going to school during the day. Nearly every one of the girls had career paths they were trying to pursue outside of the hotel.

They became my family—a family who took me in and showed me a type of love, a kind of affection and warmth I wanted, needed, craved, and desired. I don't condone that as the way life should be, but they were often penalized unfairly. I never let anyone around me talk about them in a negative way—especially the guys. I warned George that I would fire him in a New York minute if he ever mentioned the brothel or ladies even once—just once.

As the meet was coming to a close, there was a lot of talk about where to head next. I was gaining weight from growing, and it was having an impact on my rides. When I first got to Kentucky two years prior, I weighed fifty-five pounds. I was very small and didn't gain much weight until I started to build muscle. By the time I left Arkansas, I weighed between 101 and 105 pounds—nearly double what I was on the farm. I was muscular, stronger, and two years older. This was fairly typical of the best jockeys I was riding against and a little lighter than most jockeys today who weigh in somewhere between 108 and 110 pounds.

We had a tremendously successful meeting that placed me well up in the jockey standings and earnings. But those were cosmetic things. Purses were small to medium by comparison to other good meetings in the country. The success was with the wagering; we were a great team, and everyone was pleased beyond reasonable expectation.

At Oaklawn, I'd ridden a horse named Uncle Zeke a couple of times that had Kentucky Derby potential. I won the Old Line Handicap on him, which was a big race in those days. He was a large three-year-old who looked like he had a good future but went lame. It was a great disappointment because he was our Derby horse.

George, Tater, and Olin wanted me to go to Suffolk Downs in Winthrop, Massachusetts, a premier track that had one of the few turf tracks in the United States at the time. I was winning all of the right races and moving up in the rankings. Canada was cold in the spring, and Dufferin Park in Toronto was a bullring—a half-mile oval. No good horses ran there, and it was nothing but trouble for horses and riders, so I wanted to duck that meeting. We had seen a few good friends die there as a result of bad falls or being trampled afterward, so I had no desire to go.

The day finally arrived to say good-bye to the ladies I had come to love as sisters, friends, and more. They threw a going-away party for me that I'll never forget. It had to take place early in the day because they had their work to do at night. They each got dolled up in beautiful dresses and sang for me. It was sad, but it was also time to leave. I couldn't take them with me. I addressed each of them as a man—not as a shy little boy who couldn't dance, among other things. I stayed in touch with a few of the ladies after I left, even receiving a birthday or Christmas card along the way for a few years. They were good people, teachers, just beyond the bounds of earth's mores. I knew that first girl I fell in love with wouldn't be a forever thing, but it was a meaningful moment—one I will always cherish and never forget.

CHAPTER TEN

1954

When I left Canada to follow Tex without the proper immigration documents in 1952, I instinctively knew returning would become a problem. Just before the end of the meet in Arkansas, my parents came to visit me. I gave my mother a briefcase full of money to take back to Toronto with her when my parents drove back home. It was in the tens-of-thousands-of-dollars range. It was illegal to transport that much cash over the border without declaring it, but we figured no one at border patrol was going to hassle an elegant older woman or go through her luggage. I knew she'd be able to transport the money safely, and I wanted her to have it just in case my father needed it to help arrange for my documents or in the event I got killed. Besides, we'd done well in Arkansas, between my winnings on the track and our wagering, and I had plenty more left to spend. So even if they confiscated the money, it wouldn't be the end of the world. It would take some effort and pulling of strings to arrange for my papers, though, especially because I was aiming to get a work visa without being an American citizen. It was tough in those days when you didn't follow protocol in the first place.

Before heading to Suffolk Downs, I stopped in Buffalo, New York, for a few days and got a room in the Statler Hotel, where I would have to wait until my paperwork came through. I wanted to take a quick drive to Toronto to drop off the rest of my money before racing again. To expedite things, my father reached out to the most connected American racing enthusiast we knew—a man named John Montana. I rode many races for John in Canada and did very well for him.

John was a big guy who loved to dress well, mostly in sharp, dark, custom-made suits. He had a farm outside of Fort Erie, not far from the Fort Erie racecourse, which he referred to as his "getaway." He loved to bet, and I loved to win races, so we were a good team. In horseracing, if you can ride well, these types of guys think you are lucky for them. They'll do just about anything for you as long as you're making money for them at the track.

My father and I knew John was a big shot, as he was mayor of Buffalo and owned the metro transit company. What we didn't know at the time was his alleged association with organized crime. He was apparently a top mob guy in New York. I had no reason to know that, and to be frank I didn't care. There were lots of guys like that around the track. Whenever I saw John at the barn in the morning, we'd talk strategy, and then I'd apply it in the afternoon. Most of whatever we planned worked.

Our relationship was all business—always—which he appreciated from someone he viewed as a "little kid." So when my dad asked John to help me out with my papers, he immediately volunteered his "staff" to take care of it.

When I got to Buffalo, I checked into the Statler Hotel and waited to get the word that I was all set. I was told not to go across the border until John got everything straightened out. I quickly grew restless waiting. I was anxious to get to Toronto and even more so to get back to racing.

Since I always had a passion for cars, I took a ride over to the local Cadillac dealership on Main Street. Tinney Cadillac was a beautiful place. I parked, walked in, looking all of twelve years old, and sat in every car in the showroom. I was daydreaming, pretending to drive each one, making revving motor sounds, "*Brrrrrr,*" as authentically as I could.

I was sitting in a mint-green Coupe de Ville when I suddenly felt someone grab the back of my shirt and yank me out of the car and say, "Get the fuck out of these cars! Get your ass out of this showroom and don't ever come back. You are the little son of a bitch that has been stealing lighters out of these cars, aren't you?"

I was shocked and bewildered. The man who grabbed me was a good-sized guy who was at least a foot and a half taller and wider than I.

By the time I got to the door, I turned to him and said, "Well fuck you, too! I was going to buy one of these, but now I'm not."

"Yeah, yeah. Sure you're gonna buy one of these, son. Get the fuck out of here before I kick you in the ass."

I was really pissed. I was a big shot inside the gates of a racecourse, but outside I guess he didn't know who I was. Of course, he had no way of knowing, but that didn't make any difference to me. I hopped into my Pontiac that had the better part of $180,000 neatly placed under the mat in the trunk and drove away.

When I got back to the Statler Hotel, I called Tinney Cadillac and asked to speak to the manager.

When he answered, in my deepest and most mature voice I said, "I was in your showroom earlier today and saw a green Coupe de Ville with a cream-colored top. How much is that car? I'd like to buy it."

"Why don't you come on over?" he said.

"I can't come over."

"Why not? If you want to buy that car, you have to come to the showroom."

"There was a big ugly son of a bitch in there who threw me out! I don't want to be confronted like that again."

"You won't be confronted by anyone. I assure you. You have my word. But first, tell me, how do you want to pay for the car?"

"What's the price?"

"$6,200."

"I'll be paying cash, but I have a trade-in."

I counted $6,000 out of the trunk of my Pontiac, stuffed it into my pockets, and drove back to Tinney Cadillac. When I walked through the door, I asked to see Joe, the manager. When he came out to greet me, he couldn't believe his eyes.

"Hello, Joe. I am David Stevenson. I called you about the green coupe." I held my hand out to shake his.

"Oh yeah? Was that you?" Joe said, sounding as if he was somehow doubting my story.

"Yes sir. That was me."

"Well then, come on over here." Joe stopped and turned toward me, "Sonny, are you sure you want to buy *this* car?"

"Yes I am."

We walked into his office and Joe shut the door.

"David, how do you want to do this? Do we need to call your dad or somebody else? This is some kind of joke, right?"

"Joe, this isn't a joke. I am here to buy the damn car."

"Well how are you going to pay for it?"

"With money!" I was getting really angry. "How hard is it to buy a fucking car?" I asked.

"It's not hard, son, but. . . ."

"How much will you take for it right now?" I asked. I knew he would bargain with me.

Joe went into his drawer, pulled out a pad of paper and wrote down a number. He held it up and showed it to me. It read: $5,443.

"That's a lot of money, son. . . ," he said with some concern.

"We need to deduct a trade-in on my '53 Pontiac," I said.

Then I reached into my pocket and peeled off fifty-five one-hundred-dollar bills and threw it down on his desk.

"Here you go," I said. "That's $5,500. Give me my fucking change."

Joe had the same look of shock and bewilderment on his face that I had when his goon threw me out of the dealership just a few hours earlier. He was flabbergasted, and I loved it. Once we settled on the trade-in and cash for the car, we were instant buddies.

We walked out to the showroom to look at my new car. I opened the door and hopped in. Out of the corner of my eye, I spotted the big ugly son of a bitch who threw me out coming toward me again.

"Keep that fat bastard away from me!" I said to Joe.

"Don't you worry, David. He won't bother you anymore!"

Joe handed me the key so I could start the engine. The car had an electric seat. I never had one of those before. I put it up as close and as high as it would go, but I still couldn't reach the pedals.

I turned to Joe and said, "We need to do something about this. Can your mechanics rig it so I can reach the pedals?"

"We've never had this problem before, David, but let's see what we can do," Joe said.

He got one of his guys out of the back who said they could put the seat up on some wooden blocks, but it would interfere with the electric movement of the seat adjustments. I didn't care, since I knew I'd be the only one driving the car.

"Do it," I said.

I couldn't wait to get behind the wheel of that baby. When the guys in the garage were through making the necessary adjustments, I backed my old

Pontiac up to the garage doors, opened the trunks of both cars, and transferred the rest of my cash from one to the other.

A day later, I got the good news that my visa came through. It was a good thing, too, because a Canadian citizen couldn't drive an American car over the border without proper documentation, and I wasn't leaving Buffalo without that car.

Life is a game of details, I thought to myself.

I knew the green Cadillac Coupe de Ville would garner attention at the border on its own. You couldn't get that car in Canada. Add me at the wheel, and there was no doubt that I would be getting more than a second look from customs.

"Pull over there, sir," the customs official said in a commanding and authoritative manner as he pointed me toward the search area.

"Where did you get this car?"

"Who does it belong to?"

"How did you get the money to pay for it?"

The one question they never asked me was whether I was carrying any cash. And oddly enough, while they opened the trunk, they never actually searched it. I had my tack and suitcases back there, so they must have figured there wasn't much else to see. I think they were so focused on how I could possibly be in possession of the car, they didn't much care what else I might be carrying. I'd stashed my money neatly under the mat, but if they had searched the trunk, I'm sure they would have eventually found the wads of U.S. cash I was taking home with me.

The questioning went on for more than sixty minutes. They finally called Tinney Cadillac to verify my story before they let me go. I didn't really care, though. I'd put up with that bullshit and aggravation everywhere I went. I'd gotten used to it.

Once I made it back to Toronto, I remember how delighted I was driving up the Queen Elizabeth Highway. I had the seat pulled close, and I was propped up like a bird on a perch. I didn't have to shift like I did in the old Buick or coax the power out of the Pontiac because it was an automatic transmission.

When I got to my parents' house, it was a quick turnaround, because I had to be back in Suffolk before the start of the meet. I dumped the cash, giving it to my mother to deposit in our joint account. I barely had time for visiting before heading off to New England.

When I got to Suffolk Downs, I continued to do well in a very tough environment. The competition was keener there, but I got to ride with good riders. It was fun to be in the company of top jockeys in races because it helped me do better. I had the chance to ride with Tony DeSpirito, Vernon Bush, Chris Rogers, and Bob Ussery—four jockeys I admired and who helped me up my skills while riding in that meet. They each told me things that polished my abilities even more.

Riders didn't travel or crisscross the country from the West Coast to the East Coast back then like they do now. There might have been a few rare occasions for big races or for the right horse, but for the most part, it simply didn't happen. But while I was racing at Suffolk Downs, there was a parimutuel strike at the California tracks that shut racing down throughout the state. The strike looked like it was going to last for some time. That's what brought Willie Shoemaker and Jackie Westrope to Suffolk Downs to ride.

I was totally elated that I would get a chance to see Shoemaker. He was so famous. Chris had ridden against him before, but, to me, it would be a highlight of my career. As for Jackie, he had a unique style all his own. He developed the Acey-Deucey approach to riding, where a jockey uses a longer stirrup on the left side or inside leg. Before him, everyone rode with level stirrups or maybe one or two holes apart. He was extreme, which made him a novelty.

I had the chance to ride several races against Shoemaker while he was at Suffolk. When he rode, he looked like a monkey fucking a football. He was so small, stood so high, and made several colossal errors in the sport when he got Swaps beat by a sprinter going a mile and a quarter. He was a guy who made major errors in big events. He was the poster boy for the bull's-eyes placed at each finish line on every racecourse in America. Even so, he will always be beloved and remembered as "Our Little Shoe."

I laughed my ass off every time we looked at that bull's-eye—it was as if it were pointing out where the finish line was a little better just for him. Shoemaker had misjudged the wire so many times in so many races, the only words Willie uttered to me the entire time he was at Suffolk were "Pass the salt."

Eddie Arcaro was my idol. A dashing, gentlemanly rider who went on to make movies after his career as a jockey ended. He was the best horseman of the time. He was coordinated and picture-perfect on a horse. He was exactly what a horse rider should be—how a jockey of distinction should carry himself. He was totally different from Little Shoe—in all of the best ways.

Unfortunately, I was continuing to gain weight, which is never a good thing for a jockey. Although I was averaging only one thousand calories a day, my appetite was beginning to increase. There were snack bars in the jock's room, which had become a distraction—at least to me. It was a lot better when a jockey was locked up in there without anything to eat. I was definitely getting to a point where I needed to take a few pounds off. There are a lot of ways jockeys can shed a pound or two a day, which is imperative when you are racing, but I favored the hot-box-sauna-like contraption. I would sit in it and sweat the weight away. I would spend thirty to forty-five minutes in the sweatbox, sometimes next to other jockeys who were doing the same thing.

As the meet at Suffolk Downs was coming to a close, the Canadian racing season was about to start its premium meetings. I wanted to go back to Canada, where I knew I could pick whatever I wanted. There, I was king of the hill. Tater didn't take the news well, but it was ultimately an amicable parting of the ways.

I returned to Canada as a freelance rider. I had a first call with E. P. Taylor's Windfields Farm, which was a good thing to rely on. I rode for other stables that were doing well, too.

During a race at Long Branch, while riding a top-rated horse named War General, I was also engaged to ride two well-regarded Thoroughbreds, Senator Jim and Bernford, both of whom were favored for the Cup and Saucer, a Canadian Grade I race that I desperately wanted to win later in the season. The Cup and Saucer was still a few weeks away, and my focus at the moment was riding War General to victory in this race.

I could tell that War General wanted the win as much as I did. I could feel it coursing throughout his body early on. I looked at the jockey running on the inside, and I knew I had him. I gave him a bit of a grin, and then I moved confidently toward the lead. It was going to be an easy win.

Suddenly I heard a powerful *snap*.

War General had broken his leg.

When a horse fractures its leg, it's loud. Even amidst the thunderous running all around you, there is no mistaking the sound of shattering bone. In this case, he broke his leg right off. The only thing holding it on was skin.

It happened so fast, I had no control over it. I couldn't think about self-preservation because of the momentum and speed we were traveling at. The incident left little time for that kind of realization. The twelve-hundred-pound horse began to cartwheel at full gait, propelling me over his head and onto the ground. My collarbone shattered instantly upon contact. I continued to roll very quickly for about six or seven complete revolutions. All of the other horses made their way around my fallen horse with the exception of one, who stepped in the middle of my back, splitting my shoulder blade. Little did I know that two additional vertebrae—numbers 5 and 6—were fractured in the mix.

I couldn't have anticipated the bad step War General took that day. He had a lot of races under his belt. He certainly had it in him to win. All the horses were punching through three inches of soft sand and dirt at the base of the track. But he was a heavy horse. He was switching his lead on coming out of the corner, which meant I was asking him to put all of his weight on one side when he snapped that leg. It was devastating.

He was hurled to the ground, and before I knew it—I was in front of him.

I couldn't get up.

I recall trying to reach for him, to hold him down, but my limbs wouldn't move.

When a rider is thrown from the stirrups, he usually still holds onto the reigns. In this case, it happened so fast and hard, there was no way for me to do that.

When War General and I went down, we were at the point in the race with the highest intensity. We were all starting to release the horses for the home stretch, directing them to run with everything they had. I was trampled because there was no time for the other jockeys to steer clear of me.

When the dust settled, the ambulance came out on the track. I recognized the driver. His name was Frank Linette. He had buried every member of my family. I hoped I wouldn't be next.

"Dave, lie still. You're in pretty bad shape."

I had no choice but to lie still. I couldn't move my left side at all. He put me on the stretcher, loaded me into the ambulance, and drove me to the track infirmary, which was nothing more than a little room where the track doctor could examine me.

Someone cut my boots off with a pair of garden shears.

Five minutes later, the doctor told me my clavicle was broken. Although I heard him talking, my focus was on how chilled I had begun to feel. He could tell I was uncomfortable, though I didn't want to make a big fuss. My father showed up and was horrified by what he saw. He didn't say much, but I could tell it wasn't good.

I was taken to St. Joseph's Hospital in downtown Toronto. When I arrived, I was transferred onto a metal gurney. One of the hospital staff, a big fellow who didn't speak English, took my clothes off and put them under the cart. He wheeled me into a room to be X-rayed. I was met there by a couple of doctors and nurses. They were pulling on my left shoulder trying to get it in position so they could take the X-rays, but I was in too much pain to let them do what they needed to do, and I was too out of it to care.

Except for the jockstrap that I was still wearing, I was completely naked and cold. They didn't give me a blanket and they wouldn't give me anything to help wash out my mouth, which was still full of dirt and debris from the fall.

My agent, Bob Maxwell, found me in the hallway. His face was white from the site of my condition. He looked as distraught as I felt.

"I brought your clothes from the jock's room," he said.

"Good, let's get them on and get out of here," I said.

"Out of here? You can't leave here, Dave. You're in no condition to leave."

"You have to help me, Bob. Can you help me put my shoes on? I don't need my socks. . . ."

"I can't do that, Dave . . ." I could tell he was scared. Even so, Bob started to get me dressed, though he was touching me as if I were a leper.

My feet were terribly swollen, so he couldn't get my shoes on without causing great pain.

"I can get my pants on, Bob," I said, struggling to keep my balance.

Bob slid me off the gurney and draped my shirt over my shoulders. I was in too much distress to walk, so I hobbled out on my knees.

"They're never going to let us out of here, Dave."

But no one ever said a word. It was late, past dinnertime. The night shift staff was on duty, and they weren't paying much attention.

We made it past the front desk and out the door.

"Take me to my parents' place," I told Bob.

It was a long ride from the hospital to their house. I sat quietly, wondering why neither my mom nor my dad made it to the hospital. When I walked through their front door, they were horrified. I don't think they were expecting to see me. They were frantically running around in circles trying to figure out what to do. I finally took matters into my own hands. I was hungry, cold, and tired. A blanket, meal, and warm bed were all I wanted.

The hospital folks had put a bulky figure-eight sling on me that was holding some of my broken bones in place.

I was in agony for four or five really tough days. I nearly shit the bed twice. I couldn't get up to do anything. I didn't see my parents once during any part of those days. They holed me up in an apartment above the garage. I guess if I had stayed in the main house, I would have been in their way—the house that I had financially contributed to acquiring and maintaining. Occasionally, they sent someone over to see if I needed anything, but they never came to check on me themselves. I only asked for food and water—nothing else. I never saw a doctor. Never had a prescription for pain medication. Never had any therapy. I just lay there.

My physical condition before the accident was abnormally perfect. I was built like a matador—as tight as could be. I was able to ride eight races a day and get on five to ten horses in the mornings. I felt like I could literally "fly." Although my recovery was severely painful, I remained optimistic. I knew that my constitution would work in my favor. I also knew that the type of broken bones I suffered and the shock to my system I sustained were not life-threatening. They would lend well toward healing. But the pain continued beyond five weeks. I had a calendar in the small kitchen of the apartment. I looked at it every day. By week two I could hobble outside and down the stairs. I drove my car with one hand.

Six weeks later, I was back on a horse. I knew the day of the Cup and Saucer stakes was fast approaching, and there was nothing that could stop me from being there. I had a lot of work ahead of me if I planned to win that race.

CHAPTER ELEVEN

The Cup and Saucer Stakes is a Grade I Thoroughbred race held every fall at the same track where I had my accident—the Long Branch Racetrack in Long Branch, Ontario, just outside of Toronto. Open to two-year-old horses foaled in Canada, the race distance is eight-and-a-half furlongs, a long distance for such young horses in their first real test of stamina. The Cup and Saucer is also the richest race for Canadian two-year-olds, so it's a very lucrative event for owners and jockeys.

I was eager to win this race because I knew the favorites, Bernford and Senator Jim, well, and I thought I had a good shot of winning on either of them. Even though I was still sore and moved with some resistance, I made visits to the track to start conversations with the owner, Jack Stafford. I had first call on both horses. They were each outstanding, so I was giddy about the odds of our success. They were the impetus for my recovery, the urgency behind getting back on a horse again quickly.

In my estimation, Senator Jim was the better of the two horses. However, when I approached the trainer about riding him, his response caught me off guard. We had exchanged the normal pleasantries, and he inquired about my injuries. I was still visibly hurting and continued to wear the sling. While I spoke well, my neck and back indicated that I was still experiencing significant stiffness and discomfort. But I was still eager and determined to ride one of the horses in that race. I began to talk with him about the training condition of the two when he said, "I can't discuss that with you. You will have to talk to Mr. Stafford." The poor bastard wouldn't even look me in the eyes.

I went out to the barn the next morning and approached Mr. Stafford as he exited his limousine so I could tell him face-to-face that I had every intention of riding in the Cup and Saucer.

"Dave, you're not okay. You won't be okay. I can't risk it. We have to use someone else," he said.

His refusal that day was tough to swallow—it was a real kick in the ass. While it wasn't career-ending, it was humbling. The Cup and Saucer is a prestigious race. I was looking forward to riding in it because both of those horses would turn three on the first of the year, and they would move into the Queen's Plate, which is the Canadian equivalent of the Kentucky Derby. A win here meant a ride there.

Deep down, I suppose I knew Jack was right, but it was a blow to hear him say it anyway. Worse than that was the realization that the field was taking shape and I wasn't a part of it. I immediately went into the racing secretary's office to see who was going to be riding those two horses and what other possible entries there might be. I stood there looking up and down that list, shaking my head no as I read it.

Avelino Gomez was going to be on one and Jose Vina on the other. There was no arguing that they were two outstanding jockeys, but they weren't me, and that hurt.

Plus, I considered both of these guys to be friends—but that's the way the game is.

It wasn't their fault. Stafford made the decision.

As I reviewed the rest of the entries, it looked as if all of the good horses were taken already and there were none open for me.

I called a meeting with my agent, who treaded lightly with me because I was forceful at that age. I had my thoughts, and I didn't like to listen to people—especially when they were telling me things I didn't want to hear. He basically advised me to give up on riding in this particular race and to take the extra time to fully recover.

But I didn't want to give up. No way. I wanted to chew his head off for suggesting such a bullshit idea. Riding races is a contentious sport. The competition is fierce. If I gave up every time I got pushed into the fence, I'd never win a race. Hell, I'd never even ride in a race.

It was time to regroup.

Think.

Okay, so the two favorites were gone.

My agent didn't believe it was worth riding in the race, as those two favorites were overwhelmingly the best. While he didn't put it in those exact words, that is what he was thinking. He also didn't see any other horse on the list as worthy.

While I was busy looking at the situation from every angle, trainer Petey Punshon, who had claimed Small Play back in 1953, had claimed another horse for $2,500 the week before. I passed over that horse because he was considered a billy goat and was 50–1. When Petey heard I didn't have a horse to ride, he approached my dad asking if he thought I might consider taking a chance on his horse, Loyalist.

I was feeling dejected, and the stage was set. I wanted to get started again and show these bastards they had all made a huge mistake by passing me over.

"Sure, I'll give him an evaluation," I said. I was working hard to get ready for the physical exam I needed to take before I could ride again.

I went by the barn and looked at Loyalist, a tall, gangly, less-than-attractive colt.

Well, at the very least it gets me back in the saddle and on with the next step, instead of just walking around on the ground, I thought.

If I didn't like what I felt like when I rode, I didn't have to commit.

Petey wanted me to breeze Loyalist, which is giving the horse a medium workout. It is not a full gallop and not a secondary gallop. It's like putting the horse in third gear. You are letting him stretch his lungs but keeping him well in hand.

I agreed that I would ride him. I decided to breeze him with a sling on because I was afraid to take it off. If I had any hope of entering the race, I would need to get the track doctor's approval, and I couldn't risk doing anything to jeopardize that so close to the meet.

I was in a considerable amount of pain as I rode him. I hadn't been on a horse for six weeks, so my fitness level wasn't peak, either. I will admit that I was pleased with how well he breezed and responded to my commands. I got a good reaction from him, which raised my optimism a little.

"I'll ride him if I can pass the doctor's exam," I said as I gently dismounted the horse.

Petey and the owner Bill Moffat pretty much jumped for joy.

Loyalist was a longshot and hopeless—but he was also my only way into the Stakes.

We had a week to prepare, which meant we had some work ahead of us. Petey didn't really know the horse, either, as he had just claimed him.

With my mount in hand, I approached the doctor for permission. He cautiously examined me, already familiar with the injuries, as he was the attending physician on the day I got broke up. Although I insisted I was fine, he needed to officially sign off, or I'd be disqualified. He poked, pushed and prodded, checking every inch of my body. My shoulder made a little noise when he pushed on it, but it wasn't a valid reason to say I couldn't ride.

"How long did you stay in the hospital?"

"I didn't." I did my best to explain there was a little controversy around my hospital stay, but my story wasn't holding muster.

The track doctor wanted me to go through a series of examinations before he would agree to sign off on my health. Of course, there wasn't enough time to do that, so we compromised on a visit to the hospital again. If I could get the doctors there to say I was okay, the track doctor would agree to let me race.

I was up against the clock because the Cup and Saucer was less than a week away. I was considerably less than 100 percent healthy or ready to race—and I knew it. It was going to take some fast talking and some tough acting, but it would be worth it if I passed this test.

I stopped by the hospital one morning and looked up the attending physician who saw me the night of my fall. He didn't remember me because I only saw him briefly before I checked myself out.

I explained my situation to him, told him I was fine, and asked if he would sign off on my condition.

"What happened to you? Where did you go?" he asked.

"You were so busy, I didn't want to bother you. Besides, I was fine, so I left," I explained, trying to downplay the extent of my injuries.

I don't recall the doctor even glancing at my chart. He looked me up and down, shrugged his shoulders, and said, "You look all right to me. I'll 'ok' you, but you have to come back for additional X-rays right after."

Fat chance, I thought.

After the doctor signed off on the paperwork, the track doctor agreed to let me race, and the rest, as they say, is history.

First license granted to Dave by the regulatory body.

Dave while a backstretch worker at Long Branch racetrack, 1950.

First winner at
Greenwood racetrack,
1953.

First win for both Finespun and jockey, 1953 (top). Marion Heaton, Morgan "Tex"
Lewis, groom Tuckey, and Finespun in the winner's circle (bottom).

The Paddock at Greenwood Racetrack (left) and leading apprentice at Greenwood (right).

Trainer John Passero, Dave Stevenson, Lieutenant Governor of Canada Sir Vincent Massey, and owner Bill Beasley after Queen's Plate win at Woodbine, 1956.

Owner Bill Beasley and Dave Stevenson in the winner's circle after Queen's Plate victory.

Chairman of Ontario Jockey Club Bud Baker and Her Majesty Queen Elizabeth The Queen Mother talking with Stevenson, Woodbine paddock.

Greenwood | **FAIRLY REGAL** | November 30, 1977
Owner "TATTLING STAKES HANDICAP"—Purse $25,000 added | Jockey
Kinghaven Farms | Trainer - D.A. Stevenson | Brian Swatuk
2nd Emperor's Whim | 1 3/16mi. -1.59 | 3rd Screen Shot

Trainer Dave Stevenson, owner Bud Willmot, and jockey Brian Swatuk atop Fairly Regal in the winner's circle after Tattling Stakes win at Greenwood Racetrack.

Left: Woodbine racetrack's Queen's Plate program cover featuring Queen Elizabeth, 1956.

Her Majesty Queen Elizabeth II

Queen's Plate Day

SATURDAY, JUNE 16th, 1956

WOODBINE
TORONTO
Official Programme · 15c

Inscription by author Raymond G. Woolfe Jr. on the inside cover of his book commemorating Secretariat (top) and a note written by Secretariat owner, Penny Tweedy, on the inside cover of *Secretariat* given to Dave Stevenson.

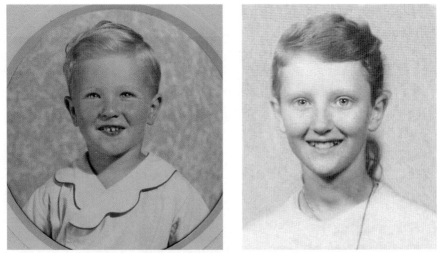

Dave at five years old, and his sister, Virginia Stevenson, at twelve years old.

Barbara and
Dave Stevenson
on their wedding
day, above, and
more recently,
below.

Dianna Stevenson (general manager HNSI), Barbara Stevenson, Dave, and Sally Hill at the opening of family-owned Hipódromo Nacional de Costa Rica racecourse in San Isidro, Costa Rica.

2010 Stevenson family photo: Dianna, Aaron, Dave, Barbara, David, Rebecca.

Inspection of La Rinconada Hippodrome in Caracas, Venezuela, following our offer to purchase discussions.

Dave's corporate aircraft MU2 refueling at Bohlke International Airways, St. Croix, US Virgin Islands.

Cockpit of N305DS Mitsubishi.

As soon as we announced my acceptance, people began speculating about the odds—not of me winning—but of me avoiding further injury before the big day.

Once I took my sling off, I began training hard. I hit the hot box as often as I could take it. I loosened up, worked out Loyalist, and strategized for the big day.

Some horses can't go eight-and-a-half furlongs, and I honestly didn't know if mine would be able to or not. My strategy was to take my horse back to last place right out of the gate and conserve everything he had until we could make an explosive bid from the three-eighths pole or the quarter pole, depending on how far out in front the other horses were at that time. None of these colts had gone that far, so it would be a test of the conditioning and the trainers' ability. If I was close and had a lot of horse, I would have a shot. I didn't know how Loyalist would act. It was a risk, but it was all I had.

The paddock scene for saddling was a little testy. I didn't go out of my way to acknowledge Jack Stafford and his team, and he ignored my presence. As we went to the post, Stafford's entries of Bernford and Senator Jim were 1–2, making them the prohibitive favorites. I warmed Loyalist up with a stiff gallop and walked up to the gate.

When the gate opened, I relaxed the horse to the back of the field and angled close in to the inside rail to save all the ground that I could. The field ran away from us around the first turn and down the backstretch. Loyalist had both eyes on the field getting smaller in front and dropped one ear back as if to listen for direction.

He was wondering what the hell I was doing, looking at the other horses and back at me, sensing we were fifteen lengths back. I knew he was confused. Loyalist strengthened his gait, and I firmed up the bit in his mouth. At the half-mile pole, I let him inch a little bit toward the field. Stafford's colors were prominent, and I could see the two favorites were laying one-two. As the drive started, and the other jockeys were asking their horses to run, we were only five or six lengths back. The pace was slowing and Loyalist was eager to improve his position. I chirped at him to pick up speed and took a fresh cross in the reins. Loyalist was lengthening stride, and I was still mildly conserving him. I saved the ground on the rail and then let him drift to the outside of the field as we entered the straightaway. I could see that Gomez had gone from a pull to a drive in his normal flurry. Jose Vina was lapped on him but giving up ground and then went to the stick and full-flight. I felt a pulse like an electric shock run up and through my arms. I had to try and subdue my confidence and not release Loyalist to expend his total reserve.

We are in good order, I thought as I let him level out approaching the eighth pole.

We reeled them in, passing the eighth pole.

I was shocked. I didn't think he had that much ability, but he did. He was determined and I was determined. It turned out we were a great match and in full sync.

Approaching the sixteenth pole, we blew past the leaders. I looked across at Gomez and Vina, who were struggling because they had shot their bolt and had obviously moved too quick. I just let Loyalist go on and win with no punishment! Loyalist was a winning claimer, and he seemed to be proud, his ears doddling leisurely, moving back and forth independently, as I let him gallop out.

I stopped him to within a four- or five-step walk while he caught his breath.

I took my time coming back to the winner's circle, and I let that skinny old bay horse gallop past Jack Stafford, who was standing trackside bedecked in his striped suit, tie, and boutonniere.

This is a fine Saturday, I thought as I gave Loyalist a few pats on the neck and a congratulatory salute for his effort. And what a fine day for a comeback!

There's a wonderful feeling that comes with riding a longshot to victory. I knew the payout would be big and my bosses were going to be happy. This was good news for everyone. While I didn't have any action on the race, because I couldn't as a jockey, my mother surely did. This was how we made money as a family. Lots of money.

Petey Punshon was drinking whiskey out of a mickey flask. His attire was not representative of a winner's circle visit. He couldn't believe what had just happened, and Bill Moffatt was beside himself. All hell broke loose. I took an extra turn just to make sure everyone got a good look at us, and into the winners circle we went. The crowd acknowledged the surprise win with much applause.

Little Davey was back! I thought to myself.

Winning that race was like turning on the fire hose, and business was booming again. My agent nearly wet his pants with excitement. After the race, later that day, I looked for Jack Stafford and shook his hand. He was white and couldn't really speak. It didn't require a lot of conversation.

"Sorry how it turned out for you, Mr. Stafford," I said.

I never apologized for beating him, but I wanted him to know I was humble and appreciative for all he had done. He should have believed in me, but he wasn't wrong to protect his horses. The important thing was that my ability was no longer in doubt. I was back and better than ever.

CHAPTER TWELVE

With my win in the Grade I Cup and Saucer stakes fresh in everyone's mind, I was finally hitting the big time and attracting the attention of big stables as well as fans. I finished the season at Long Branch racecourse in grand style, with a lot more wins and a lot more money in hand. In the grandstand that day was trainer John Passero, who would go on to become a future hall-of-famer. Johnny had been a jockey earlier in his career, but he was the head trainer for the fast and powerful growing stable of Bill Beasley. Beasley was known as "Bingo Bill" because of his gigantic bingo and recreation operations at the Canadian National Exhibition and Centre Island locations in Toronto. He was wealthy, handsome, and an extremely gregarious personality who lived to win a bet.

When Beasley got into horseracing, he vowed to upset the extremely conservative establishment, known in our region as Canadian Royalty, that had cornered the Thoroughbred sport. The establishment had shunned Beasley, it was said, because of his willingness to place bets with "bookmakers." In fact, he was never asked to become a member of the Board of Directors at the Ontario Jockey Club or other prestigious Toronto-based fraternities because of his love of betting outside the tracks.

His team was purchasing very good bloodstock wherever they could. They had even shopped at E. P. "Eddie" Taylor's yearling auctions that represented the best pedigrees in the land. In the ensuing weeks after my major victory at the Cup and Saucer, Johnny Passero approached both my agent, Bob Maxwell, and my father with a proposition to join the Beasley stable.

When the proposition was presented to me, I said, "It sounds like a match made in heaven."

Our meetings went well. I was armed with what I referred to as a live-stock business plan that stretched out over two years. Passero acknowledged that my riding style "was fiercely competitive and a perfect fit" for their stable.

I already knew that. I didn't have to hear it from him.

Even so, being asked to ride for Beasley was awesome—and more than that, it was positively predatory! I accepted the terms, which allowed me to ride first call and anything else in races when the stable did not have an entry.

Ironically, less than a week later, Joe Thomas, the racing manager for E. P. Taylor's sixty-horse Windfields Farm presented me with a similar deal. Although I was flattered, I had to let them know I was already committed someplace else.

Disappointed, Joe proposed a "second call" arrangement for $2,000 a month. I didn't expect that, and I couldn't ignore it, either. I consulted with the Beasley group and was given permission to accept their offer. I was told this was an unprecedented arrangement, at least in Canada. The top American jockeys were getting anywhere from $3,000 to $5,000 as a retainer. While my deal wasn't quite there, it was big for a Canadian stable.

As soon as the season came to an end, I got ready to ship to Florida with Beasley and my new stable.

Racing at Hialeah Park was a very different scenario for me. It was extremely upscale compared to the other tracks I'd come to know. I loved it from the moment I arrived. I quickly found a house to rent near Gulfstream Park in Hallandale, Florida, and decided to bring my mom, dad, and sister, Ginny, down for the winter. They never took a vacation or had time off for the holidays, so I thought they should enjoy the warm Florida sun and take a break from the frigid Canadian winter. It worked to have them with me for a while, but it wasn't the best arrangement because my dad quickly started dictating policy to me again. He treated me like a little kid in my own home. I don't know why I thought things would somehow change, when, in fact, they always stayed exactly the same. Einstein said that the definition of insanity is doing the same things over and over again expecting a different result. If that's true, I was definitely on the road to insanity.

Prior to arriving in Florida, Beasley had purchased a horse named Little Wolf for $17,000, which was a lot of money for a horse back then, but considerably less than he would have paid had the horse not been such an undisciplined rogue. That horse was a mean bastard. He was determined *not* to do whatever we asked of him. He would flip over in the starting gate and do whatever he could to throw me off. We spent a lot of time trying to school this damn horse, especially in the starting gate because he needed it. The idea, though, was simply to not get hurt.

The more time we spent with Little Wolf, the more potential we saw in him. We breezed him in the dark of the mornings, thinking it made him easier to handle. The early hours also worked in our favor because there were no clockers to time the horse. Although this practice is frowned upon today because handicappers want to know all the speed and performance statistics in advance, this was a rather common practice back in the day. We didn't do it all of the time, but we opted to do it this time because we didn't want other trainers to know how fast he was before race day. It also maximized the mutuel price at race time since there were no "published workouts." Doing this was another way to make more money wagering. I could make decent enough money riding, but there was no better way than through wagering to make real chunks of cash. Purses were still smaller, even at the top tracks, unless you won a stakes race. And it was better than the bonuses owners handed out—when and if they handed them out. However, my situation in Florida was good because of the nature of our agreement.

We hid Little Wolf from everyone until race day. Being covert about a horse can be really exciting and fun. Some people would say it is devious; I'd say in the right circumstances it's just smart and calculating. It definitely gave us a competitive advantage.

Look, I was a stranger in a strange place. I was going up against a mountain of major competition. Every prominent rider in the sport was at Hialeah Park during the winter of 1955. It included every great horse and jockey in training: Eddie Arcaro, Eric Guerin, Teddy Atkinson, Chris Rogers, Walter Blum, Johnny Adams, and many more. These rare circumstances were precipitated by the fact that there was no winter racing in the North, particularly at the big tracks in New York.

It was electrifying to be around such legends, especially Arcaro, who was riding all of the top horses—like Nashua and Citation. Plus, he won three triple crowns for Calumet Farm. He was a true celebrity. People surrounded him wherever he went, asking for an autograph or to have their picture taken with him. He was very articulate for a jockey and, yet, often extremely brazen, too. He would say and do outrageous things, such as breezing horses in a tuxedo the morning after a black-tie party and riding up alongside of a leader and then slowing his horse down just to intimidate the competition. We both spent time in the same locker and had the same valet, so we'd strike up good conversations here and there. He told me to tuck in a little bit more when I was riding, and he showed me how to switch a stick more efficiently. He had the best seat and hands on a horse that there ever was. He took the time to be complimentary and even mentored me in the brief exchanges we shared. Though our time together was fleeting, I've never forgotten it or the impact it had on me as a jockey.

We never had long conversations, and I am not even sure he knew who I was, but I was inspired by his determination and commitment to the sport. Every now and then, he was said to be seen late at night working horses in his tuxedo because he never went home after a party or fundraiser. If anyone else stayed up all night, drinking champagne, the stable would fine him. Not Arcaro. He made a joke out of it, but he also performed at the highest level. He was a true superstar who always brought in the crowds. It was great theater whenever he performed at the track. Eddie Arcaro was an incredible inspiration to many, but especially to me.

Our horse Little Wolf was a first-time starter. He continued to train well and didn't manage to kill me, even if he did try most mornings. As difficult as he could be, he was a piece of cake compared to the six- and seven-year-old maidens I spent breaking on the farm every day with a lot less expertise than I had now. He spent more time on his hind legs than Trigger, but fear was never my problem. I knew he was going to be fast, but I didn't know how he was going to act in front of thousands of people in the noisy afternoon or in the starting gate, which he vehemently detested. He continually tried to flip over backwards whenever we schooled him. Even the starting gate crew was afraid of him. They'd apply the ear tongs on him while two others held onto his tail to try and keep him from going over backwards. Nevertheless, Little Wolf was getting fit and working faster each time we let him run.

Prior to deciding whether to race the horse, our meetings were open to only four of us: Bill Beasley, Johnny Passero, assistant trainer Bobby Bateman, and me. I was really the only one who knew how fast he could run because I was the only one who rode him in his works. The others knew how crazy he was in the gate because he was schooled at the starting gate in the daylight but not allowed to break from it. Although I attempted to tell the others how fast he was at our meetings, two of the four of us had serious reservations that he would ever get out of the gate in one piece or, at least, with me on him. Bill Beasley listened intently and was fully committed to my discourse.

I looked at the racing form entries the day before the race and saw one horse, Well Done, owned by Alfred Vanderbilt, who had one of the top stables in racing at the time. Jockey Eric Guerin was named to ride him. The horse, although a maiden, showed a lot of early morning ability in his works. Well Done drew the one post and Little Wolf drew the number two post position. I felt we were in relatively good shape considering there were seven horses in the race. Normally three-year-old maiden races had twelve or more horses this time of the year, so it was a relatively small field. I figured the horsemen were staying away because of Well Done's ability. No matter what, I wasn't backing off. I knew my horse could run like hell, and the fewer horses I had to beat, the better. But word had traveled quickly about how bad my horse had acted at the gate, thanks to the starting gate crew—not how fast he was. That was news to me.

As I lay in my bed early that night, thinking over my strategy for the next day, a smile crossed my face in the dark. I sprung bolt upright in bed, delighted with the thought my mind had produced: fear would provide my advantage! Jockey Eric Guerin was much older than I, rich, and very careful. I finally fell asleep plotting and rehearsing my script for tomorrow.

After my early morning workouts and discussions at the track, I returned home and instructed my mother to sit down at the table and listen very closely to everything I was saying. I even asked her to repeat it very slowly.

"There is somewhere around $3,000 cash on my dresser in my bedroom. Go to the racetrack at least forty-five minutes before post time for Little Wolf's race," I told her.

My mother was a two-dollar bettor who was familiar with the pari-mutuel location at the track. I explained that when the pari-mutuel windows open thirty minutes before the race, there are at least ten twenty-dollar windows, a dozen or so ten-dollar windows, and thirty or more five-dollar windows. I told her that there is a fifty-dollar window but *not* to go there.

"Why not?" she managed to ask as I rapidly fired off what I wanted her to do.

"Because the higher denomination windows are manned by mutuel clerks who accept bribes from their regularly established customers to place their bet where the 'smart' money is being wagered. I don't want to knock the price down!" I said in a very demanding voice.

"Bet the entire amount at at least ten different windows and bet it all to win. If someone asks you why you like the horse, tell them it is your favorite number. That's all. Don't visit. Don't have any discussions!"

My mother looked at me with a blank stare. I think she was stunned, scared, and rendered completely speechless by what I was telling her to do.

"Start early and don't wait too long. It can get busy, and there will be big crowds today," I said.

"I CAN'T! I WON'T!" She blurted with a look of terror in her eyes I'd never seen before. Her face turned white, and her grimace actually made her look ugly for a moment.

"I'm not going to be a party to that kind of loss," she started to ramble.

"HOLD ON!" I raised the volume and the tone of my voice about a half an octave. "We've been through this shit before, and that's why I don't want you around when I'm doing business! Now, I haven't got much time because I have to get to the jock's room before the race. I don't want to argue about trying to be successful."

My mother had a tendency to be a pessimist about a lot of things, but money made her tick, and I'm sure she would have liked me to give the money to her instead. She was domineering and managed my money as if it were hers anyway, offering my father a weekly allowance like he was a kid.

Still nervous about betting so much money, she did her best to try and talk me out of it. I heard a dozen "what ifs" in ten minutes.

When my father got wind of the wager after he came in from the store, he wasn't very happy about it, either.

"Shorty"—that's what he called me when he was pissed—"you don't want to do this."

"I am going to do it, and I'm not going to hang around here debating success and failure and suffering through another version of the Great Depression." I think they got my point loud and clear. They could see by the look on my face and the tone of my voice that I was on the threshold of some very ugly decisions.

There was nothing they could say or do to talk me out of it, though I will admit now they were getting to my confidence a bit. That was the last thing I needed before post time.

"Okay, I'm going to make other arrangements!" I said, turning my back as if to walk away.

"Why don't you bet most of the money to place and show?" they tried to reason.

"NO!" I hollered.

I knew it was a lot of money to them, but to me, I didn't give a shit. I never cared about losing money, and my mind was made up.

"We're just trying to help you, son!" Mother shouted out through tears. "But, okay, I will do it," she said with more tears in her eyes.

"Okay, you little son of a bitch, I'll go with her, but don't say I didn't warn you," my father threatened.

The discussion was over.

We went over the procedure one more time while my father was in the room just to be certain everyone understood what they were supposed to do.

I marched across the Hialeah paddock from the jock's room to find Bill Beasley. I wanted to talk to him about Little Wolf before post time. I was going to express how I thought he was a really good horse and worthy of a substantial wager. I explained how I felt about Well Done and that Eric Guerin was one of the favorite jockeys and a supposed superstar. He was riding an Alfred Vanderbilt horse that day. I wanted him to know everything. But Beasley wasn't there. The trainer Johnny Passero intercepted my search in the paddock.

"Where's Mr. Beasley?" I asked.

"He flew to Toronto last night," Johnny nervously said.

For reasons I never quite understood, Johnny was always a worrywart.

"Riders up!" called out the paddock judge.

"Lay close if you can, Davey," Johnny said in a hurried voice. Little did Johnny, or anybody for that matter, know I already had my own strategy. I didn't want his input anyway.

When I arrived at the jockey's room that afternoon, I grabbed a program off of the clerk of scales desk and saw that Guerin didn't ride the race before our event. Guerin was known for his timidity. He had ridden more than a thousand winners and a great many classic races, and the older and richer he got, the more he seemed to favor the overland route to safety, meaning he liked to stay on the outside and out of the way of any danger. I found him trying to snooze in a bunk. He had a T-shirt and ascot on as well as boots. I wanted to appear subtle when I tapped him on the shoulder. He rolled over and faced me.

"Hi," he said rather sleepily. "What's up, kid?"

I put on my innocent little boy look and said as respectfully as I could, "Mr. Guerin, I just wanted you to know the horse that I ride in the third race is one bad son of a bitch."

He sat up immediately, giving me his total attention. "What can I do about it?"

"Nothing," I said. "I just wanted you to know this bastard will try and flip over backwards in the gate. He's never run before. He tongs and tails, and I don't know what the bastard will do when the gates open! He's liable to be upside down or try and tear the doors off leaving there. I'm going to have my hands full. I just wanted to let you know because you are on the inside of me."

"Why do they let a son of a bitch like that run anyway? Especially with a kid on him?" he asked.

"I don't know. . . ," I feigned with a slight murmur from the most childish face I could muster.

"Thanks. Thanks a lot, kid."

When it was race time, Johnny got permission to send a pony with Little Wolf and me as a safeguard, but the pony had to turn him loose a couple of times in the post parade when the studdish bastard tried to mount him, causing a mini-commotion in front of the grandstand. I could see Guerin's face frown as he watched our antics while we made a turn toward the starting gate. As we straightened out to gallop, I caught a good look at the odds board numerals in the centerfield.

Well Done was 1-2 and I was 40-1.

How could that be?

I didn't care about the rest of the numbers, but I was somewhat perplexed at the price on my horse. It finally hit me like a ton of bricks. Bill Beasley is not betting here through the mutuels; he's betting in Toronto with the bookmakers! I could hardly control my laughter. I was smiling like a jackass eating briars. The pony boy with me must have thought I was going simple.

I could hardly control myself as he handed me off to the assistant starters. They loaded me last, knowing what a rogue this bastard was. I had my half-cross and a forefinger full of mane in my left hand and my stick hand (right one) free. We hardly got into the gate when Little Wolf tried to break and ended up bouncing off of the iron front doors. It made a hell of a racket as the starting gate rocked heavily from the impact. I caught a glimpse of Eric watching the shit show with mild trepidation. I had one assistant starter with tongs on the horse's left ear and his head cocked sideways and two assistant starters each with a handful of red tail. The doors banged open loudly with a little recoil from the steel.

"THEY'RE OFF!" the track announcer said over the loud speaker.

Scaring the hell out of the seasoned rider was the only way I was going to help influence the outcome of this race.

Little Wolf broke clean, and I was about a half-length in front of Well Done soon out of the gate. I looked across at Guerin, and he looked at me, then he steadied Well Done to about a length and a half back. I dropped right over to plug the hole. Well Done was back behind me, and I had him boxed in—exactly where I wanted him. The rest of the field scattered on the outside of me. Three of them were under direct urging just to keep up. Little Wolf had one ear cocked facing forward and the left one laid back and ready to listen. He was in control and running easy. We were clear of Hialeah's flying black dirt, and I needed no adjustments to our trip at this point. Having Guerin and Well Done inside and behind me, we had run the first quarter in about twenty-three seconds, a comfortable pace.

We went to the turn, and I was sitting with a lot of horse still to let out. We started to go around the turn, and Well Done still couldn't go anywhere. There were a few horses on the outside that started to drift. When we straightened out, approaching the eighth pole, I had a quick flash of goose bumps. There was no Well Done in sight. I let Little Wolf out another notch; he accelerated briefly; I shook the stick at him on the right side and watched both his ears lay back. He wasn't focused on the crowd. There was nothing else to do but stay vigilant and sustain the pace of acceleration to the finish.

Well Done had come *undone* as I confidently completed the journey!

It was a hell of a race, and my most lucrative payday as a jockey, I thought as I galloped out around the turn.

It was a big accomplishment, as Little Wolf paid $83.80 for the win.

It is a game of details, I thought, pulling my tack from his back in the winner's circle! Johnny and the groom's eyes were as wide as saucers to me.

It was like a day with no end.

Just to win at Hialeah was a big stage accomplishment for a little kid from Canada.

While there were plaudits from several jockeys, saying things like, "Where did that son of a bitch come from?" the others were mostly stunned into silence. Upsets like this were unusual at Hialeah.

As it turns out, Johnny Passero got cold feet and didn't place a bet on the horse, and he was pissed.

Beasley, who only bet with the Canadian bookies, "broke every book-maker from Montreal to Vancouver," he quipped upon his return two days later.

Bobby Bateman had bet twenty dollars after I talked him into it *and* guaranteed it.

My mother was a nervous wreck, because she was still holding some of the winning tickets on the wagers she had placed. She had started cashing tickets right after the race but stopped when her purse was full. My father was no more composed, although he figured out that they could come back the next day and cash the balance at the "previous day ticket window."

"What do I do with all of this money?" she asked.

"It's a high-class problem!" I retorted.

I could never figure out how they always managed to turn a wonder-ful experience into shit—but they did. I appealed to their British pluck by congratulating them on their bravery and cooperation and let it go at that.

By my calculations, we had won somewhere over $125,000.

That's horseracing at its finest.

CHAPTER THIRTEEN

1956

Being a trainer is one of the hardest professions in horse racing. The hours are long, often demanding that you be at the track day and night. The mornings are especially lengthy. And time off is rare. If you're training, it's hard to miss a day. You don't want to risk seeing that turning point in a horse's career. When the horses are young, their characteristics can change fast, and the learning process can take time. A great horse trainer can lie in a field, simply watch his horses move, and then pick out the potential winners because he has the ability to spot the ones with the best leadership qualities. Trainers know what every nuance means. That's how they tell the talented ones, or those who have something special, from the rest.

To train a stable of ten or more horses requires a lot of attention to detail. Each horse is an individual and needs its own assessment, programs, feeding regimen, shoeing, working, galloping, training, and care. It's the same intensity as training an elite athlete. While some of today's trainers are working with up to two hundred horses, they also have a dozen assistant trainers who attend to the actual day-to-day training. Every horse is still getting that customized attention; however, the trainer is the director in that grand production.

A trainer assesses the ability of the horse. An owner will sometimes buy a horse without involving his or her trainer, but that rarely happens. They usually want the trainer's expert opinion—their knowledge of conformation and pedigree—to help ensure that their money is being spent wisely.

Sometimes an agent will act independently and buy a horse based solely on pedigree, but that, too, is unusual. Owners rely heavily on the judgment of their trainers. That's the pure and simple truth.

When a trainer is working with a horse, it takes at least thirty days to get into that horse's head. He has to see if he has the temperament as well as the mechanical ability. Sometimes it takes longer, anywhere between sixty and one hundred days to get to that point. Horses don't talk, so there's a lot of intuition in play. A good trainer needs to rely on instinct, because there is no other way to communicate. He is at the mercy of the components—the jockey, the grooms, the exercise rider—because they are the pit crew that tells the trainer how the horse is doing that day. The trainer is dependent on the knowledge and observations of these people. A good trainer will always pay attention to the feedback he hears because they offer a wealth of skills and understanding to draw from. He selects his team carefully knowing that every member contributes to the outcome, and helps to keep them in sync, for that winning combination.

The relationship between a trainer and a jockey, however, can often be contentious. The jockey will usually blame the trainer first if a horse's performance is not what he thinks it should be. Bettors, owners, and the public blame the trainer, too. The jockey is usually the last person on the food chain to take the heat, although there are lots of exceptions.

The trainer, of course, has a different perspective. He will always say it's the jockey's fault if a race is lost on a good horse because he was the last to touch the horse.

To be fair, sometimes the relationship between a jockey and trainer is good—especially when they are able to work as a team, like a race-car driver works with his engineer or crew chief. As long as you are doing well, conforming to the wishes of the trainer, and he believes you are following his instructions, life will be fine.

I seldom followed what the trainers said verbatim. And that is why I had trouble many, many times. Not so much because the outcome was different from what we both wanted, but because we differed in ideas about execution.

A race is very complex in terms of the incremental developments during the event.

In cases of an established stakes horse, fixed agreed-upon strategy is good policy. A stakes horse generally has developed a successful running style, either close-to-the-pace or come-from-behind. It is referred to as tactical speed;

however, most horses can maintain full gait for an average of three furlongs. It is unusual, but the good and great horses sometimes will exert a full gait for four furlongs. Then we can inject those incrementals, which can result in being badly or moderately impeded at some point in the race. This calls for PIC, or "pilot in command," to make or break decisions on how to "use" the horse's resources without depleting them too early. It is critical to be a finely tuned athlete with tremendous strategic abilities and knowledge of the anatomy of the animal.

Few have that combination of skills!

The fact that Johnny Passero didn't bet on Little Wolf that day at Hialeah bothered me. It indicated confidence problems in the horse's abilities that were never explained. That is not a great combination. However, despite our differences, Johnny went on to be in the hall of fame.

By the time we got back to Canada, it was time to prepare for the Queen's Plate. I would be riding Canadian Champ, the same horse I rode when he was a two-year-old to win the Cup and Saucer for the second time in 1955, the Grade I Coronation Futurity, and other top stakes in Canada, where he remained unbeaten. We shipped to New York, which, at the time, was considered the racing capital of the world, to get in a few races before the Queen's Plate. "The Champ," as I called Canadian Champ, was second and third to Career Boy, Nan's Mink, and Head Man, three of the top two-year-olds in the world, who would later go on to become Classic winners. This was one of the only times a Canadian-bred showed this level of ability until Northern Dancer came along.

Now three years old, Canadian Champ had established himself well and was living up to his name. I thought we had a good shot at winning the Queen's Plate, Canada's oldest Thoroughbred race and the oldest continuously run race in North America.

It was getting close to race day. There were three or four come-from-behind horses that some people were speculating could catch Canadian Champ; because at a mile and an eighth, it was a slightly longer race than he was used to running.

In 1956, the Queen's Plate was moved to the new Woodbine Racetrack outside of Toronto by the airport. The racetrack was considered a masterpiece for the times. But the track wasn't quite ready in terms of depth and consistency, so they shortened the Queen's Plate that year to a mile and an eighth from the traditional running of a mile and a quarter. Everyone had concerns about the race. If they were going to beat our horse, it would definitely be a track-related situation because the dirt track was a mess.

We spent several weeks breezing Canadian Champ in advance of the race at Gulfstream Park and Greenwood track at the east end of Toronto. I was on him each time he would breeze or work, though I never let him work to his maximum ability. I kept a hold of him and let him out a little, and he was wonderful every time.

After the final mile work, however, Passero flipped out. He was angry because he wanted to make the Champ really work and run hard, but I had reservations. I never used top gear unless he needed to win. I thought what I was doing was acceptable. But not doing what Johnny wanted pissed him off. Although we had never had a serious debate before then, I knew Passero was a hot-tempered guy. I also knew the horse could not be short because of the come-from-behind horses. Johnny was a former jockey under a lot of pressure who thought he knew more than I did. And maybe he did. But at this moment we were both entrenched in our positions.

The next morning, still infuriated, he commanded that we go out and work Canadian Champ another fast mile, an unusual step for a trainer.

I was flabbergasted by his audacity.

And pissed.

We were barely talking after that. I was concerned that he underestimated what the horse was getting out of his works.

Most horse trainers would agree that it was wrong for me not to take Passero's direction—they'd say I should have done what he wanted. But I didn't. Instead, I commenced to just work the Champ hard on the second day.

We were two bullheaded guys trying to prove we knew more than the other.

But the acrimony didn't end there. We were pointing for a seven-furlong prep for the Plate at Greenwood, which would set the Champ up for the big race. Being only seven furlongs, we encountered half a dozen sprinters, one of which was Laurie's Dancer, an extremely fast horse and an American bred.

Johnny's orders in the paddock were to take and maintain the lead at any cost. I knew the early fractions would be "sizzling," having studied the racing form and watched Laurie's Dancer win other short stakes before. But I also knew the longer we ran in this seven-furlong race, the more "in command" we would become, because Canadian Champ had both speed and endurance.

I had spoken to the rider of Laurie's Dancer before we went to the paddock for the race. He stated he had no other choice but to fight for the lead. I believed him and would have thought the same based on the past performance of the horse. I was perplexed by Johnny's orders, especially knowing and feeling the circumstances of Johnny's and my differing opinions.

I had to think "down the road."

Not only did we face the Queen's Plate, but we also had a lot of races left to run the rest of the year. I told myself his advice was a suicide mission.

I was riding in the post parade weighing the circumstances, when I came up with my answer.

I'd see how the field broke from the gate and, more particularly, how Laurie's Dancer breaks. If he stumbled at the start, it would be easier for me to take the lead—*if*. . .

I'd run out of time to figure out the rest of my options.

I was at the starting gate.

In we went.

I managed to have the Champ's ass backed into the rear doors and to have him take a step as the gates sprung open.

Bang!

Clang!

We outbroke the field by about a neck. I had the Champ in slight check to maintain the advantage. The jockey on Laurie's Dancer cocked his stick to an upright position and struck Laurie's Dancer three times with lots of slack in the reins. After registering those data, I instantly and instinctively checked the Champ.

We relinquished the lead.

The Champ relaxed as soon as he received my transmission to wait.

This was a "push button" horse. He was incredible!

Laurie's Dancer opened up a length and a half and then two lengths as a result of his momentum away from the gate and into the first three-eighths of a mile. I was 100 percent confident in our ability to reel the leader in but now had no desire to do it this quickly.

It was too early!

I could tell the fractions were on the outer edge of insane, and we were just fine.

Leaving the half-mile pole, I could see the leader was under no restraint and had no residual. We were gaining with no dramatic change in energy.

At the three-furlong marker the contest was ours to claim. I transmitted that desire to the Champ, and he lengthened his stride to win openly.

I knew, pulling up and galloping back after the race, that I'd have to explain my decision to alter Johnny's strategy, but I wasn't ready for the consequences that met us at the winner's circle.

Passero looked like an Indian doing a war dance as we jogged up to the entrance. Just looking at him, there was concern on my part that he'd risk a heart attack. He was gray, drawn, and livid to the point of hurling verbal abuse at me. He claimed I was intentionally defying him. It didn't sink in immediately that he was still riled by our disagreement a week and a half ago. He actually thought my actions in the race were intended to challenge his judgment. Nothing was further from the truth, but it was not the time or place to have that debate.

I know, without a doubt, if it hadn't been for Bill Beasley's intervention, Passero would have wanted to take me off the horse in the Plate. Days later, when I tried to explain the circumstances of pace, strategy, and possible injury and defeat, Passero became violent again, maintaining his position that I willfully ignored his directions.

He never got over it and carried his grudge well into the fall meet. I later learned that Beasley tried to make the point that the horse ran better for me and that it was high-risk to change jockeys. No matter what I did to make things right between us, our relationship would never be the same.

After that race, we had to put our differences aside so we could get through the running of the Queen's Plate. The Woodbine racecourse was far from perfect, and there was a lot of concern about the conditions. The main dirt track had some questionable mixes of soils and was too deep. It appeared as if there were too much clay and not enough sand and silt. But the course was Chairman E. P. Taylor's pride and joy, and it had to be open for the Queen's Plate.

The entries for the Queen's Plate drew a good field, including one other horse, O'Morrissey, that had a lot of early speed to be aware of, but I didn't think there would be any real competition. I didn't know the exact conditions on the track, but I expected the dirt to be on the deep side, favoring the plodders and come-from-behind contenders.

There were thirty-five thousand people in attendance the day of the race, a large turnout for Canada. It was thrilling and exhilarating, though sometimes that much noise can spook a horse. I didn't want anything to interfere with my odds of winning on that glorious afternoon.

The pomp and pageantry of the Queen's Plate is second to none. The gift of fifty guineas from her majesty dates back more than a hundred years and has done a great deal for Canadian pedigree, which is its purpose. Historically, Canada fields one or two horses a year that rank in the top ten horses in North America—wonderful for a country that breeds an average of two thousand foals in comparison to the U.S., which accounts for over twenty thousand annually.

Canadian Champ put on his normal show, rising on his hind legs in the paddock to demonstrate his soft dominance. The large crowds had become accustomed to his prerace performance, and he seldom disappointed.

The Champ broke from the gate a little tardy, due to an assistant starter who insisted on being in the gate with me with a hold of the left rein. He placed his body in front of me and the horse's neck, retarding the chance for a clean break. My right knee and shoulder raked against the side of the gate. It was just for an instant, but it was enough to slow us down. I can't say for certain if it was at all intentional, but it felt like it. Bookmakers had a long reach in those days, and I always had my suspicions.

After the break I let the horse straighten up, and we were neck and neck going into the first turn. There were three of us vying for the lead. The agreed-upon strategy was to be on the lead. Johnny's instructions were short and to the point.

I steadied the bay colt around the first turn and into the backstretch. I let the Champ lay head-to-head with no additional urging. I kept him there and didn't let him open up until the time was right. I could hear the other horses breathing heavily as they galloped just at our flank. As we straightened down the backstretch, he opened up on the field with his normal ability. Leaving the four-furlong marker, he continued his dominance without urging. He was handling the laboring track with little problem. This horse was so tough, he would run on broken beer bottles if asked. From the quarter pole, my horse was pricking his ears and paying close attention to what was in front of him.

As we neared the grandstand, the roar of the cheering crowd reached a crescendo—a sound much louder than the Champ had ever heard before during a race. Horses can sometimes hear an echo, which we had endured before, so I opened up a little bit more but still well within himself. Two horses, London Calling and Argent, were making an expected bid but were too far back for me to see. If they were going to catch us, they were going to have to be right at us by the eighth pole, because we were only at half throttle. There was no further challenge, and Canadian Champ convincingly crossed the finish line, magnificently triumphant. It was all his game. He was a true champion!

This was beyond exciting because the international recognition and prestige of winning this race put me in a whole new category in my career.

I took a deep breath to inhale this victorious moment of joy.

Everything I worked for since I was a boy climaxed in this race!

Best of all, my entire family was there to see me win. I thought I had finally made them proud.

It was gratifying to know that I had carried on our family legacy in horse racing and had accomplished something no one else in our history had ever done before.

I let the Champ gallop out around the turn and pull up slowly after the race. I took my time to take in some of the faces of the hundreds of people who had gathered on the backstretch. They were looking, clapping, and cheering for Canadian Champ and me. I let the horse gallop out by them so they could get an up-close look, which is something I believe the backstretch people deserve. They are not the people who pay the big dollars to get into the grandstand area. They are there for the love of the sport and are just as entitled as the others to see us.

Out of the corner of my eye I caught a glimpse of an old familiar face under a cowboy hat perched on a tall frame.

"Hi ya, Dave," he said.

It was Tex.

He had his same old hat on and that big fat half-chewed cigar in his mouth.

Admittedly, I was a little melancholy when I saw him. I had just accomplished the greatest victory in Canadian horse racing. I was enjoying the moment, and he was applauding like everyone else. It was bittersweet to have him there.

I took my hand, extended it toward him, and said, "Thank you, Tex. Glad you could be here."

I suppose he could have been in a bar somewhere drinking a boiler-maker, but he wasn't. He had followed what I was doing. At least, that's what people later told me.

The winner's enclosure was special.

It was "David's Day," I thought selfishly as I paraded around among the cameras.

Bill Beasley was handsome and glowing. He had finally bumped the establishment and taken their perch. Not just today, but that whole year we rode together. We had become a formidable force in Canadian racing!

The trumpets and French horns struck a penetrating imperial chorus amid the military snap of one hundred drums. The decorations and trophies were presented by Sir Vincent Massey, the lieutenant governor of Canada. The handshakes were abundant, and then it was over.

Upon reaching the jockey's room, I was greeted by Jim Vipond, Milt Dunnell, and other senior members of the press. We had spent many hours over the years discussing the results of stakes with the media, but this was different because of the gate incident, the distance, and the magnitude of the event. The interviews were hastily interrupted because I had to attend the award ceremony later that night.

I quickly donned a rented tuxedo that was hanging in my locker, escaped the congratulations and slaps on the back of the many well-wishers around the track, and was guided to a waiting limousine that ushered me off to the swank Toronto Club, where once again the lieutenant governor greeted me amidst great pomp and pageantry and glove-wearing swells. I'd come a long way from the turkey house in Versailles. It was an extraordinary night for this miniature intruder. But I welcomed its conclusion. It was a world I never knew and didn't much enjoy. I wasn't sure I deserved all of this attention for winning a race.

The next day, I walked around the backstretch to visit with some of the old timers I'd known from the days when I used to sneak into the old Woodbine track. I had, over the years, developed a small fan club of guys that I had ridden for who had nothing but their asses and elbows. I was a popular guy because of the years I had spent with them in the backstretch—and they were all still there. To them, I was the first Woodbine-born-and-bred Queen's Plate winner, and I never forgot where I came from. They appreciated the time I took that day.

A few years later, Tex paid me a visit in Toronto. He'd gotten married to Gladys the hatcheck girl from the Long Branch Hotel near the racetrack. I thought that was amusing. He and Gladys came by the house for dinner and talked about old times. It was nice to see Tex happy and in love. Gladys was good for him, and he seemed genuinely happy. I suppose that night healed up any old wounds that remained festering for me.

We said our good-byes and fond farewells, as Gladys and Tex headed out to Ohio in the same old Buick he drove when I was with him. They looked as though they were dressed for their honeymoon. I later heard the old car gave out on the New York State Thruway. While Tex was standing on the side of the road with his head under the hood, a semitrailer truck hit the car from behind. Gladys was killed instantly. Tex was left in bad shape. He was comatose and wasn't expected to recover.

Tex's 90-year-old mother drove from Pecos, Texas, to take him home. I offered to help her in any way I could, but there wasn't much anyone could do.

In all of the years I knew Tex, I'd never heard him talk about his mother. In fact, he never went back to Texas or even wrote a letter home as far as I knew. I volunteered to drive him back for her, but I never heard from anyone with more details. She just made the trip herself. I don't know what happened to Tex after that, but I assumed the worst. To this day, I can never completely remove his imposing presence from my mind.

Despite my winning the Queen's Plate, the relationship with Passero was in decline. There were deep-seated issues between us that were never going to be resolved. Shortly after the Queen's Plate win, he entered Canadian Champ in the Ohio Derby without telling me. I had never been off that horse. I don't know if Passero did it out of jealousy or spite, but our feud seemed to have escalated without my input. Jealousy and animosity are so destructive. It has always been known that acid will destroy the container it's held in! I found out soon that Johnny engaged another famous jockey, Hedley Woodhouse, to ride the Champ. According to his groom, Bruce Naylor, the horse did his customary raring up routine in the paddock. Woodhouse became terrified of him. The Champ bolted, turning into the backstretch. According to the racing form chart, he came in last place to a very mediocre field. That loss made things worse than ever. Johnny's greatest fear had become a reality: now it was Johnny's future that was questionable. Bill Beasley was furious with him over his careless and selfish decision.

Soon after that race, I was contracted to ride the Champ in the Prince of Wales Stakes, which is the second leg of the Canadian Triple Crown. We won with gusto!

Canadian Champ and I were an established team—you can't break up a team and think they will perform the same as before.

I won many stakes under our agreement, but in the Canadian Breeder's Cup, Passero told me that if I rode the Champ, I couldn't take a commission. He was giving it to the stable help. He was still so bitter. It took me a long time to figure it out, but I finally realized that his anger was really over Little Wolf.

There comes a time when all good things must come to an end. My relationship with Passero was beyond repair. There was nothing good left to hold onto or worth saving. There was a lot of spite that couldn't be negotiated. Worst of all, the main victim in this case was Canadian Champ. His form was being compromised because of silly machinations. It was really a bad and disappointing situation. Fans and people were complaining, and that was leaving a bad taste in my mouth. Beasley didn't have a stud for him, so he was sold to Windfields Farm, where he produced two "horse of the year" colts, including a Triple Crown winner in Canada. Later he was sold to Japanese interests. Secretly, I was happy he reproduced himself with great distinction. He was a true Canadian breed.

While Canadian Champ went on to greener pastures, it was time for me to consider doing the same. In 1957, I left Beasley and Passero to ride for True Davis, Jr., a wealthy pharmaceutical executive who eventually became the Canadian ambassador to Switzerland and who, at the time, was the assistant secretary to the treasury. Unfortunately, that arrangement turned out to be rather short-lived.

A good friend of mine from my Oaklawn Park days was training for Davis in New England. I realized pretty quickly that I wasn't happy with the trainer's assessment of the stable. I knew he was a great trainer who had a terrific career, and I didn't want to second-guess him. True Davis was a nice man whom I considered a friend. I didn't want to waste anyone's time, money, or expectations.

At the time, I was seriously struggling with my weight. I was starting to get mean with horses and to lose my congenial personality. I had done enough, won enough, lost enough, and witnessed enough from the saddle. My jockey days were over. It was time to quit. I didn't know what I would do or where I would go next, but I definitely knew it was time to pull the plug. I didn't want to wait to hit bottom. I preferred to exit with grace and dignity.

I called my father and told him I was returning to Canada.

The day after I said good-bye, a horse I was scheduled to ride broke his leg and fell. The jockey who replaced me was critically injured and never recovered.

They say, in life, everything happens for a reason. While I felt awful that the jockey who rode that horse was hurt so badly, I knew in my gut it was a sign. It was definitely time for me to hang up my boots and switch. That could have been me—would have been me—if I had ridden just one more day.

CHAPTER FOURTEEN

My decision to quit racing in 1957 came with a lot of mixed emotions. On the one hand, it was a tremendous relief. The mounting pressure of maintaining a constant weight was getting to be too much. I was always so preoccupied with losing weight. But quitting was also perplexing because of the incredible amount of information, skills, and athletic perception I had acquired over the years. It seemed as if I couldn't apply that knowledge to anything else. Outside of the racecourse, I had no real life. I was always in training and maintaining mode, so I had no social life to speak of. When I was riding, most of my evenings were spent going out to dinner, but not eating! I was always in the company of men, and always talking about racing or debating the virtues of various horses. It was "all business, all the time." It was hard not to share all the accumulated information I had to offer. It was constantly running through my head. While it was still extremely prized, it had to come to a point where my body was fighting against my ambitions.

So as I drove my Cadillac in silent contemplation from New England back to Canada, I was resolute about my decision to leave riding for good. What I wasn't sure of was what I'd do next. I didn't have an exact plan. I figured I would see what was out there and look for something that felt right for me, whether it was as a trainer or racing official.

I struggled with my demons for a couple of months. I went to Florida and galloped a few horses for two trainers I knew and liked just to stay connected to the sport. Their horses were really nice, and I must admit it felt good to be in the saddle. I don't know any elite athlete who truly walks away from their sport without wondering what it would be like to make that great comeback. I was no exception. I played the "what if" game in my head over and over.

"Dave, why don't you ride for us?" one of the trainers inquired.

The thought had surely crossed my mind more than once. I was only ten pounds above what I could ride at professionally, and I knew I could shed that if I wanted to. As tempting as it was, there just wasn't enough on the table or in the future to convince me to rethink my decision. There would be nothing worse than to come back and lose. I had to put my glory days behind me and look toward the future, even if I didn't know what was in store for me.

The more I thought about it, the more I realized that exercising the horses and being around the track placated me to some degree. I didn't need to race to fulfill my desire to be around horses. Of course, I knew I wouldn't make a great living as an exercise rider, but I had plenty of money, so that wasn't my motivation anyway.

What I had a lot of was information. I had a great knowledge about horses, more than most trainers I knew, so I thought training horses might be the right avenue for me. In many ways, it would have been the sweetest revenge on all of those trainers I'd come up against as a jockey, who I thought didn't know shit from Shinola. But I wasn't certain revenge was what I was seeking. What was the point in that? I'd had a great career as a jockey. Did I really have anything left to prove as a trainer?

Probably not.

While I was contemplating my next move, I received an unexpected job offer to become a racing official with the Ontario Jockey Club, the Canadian organization that controlled racing and owned the racecourses, which consisted of Woodbine, Fort Eerie, and Greenwood. It's a very large and prestigious operation. I was quite flattered to receive the call. George Hendrie, the acting president, thought I had a bright future as an official because I understood the sport from the other side. I certainly knew every inch of the track, which gave me great perspective. I was bright, had a little bit of a celebrity status, and knew all of the jockeys and trainers, too, which gave me some clout with the organization and the stables. Although it was a menial position, I took it because I knew I could rise quickly up the ranks into management and operations. I had ridden for a lot of the trustees and directors in the organization, and knew they carried a lot of influence in Canadian racing.

And so my journey from jockey to official began. The position the Jockey Club created for me was called "reporting claims of foul," which refers to when jockeys pull up in the turn to launch an objection or a foul against one another rather than waiting until the race is over. I had a hotline directly to the steward's stand to accelerate the process of looking at films, which had to be developed back in those days before anyone could review them and come to a judgment. We didn't have instant video playback then the way we do now.

It was an ideal position for me because I knew the language of racing. I could communicate with the jockeys and the officials in ways both would understand. I could offer my expert opinion on any given scenario. Jockeys, in general, are hotheaded, so they can become hostile when they don't have the details about the conflicts that occurred during the running of a race. Speed and accuracy are essential to maintaining harmony on the track and to pacifying the wagering public.

I was quickly moved into a patrol judge position, which is someone who can be moved from one location on the track to another depending on the length of the race. The quarter-pole position is where most incidents happen because it is where the horses are beginning to make their move. If a patrol judge spots a conflict from any of his vantage points, he reports it to the stewards overlooking the finish line before the race is over.

I spent a year rotating between the three racecourses the Jockey Club controlled and owned before being moved into the racing secretary's office to work in the mornings during entry time.

Compiling information for the formulation of each race is a major function of the racing secretary's office. The oversight of races in the afternoons completes the learning curve and provides the bridge between the Jockey Club and the racing secretary's office. Accuracy in the process is absolutely essential to provide a fair playing field among the horsemen and the horses.

Whenever I was in Fort Eerie, I bunked with my former valet and friend, Ronnie Robinson, instead of staying at a hotel. Ronnie was married, so he suggested I look into a local boarding house owned by Mrs. Bikey, a lady who always had the local priests and bishops over on a regular basis. Mrs. Bikey's husband had died some years back, and I knew her daughter as an acquaintance.

One morning, I noticed a cute young girl helping with chores at the boarding house. I'd come back from the racetrack early and found her making my bed. I was caught off guard by her presence in every way. I innocently said, "Hello." She talked differently from the other girls, which I liked—but I also realized she was too young to pursue in a romantic way. Besides, at the time, I was dating Miss Toronto. Even so, I thought there was no harm in getting to know the young bed-maker.

"Who is that?" I asked.

"Her name is Barbara. She's my daughter's best friend. They grew up together," Mrs. Bikey said with a knowing look on her face.

"Can you introduce me?" I asked.

I took Barbara out on a date to the drive-in movie shortly after.

There seemed to be chemistry between us. She was likable and nice, and I was attracted to her. But she was just 16, and I was 21, which made her too young for me. Besides, I was leaving for Toronto at the end of the meet, and I had a steady girlfriend.

By the time I returned to Fort Eerie for the next summer meet, Barbara and I had spent some time exchanging letters and really getting to know each other better. That became the glue. When we went to dinner, I'd order steak and she'd order a hamburger and French fries. She was casual in the way young people are, and I felt older—maybe too old. I wined and dined her, even though she couldn't drink alcohol. We went to fine restaurants night after night. I never noticed that she wasn't eating the food on her plate—she was just moving it from side to side. Here I was, showing off by paying for fancy meals, and she couldn't have cared less. I'd forgotten she was still in high school.

The summer season came to a close and for the moment, so did my relationship with Barbara. It wasn't until the following spring meet that we met again while standing in line at the bank. We didn't say much to each other. What was there to say? I hadn't called, written, or come to take her out in over ten months. As I walked away, I realized how I really felt about this girl.

I called her house and spoke to her stepfather, who answered the phone.

"It's Dave Stevenson. May I speak to Barbara?"

"She's not here," he said coldly.

When Barbara called me back, she flatly refused to go out. I was upset. But she was still just a teenager and in high school. I suppose I understood her reaction.

In the meantime, I was doing several jobs with the Ontario Jockey Club, and I was also getting a master's-level education in racecourse management. That education would become invaluable as I grew into my career in racing operations.

Since Canada is geographically isolated in many respects and purses are much smaller than in the U.S., it was always a struggle to get big-name horses to come to our tracks. The program was also limited to Canadian-bred horses, which made things even more difficult. Cheap and beaten claiming horses dominated the herd and drove down handle.

Monetary differentials also played into our challenges, as the American dollar was worth twenty cents more than the Canadian. The Ontario Jockey Club and horse owners were trying to elevate their stakes ranks and contenders, but the policies and system worked against the change.

Knowing the odds were stacked against us, I concocted several plans to rebuild and reconfigure the herd, and to radically change policies governing our growth. First, we eliminated beaten claiming races and minimized Canadian-bred claiming. These changes narrowed the options, so there were no longer too many categories and selections. By eliminating categories, we effectively channeled more horses into fewer types of races, creating a greater volume of horses to fuel open-claiming and allowance races. I was always prone to looking at ways to help the operation improve. I saw things differently because of where I had been; I had slept on dirt floors and was housed in fire traps. I knew the areas of the tracks that few others ever looked at. Nobody cared much about the backstretch or the rules and regulations there. When I rode, I benefited by officiating, but I was also a victim of it. The industry needed to make changes with the help and leadership of someone who understood what the game was about. It had become "us and them."

I was articulate and could put together the right people, those who had the power and ability to make the decisions to get things done. For a jockey, that was a lot of power. Although I no longer identified myself as a jockey, I was still being lauded for what I was doing for racing by many in and around the sport. This recognition gave me opportunities to advance quicker and to accelerate my experience, which I fully embraced. I was far better off supporting and working within the track than living outside of it.

The one area of my life that needed attention now was my love life. After much pursuit, Barbara finally agreed to go out with me. She smartly played hard to get, and it worked. After she graduated high school, she started coming to Toronto on the bus to visit me. Friends of mine had a house where she stayed. She couldn't stay with me because I was still living at home with my parents. I was desperately seeking more independence from them as our relationship grew. Barbara and my romance was developing quickly, and that made some people uncomfortable—most especially my parents. I was terribly unhappy in their home, again, which may have been one of the reasons I was now looking to accelerate things with Barbara. And for a period, as a way of dealing with my angst, I began to drink too much. I started by drinking gin and lemon—a kiddie drink, but then moved into rye, Canadian Club, Seagram's V/O—just about anything I could get my hands on to help stabilize me, which of course, is never the answer. I was at my wit's end and was using alcohol as a way to cope and escape. Barbara didn't drink, so most of the time I was drinking with my buddies or, worse, alone.

Frustrated, I left their house and headed where I was the happiest—with Barbara. When I walked through the door, she could tell I was mad as hell. I pulled a red velvet box out of my coat pocket, handed it to her, and simply said, "Here. See if you still think I am such a bad guy."

I was probably planning something nicer, but in the moment, that was about all I had up my sleeve for romance. We had talked about getting married; I knew we would. Though, to be certain, there were a few people trying to talk me out of it because they thought I had such a great life and that my relationship with Barbara was somehow undermining it. But my mind was made up. I looked to her for the future. Hell yeah—this was the girl I was going to marry.

Barbara and I wed a few days before the summer meet in Fort Eerie on July 16, 1959. No one from my family came to either the ceremony or reception except my sister, Ginny. About a month before the wedding, the others made it known they would just attend the next one!

When my parents made it clear that they weren't going to be there, it was crushing. They did everything they could to break up our engagement— and as far as I could tell, it was over money. To them, money was God. They saw Barbara as "that little girl from Fort Eerie." They never really looked at her as worthy enough for me or them. That kind of rejection of the woman I planned to make a life with was the final nail in the coffin. I had no choice but to disown my parents in every way. If I wanted to make a life with Barbara, I had to let go of my life with my mom and dad once and for all. I was livid, hurt, and full of hate.

Barbara and I never spoke about their refusal to come to our wedding or to accept my relationship with my wife until they found out Barbara was pregnant and ready to have the baby. It was very hurtful to both of us. It would take many years for Barbara and me to heal from the pain and hurt that the dismantling of our family caused.

The real reason for the rift was that they somehow thought Barbara was affecting their financial security—through my elimination of the joint account with my mother and also the ownership of the Florida house. They relied heavily on the one hundred dollars per week I paid and the various other contributions I made to the upkeep of their home and cars. I finally just gave them the house at our last meeting. After that, Barbara and I rented our own place in Florida as far away from them as we could get without being too far away from the track in south Florida. It was a very bitter time. They could see I was gaining in stature and would soon be my father's boss, which eventually happened. This development put me in charge of his employment and his pay scale, which became as emotionally devastating to them as my disowning them was to me.

CHAPTER FIFTEEN

1963

Marge Everett was a well-known, wealthy socialite from Chicago. She was a Russian Jew adopted by Benjamin Franklin Lindheimer. In the world of Thoroughbred racing, there was no one who moved with more magisterial calm or exercised such great power more ruthlessly or more tactfully than Lindheimer. Though he was thought to have ties to the mob, no one could ever prove it. When he died of a heart attack at age 69, Marge took control of the two racetracks Lindheimer owned at the time: Arlington Park, long considered one of the finest tracks in America, and Washington Park, both just outside of Chicago. In the process, she also inherited Lindheimer's enemies—political and otherwise.

Marge was no stranger to the racetracks. She starting going there when other girls her age were home playing with dolls. In her teens, she mingled with the crowds at her stepfather's venues until she was old enough to start working at both. She learned everything she could from running the switchboard (not something she was particularly well-suited for due to her lisp) to eventually becoming his chief assistant in 1949, after he suffered his first heart attack. For years, Marge operated as a behind-the-scenes boss, overseeing the administrative details of both tracks and never missing a beat.

She had developed a shrewd work ethic similar to Lindheimer's but lacked his polish and tact. She was tough, brash, and made a lot of enemies as she clawed her way to the top of the boys' club. She was a unique woman who was both cunning and brilliant.

In need of someone with my background, Marge sent a fellow named Larry Marsh up to Toronto to talk to me about coming to Arlington Park and working for her as the racing secretary there. It was a prestigious position. Larry was the son of the CEO of the Santa Fe Railroad. He was a young, handsome guy and a real smooth talker. Standardbred racing was his passion. I'd just finished a season on loan to Assiniboia Downs in Winnipeg, working primarily as steward and racing secretary and dealing with a large Indian nation. I'd definitely had my fill of colorful characters and wasn't sure I wanted to take on another similar post. I knew how tough Marge was to work for and how eccentric she was to be around. I heard lots of stories from the many horsemen I'd met over the years. But even so, Frank Merrill, a former leading American trainer for whom I had ridden successfully from time to time, urged me to take the job.

By this time, our son, David, born in 1960, was three years old, and our daughter, Dianna, born in 1962, was still just a baby. Every time we moved, it meant uprooting the kids and starting all over. Living the life of a nomad is one thing when you're on your own, but now, as a family man, there was a lot more to consider. Barbara and I talked it over, anyway, and we both came to the same conclusion: this was a once-in-a-lifetime opportunity that we couldn't pass up. So I accepted the position.

We moved to Chicago and initially lived at the Inn, which is the clubhouse Marge had built into a house—a mansion really—right at the racetrack at Arlington Park. It overlooked the finish line and was the place Marge also called home.

We were immediately thrust into the high life, with big parties and celebrities coming and going every day and night. We felt like a couple of country folk who landed someplace we clearly didn't belong. Every time I turned around, I saw and met people I recognized from the movies. Cary Grant, Roy Rogers, Jimmy Durante, Dale Robertson, and Elizabeth Taylor were all regulars at Arlington and often stayed at the Inn at the same time.

Marge never had any children, but she loved her dog Biff, a boxer, like he was her child. She was eccentric as hell, so she often threw lavish parties for Biff, dressing him in costumes, clown suits, and even pajamas at night. His favorite evening dish was meat loaf, prepared and served by a staff of six.

"Biff would like you to be at his birthday party today," Marge said to me one afternoon.

At first I thought she was joking, but then I realized she wasn't. She was dead serious.

I had only been on the job for a couple of weeks, so I dared not refuse the invitation. I had to go. When I arrived at the party, all of Marge's secretaries and staff were there. Biff was sitting on a chair with his birthday party hat perched on his head. He was used to wearing such attire, so he didn't knock it off.

What do you bring a dog that has everything? I thought.

Dale Robertson, of Wells Fargo television fame, gave her a full-size oil painting of Biff wearing a clown suit and a tuxedo by a leading artist.

I wasn't that clever.

I brought a large Milk Bone biscuit.

We sat through twenty minutes of Marge reading telegrams from celebrities and friends wishing Biff a happy birthday. There was even a singing telegram delivered from a high-profile movie star in L.A.!

"Happy Birthday, Biff! Woof, Woof!"

The birthday cake was made of dog food and shortcake. Biff dove in. Every once in a while he would come up for air, "woof" happily, and lick the food from his face.

"Oh, Biffy boy!" Marge squealed.

All of the women who worked for Marge were afraid of the big son of a bitch and would practically wet their pants with fear every time he came near them. He drove the girls crazy because Marge would make them take him for walks, or she would have him sit in the reception area of her office during meetings, and he had terrible gas problems—I presume because of the homemade spicy meat loaf he ate. Whenever Marge would have Biff come back into the office, the people walking through the reception area would look at the secretaries and wonder who had passed gas.

You had to be careful talking badly about Biff behind Marge's back. If she caught you, she'd have you fired on the spot. To be certain, Marge fired people on a daily basis for far less significant reasons.

There was a rumor for years that Biff was worth a cool two million in ransom without a call to the cops if he went missing. It was half rumor and half reality, because a lot of people hated Marge. There was no doubt there was a bounty on that dog's head.

As I got more comfortable, Marge introduced me to everyone. One night, she told me to take care of one of her guests.

"Get him anything he needs, David," she said.

It was Jimmy Durante. I was thrilled because I was a huge fan of his. I took him to the racetrack, to lunch, and to the nightclub at Arlington Park, where he had been booked to perform. I was his official guide and chaperone whenever he was in town. My sole responsibility was to make sure he was well taken care of and had a good time.

The track had an alphanumeric board that was sponsored by Coca-Cola. At the time, it was one-of-a-kind. I was the only guy who had the key to unlock it. Whenever we were expecting high-profile guests at the track, Marge liked me to welcome them on the board.

"Welcome, Mayor Daley," and so on.

The employees at the track used to joke around, saying that if they got fired, they would pay me $1,000 to put up a big "Fuck You, Marge" message on the board that day.

I always laughed and said, "That will be on *my* last day!"

We all knew Marge had tentacles that extended a long way.

Working for Marge required wearing many hats and working your ass off. It was a twenty-one-hour day—every day. During the Washington Park harness meeting, I worked in publicity there from 7:00 to 11:30 p.m., after working in the racing office at Arlington Park from 6:00 a.m. until 6:00 at night. But I loved it. I really did. It was exciting and different.

When it looked like my position with Marge was secure, Barbara and I decided to buy a house and settle down. We needed a break from the track, and the kids needed room to play. We went over to look at a home in a new upscale neighborhood called Plum Grove Estates near the racetrack in Arlington Heights.

Barbara and I loved the house, but it was a lot more money than we wanted to spend. Marge knew we were in a quandary about our decision. Never one to let something like money or price get in the way of getting whatever she wanted, Marge picked up the phone, called the builder, and said, "Hello, my boy David is here and wants a house you've got for sale in Plum Grove. You are charging him way too much. Who do you think you're fooling?"

"Who is this?" the builder asked, taking great exception to the call.

"Marge Everett."

That's all she needed to say.

"Oh, sure thing, Mrs. Everett," he said and then knocked a lot off the price for me.

She was a woman of great influence, wealth, and prestige. It seemed everyone knew Marge and the massive power she wielded. Whether it was her alleged ties to the mob or just her larger-than-life persona, no one said no to Marge Everett.

Once we settled into the house, I began to get nervous because I had applied for my green card and received notification that I had been denied due to the quota system. No Canadian had ever held a position of this stature outside of Canada. Barbara was getting antsy, too. She had just given birth to Rebecca and didn't want to face packing up the home we had just moved into.

I decided to go to Mrs. Everett with my problem.

"I have an issue that isn't good," I nervously explained.

"David, you make big things out of little things."

"I hate to disagree with you, ma'am. This is big to me."

"Get Hubert on the phone," she barked out to one of the several secretaries who sat outside her office.

"Hubert? I've got a boy here, David Stevenson, and he needs a green card. They say he can't get one. You tell them they can do it. Tell them I don't want any nonsense. It's interfering with his thinking. Call me back, and, when you do, don't tell me you can't. Bye, Hubert." She spoke without ever letting the man get a word in.

"Mrs. Everett, I don't know who you just called, but I—"

"It was Hubert Humphrey, David."

He was the vice president of the United States at the time.

I had my green card in three days.

Marge certainly had friends in all of the right places. Her lawyer eventually became a Supreme Court justice. She contributed to every politician's political campaign—local and national—so when the time came for her to call in a favor, she had every single one of them in her pocket. No one could ever say no to that woman, and, for as long as I worked with her, no one ever did. You couldn't cross Marge, and anyone who knew her knew not to try.

Arlington Park had been my home for three wonderful action-packed and unforgettable years. Being there gave witness to some of the greatest people and horse races that I had ever seen. I always looked forward to the Arlington Classic, one of the most prestigious events in horse racing. During my last Classic as an Ambassador for the track, I spent most of the day in and out of box seating mingling with the hoi polloi who frequented this glorious event, and having lunch in the presence of the legendary actor John Forsythe. I watched in awe with the rest of the world as the powerful Phipps family's mighty Buckpasser broke a world record for the mile around our track, circling it in a staggering 1:32 and 2/5—defeating the Kentucky Derby and Preakness winner (and Triple Crown hopeful) Kauai King in the bargain. There was audible disappointment among the crowd when Kauai King lost that day and deafening victory cheers among those who had bet against him. Hall of Fame trainer Bill Wimfrey shipped him back to Arlington in August and won the American Derby, breaking the track record for a mile and an eighth with stable mate Impressive setting a record-breaking pace for the mile.

Those were heady days at the races, followed by grueling evenings when I would drive to Washington Park harness track to fill my additional role as the acting assistant publicity director. My slate was full—too full—but I was in the presence of the greatest trotters and pacers in the world. Watching Dancing David, Adios Vic, Cardigan Bay, and the Farrington brothers made the journey thrilling. Bob Farrington drove and made harness racing every bit as spectacular and exciting as the best jockeys I had ever seen made Thoroughbred racing. Most of the time, those twenty-one-hour working days were some of the happiest in my life.

As much as I enjoyed working for Marge and her organization, toward the end of my run I knew it was time to get out. Things were beginning to get ugly, because I could see she was in cahoots with the racing commissioners and Mayor Daley. I overheard too many conversations about borderline illegal activities, and I knew I'd end up being subpoenaed if the heat got turned up. I sat in on a conversation indicating Secretary of State Paul Powell had $2 million behind the wallpaper in his office. During his years as secretary of state, Powell was investigated for corruption, but he was never convicted. The truth didn't come out until after he died of a heart attack in 1970. His death was kept a secret for more than twenty-four hours, while aides removed incriminating papers from his office. Unfortunately, there was so much to incriminate Paul Powell that they couldn't collect everything. After Powell's funeral, his friend John Rendleman, chancellor of Southern Illinois University-Edwardsville, opened the secretary of state's Springfield hotel room and found $800,000 in cash packed in shoeboxes, strongboxes, and briefcases, all hidden in the closet. Clearly, he was into some things that weren't "kosher."

I could sense things were finally getting too hot when I was approached by an employee named McKinsey at the track, asking if Joey "Doves" Aiuppa could come to the track. In September 1962, as part of Robert Kennedy's crackdown on the Chicago Outfit, FBI agents in Kansas searching Aiuppa's car discovered 563 frozen doves. While awaiting trial, Joey had to lay low. He couldn't do much of anything, but he loved the horses. He and a trainer named Arnold Winnick wanted me to approach Marge about Joey coming to the track. I didn't want to do it. I thought Joey was just some local thug. I didn't know he was a big-time mafioso. I also didn't realize Joey had some horses that Winnick was training but running under another name. None of that really mattered anyway, because when I brought his name up to Marge, she simply said, "No Joey Aiuppa."

I knew Marge wasn't a proponent of the Mafia, but I had never seen her so adamant. Everything she was doing was cooked, and, yet, the mere mention of this man's name made her blood run icy cold.

That night, I realized it was time to get Barbara and the kids out of Chicago and wind things down for myself. I wanted to be gone before the situation got out of control.

The next day I told McKinsey that Marge wouldn't honor Aiuppa's request.

He must have gone back and told Winnick that I wouldn't do it.

About a week later, I got into my brand-new shiny Pontiac. I'd just bought the car a couple of days earlier. It was flashier than I usually go for but really nice. When I turned the key in the ignition, I noticed the engine was having trouble. Smoke began to come out from under the hood.

I quickly called the dealer where I had bought the car, and he came right over with a tow truck.

"Sorry about that, Mr. Stevenson. We'll take it over to the shop and let you know what we find," he said.

About an hour later I received a call from the dealership.

"I don't know how to tell you this. There is an apparatus in the car that appears to be a bomb." His voice was trembling as he gave me this disturbing news.

This *was* new.

"Be careful, Mr. Stevenson," he warned.

It wasn't hard to figure out which car was mine at the track. I had a parking spot with a sign that had my name right on it. It was nothing for Aiuppa to put the hit out to blow me up.

I told Marge what had happened. She brought in extra security, but it wasn't enough to make me want to stay. I had kids and a wife. Besides, the Jockey Club in Ontario wanted me back, offering me a job as the director of racing.

The time had come to say good-bye.

"Marge, thank you for the opportunities you gave me here during these three wonderful years. I will never forget what you've done for me. My experiences in Chicago were a time of great prestige and pride. I dealt with Kentucky Derby winners and all of the major stakes winners."

"David, I understand your feelings and that your wife is gone. . . ." She thought Barbara had left me. She didn't know I had sent her back to Canada for her own safety. I didn't feel the need to explain myself any further.

Many years later, when I was vice president of the New York Racing Association, I received a telephone call. It was Marge. She told me she and Martha Kilroe were coming to Belmont Park racecourse in New York, and she didn't trust anyone else to make the arrangements for her. I was delighted to accommodate her and have the chance to reciprocate all she had done to advance my career.

When Marge arrived, we had lunch. After, we chatted and caught up, then enjoyed a great day at the races.

"I'm proud of you. You're one of my boys!" she said upon leaving.

It was a softness that I had never seen Marge show and was completely out of character. The fact that I could please her was astounding. *She is human!* I thought.

That was the last time I saw Marge Everett, and it's the fond way I want to remember her.

CHAPTER SIXTEEN

1967

When I returned to Canada as the new director of racing, I had a single goal in my mind—to improve the conditions of the Ontario tracks and to bring champion horses into Canada. I really wanted to put Toronto on the map for Thoroughbred racing. I spent the next several years trying to recapture and build upon what I had seen and experienced in Arlington, New York, and other bigger and better venues in America. Toronto had a world-class facility in Woodbine. In an effort to follow through on these ideas, in 1971, I made an appointment with Jack Kemp, a congressman from New York, to start discussions about interstate commerce. I aimed to address the heavy taxes being placed on the horses coming in and out of Canada, including the U.S. horses being transported through Buffalo and Fort Eerie, as well as those going to or coming from Woodbine. These meetings allowed for permanent and positive change; the volume of horses that went back and forth was dramatically increased, and Canadian racing, particularly Ontario racing, was placed on an attractive plane with regional racecourses within a three-hundred-mile radius. Solidifying these policy changes was no easy task because it required both governments to agree that this import/export tax on horses should not exist. Through lots of long hours and discussions, I negotiated a reciprocal arrangement eliminating the tax altogether, which came as a great relief for horsemen in both countries.

When I was able to get that law changed, I realized just how important my voice was in a sport that needed an advocate to help clean things up. I knew from a very early age that although the tracks were run pretty well, there was always room for new ideas and a better way of doing things. I wanted to make it even better.

There was a good team in place at the Jockey Club when I arrived, but I wanted an even stronger one. I was quick to change racing conditions over the next year or two to make the Canadian International Championship the focal point. The Canadian Championship had been in existence for years, beginning at Fred Orpen's Long Branch Racetrack. The "International" title was added when consolidation brought all Ontario Thoroughbred tracks under the banner of Ontario Jockey Club.

I knew I couldn't make substantial progress on a daily basis, but I could certainly improve a single race to attract the high-profile global candidates I wanted to bring in. It would take time, but it was doable. We had to increase the weight spread between three-year-olds and older horses to encourage the younger group to compete.

Lucien Laurin was a French-Canadian trainer who had gone to the United States to train a string of very successful horses for several top owners, including a woman named Penny Tweedy. Penny hired Roger Laurin, Lucien's son, to train and manage the Meadow Stable horses, the Thoroughbred operation and horse-breeding business founded by her father. When he was hired, Laurin helped Penny cut costs and returned the operation to profitability before leaving her to train for the powerful Phipps family stables.

In May 1971, Penny hired Lucien to take over. In 1972, they guided the Meadow Farm's colt Riva Ridge to victory in the Kentucky Derby and Belmont Stakes and an unknown two-year-old named Secretariat to be named the 1972 American Horse of the Year. The following year, Secretariat captured the imagination of racing fans worldwide when he became the first Triple Crown winner in twenty-five years.

I'd met Lucien and Roger over the years but became better acquainted with Lucien when I started the mass solicitation of nominations for a purse program and a stakes program we constructed for Canada.

When we got the nomination, it was a big score. Before then we couldn't compete with New York, whose handle was gigantic compared to ours. We would usually bring in less than $100,000 a day combined, which meant there was never enough money in any single race to justify bringing in any of the big-name horses. But the Canadian International Championship would be a $150,000 purse, the largest in the track's history—in Canadian racing history!

E. P Taylor was a brilliant industrialist in Canada, who was now known internationally as a major breeder of racehorses, with the development of Windfields Farm and growing success stories precipitated by top filly Canadiana and North American champion colts Nearctic and Northern Dancer. This success laid the groundwork for us to grow our international identity and ultimately helped convince various trainers and owners to come to the 1973 Canadian International Championship.

Penny Tweedy was a gracious woman who was always kind on the many occasions I'd met her in the barn areas from Saratoga to Belmont and beyond. She was a hands-on owner who had horseracing in her blood. She was accessible and classy at all times.

We had set the foundation for the race on paper, but it was a long shot to attract Penny, Lucien, and Secretariat to our race, and we knew it. We had to zero in on what would be the reason for them to say yes and then make it happen. A champion horse like Secretariat running in our race would generate such excitement and put Canadian racing on the map for the entire world to see.

Penny had said she would race Secretariat until he was four. What was little known at the time was that her father had died with no will. His estate had gone to the United States government in taxes, and she was desperate for money to maintain the stable and farm. It wasn't a great secret in horse circles that Penny was in need of cash. Time was running out, and there was a good chance she could lose everything.

Decisions were being made about where to run Secretariat based on how much money he could make in his final year. She put together a syndicate of high-profile members who each had a say in the matter, but, ultimately, she had the final word as to where he would race. The syndicate was anxious to end his career in glory and retire him to stud. They believed it would be counterproductive to send him to Canada, because Canada was considered a secondary market—one that wouldn't help his stallion career. Compounding their decision was the fact that the horse had never won on grass—he was a dirt horse—and the Canadian International Championship was a turf race. Finally, the race was a mile and five furlongs, which is the longest major grass stakes race in North America. It's not appealing to most breeders and buyers of yearlings because of the distance. Now we had three strikes against us. The syndicate didn't want to take what they saw as unreasonable chances.

In fact, the mere thought of Secretariat racing in the Canadian Championship was ludicrous.

On the other hand, Penny retained all of the purse earnings but didn't get the $6 million she syndicated him for until he actually went to stud. She couldn't wait that long. She needed money fast and was looking to race him more because she needed the immediate income. Because of this, she was at constant odds with her syndicate over their decisions.

Despite knowing all of this, I was still convinced that if I could get Secretariat to Woodbine, other great horses would follow. It would put us on the global map. I made it my number-one priority.

By this time, I had my pilot's license and had purchased my own multi-engine plane. I started flying to New York on a regular basis mainly to meet with Lucien and occasionally Penny to discuss the idea. It began as monthly visits but quickly turned into weekly and then daily conversations. I was very determined to get them to say yes. I hung around the stable, doing my best to talk my way around the three strikes. The fact that I was a fellow Canadian helped me bond with Lucien right away. I knew his son Roger quite well, as he brought the classic filly Drumtop to win the same race in 1970. Roger became a fan of our operation, the racecourse, and its idiosyncrasies. Lucien never had a doubt that the horse could go the distance, but the grass was a challenge because it was a totally different footing. It was deeper sod, which made the going slower than the New York tracks. He had no idea if the horse would like the feel of the surface and the depth. Secretariat's arsenal contained push-button speed that could be utilized at the rider's command. There were far more questions than answers at the time.

Deep down, I think Lucien wanted this to happen because he was Canadian, and he was proud of where he hailed from. He wanted to bring that horse "home" before retiring him. Lucien always said Penny promised him he could race Secretariat in Canada. Although I can't vouch for that, I wanted to believe it every time he said it. The more we talked, the more he—and I in a support role—became determined that Secretariat was up for the challenge.

The only problem we still needed to address was the amount of the purse. It wasn't exactly where it needed to be to get Penny to say yes. Knowing this, E. P. Taylor, in all of his greatness, said he would make it $125,000—a record Canadian purse and far beyond the OJC budget—which he person-ally met to give us the leverage I needed.

E. P. Taylor telephoned Penny directly to invite her to Canada and to advise her of the purse increase.

After many days of endless dialogue, Penny tentatively agreed to bring the horse for the race. Even so, she had reservations about her decision. She was constantly asking questions—good and fair questions—about the sur-face conditions, the weather, the time of day the race was to be run, and more. She was smart and always on top of the important factors when it came to her horses.

I got the written nomination, which was a first step in a long road, but by no means was it a guarantee of commitment.

Once Secretariat was on board, others soon followed. In fact, it drew the largest field that ever ran against Secretariat, including Big Spruce, a graded stakes winner on the grass who could go long. Big Spruce was trained by Lefty Nickerson, who was quoted as saying, "I am not afraid of that big red son of a bitch," referring to Secretariat. Kennedy Road, a local champion who had a ton of speed and had set track records, was also among the com-petition. Trainer C.D. Whitaker said at the time, "Our horse is going to burst out of the starting gate, his eyes are going to be bulging out of his head like the Wild Man of Borneo. He's going to be GONE!" These horses were not "cannon fodder."

On paper, the odds appeared so stacked against Secretariat in this race that all of the other owners figured they had their best shot of upsetting the great champion.

In an effort to prep Secretariat for the Canadian Championship and to see how he would do on the grass, Lucien ran him in the Man o' War, a turf stakes race at Belmont Park in New York, which he won. With that victory, interest was heating up. John Shapiro began to court Penny to run in the United Nations, a mile-and-a-half turf race at Laurel Park in Maryland with a bigger purse in a much more established race. In my mind, I could hear Shapiro laughing at me, thinking, "If that horse is going to run on the turf, he is coming here."

The New York Racing Association (NYRA) wasn't happy to hear Secre-tariat was racing in Canada, either. They wanted him to stay in New York, home of some of his greatest races on dirt. There was a lot of politicking going on behind the scenes because the syndicate that had put up the six million to buy him when his career ended thought it was lunacy to have him race in the Canadian Championship. In their eyes, a win didn't necessarily enhance his value, and a loss would have a major negative impact.

I won't lie. I was nervous when I heard about that offer, because I'm sure Lucien and Penny seriously considered it. They could run the horse close to home. At the very least, it meant they wouldn't have to ship him to Canada, and, at the most, it was a lot more money in Penny's pocket and a much shorter distance over a course with fewer encumbrances.

We were on very shaky ground!

The press was demanding. They had been on board since the early thought of the horse's possible appearance in Canada. I had flown Ray Timson, executive manager of the *Toronto Star;* Bruce Walker, publicity director for OJC; and Jim Proudfoot, award winning sports editor of the *Star,* to New York to see Secretariat. They got to be up close and personal. Lucien thrilled the group with a petting session with Secretariat. The die was cast. When we arrived at the airport to depart, Art Stollery, wealthy owner of many good horses, including Kennedy Road, who would compete against Secretariat in the very near future, and jockey agent Colin Wick were preparing to board Stollery's Turbo Beaver that was parked next to my Piper Aztec. That's when the stories and challenges really began.

Many drinks had been consumed.

Stollery vowed his plane would beat us to Toronto and would run away from us like Kennedy Road would do to Secretariat.

The bets were on.

Money changed hands.

The Beaver taxied out in front of us and was gone.

They were lighter with only three passengers on board.

The rest of us climbed into my Aztec and proceeded to climb to 10,000 feet in the darkening sky, monitoring the progress of their Beaver, which was at 6,000 feet and slightly ahead of us. Their choice of altitude gave them an early edge. I had chosen a higher altitude because we had to cross Lake Ontario, and that gave us a cushion. We were at a compatible altitude for circumventing departing Toronto traffic.

Our progress excited my passengers, who had consumed the contents of two bottles of Canadian Club that were now being set up as faux machine guns atop the counters on the window side where the Beaver was spotted.

The antics were loud and demanding; the rivalry intense.

"We can't have defeat on our record! I demand emergency action!" Timson hollered.

The drive to win was mutual, as Stollery was on 1.21.9, the emergency broadcast channel used by pilots, spouting words of (premature) victory.

The Beaver was at 6,000 feet, though they were asking for permission to go to 2,000. We were at 10,000 asking for 4,000 as soon as possible.

We could see the lights of Toronto International just ahead. Permission was granted for us because of our altitude. I put the Aztec into a steep descent, which added about twenty-five knots to our descent rate and near redline. I asked Toronto approach to expedite my arrival due to circumstances onboard. They put the Beaver into a holding pattern at the outer marker, as we blew by them making the turn onto the ILS—pilot talk for the instrument landing system.

I reported the circumstances to my amiably incandescent cohorts on the taxi into customs. The victory applause, hoots, and hollers were deafening. To them the race had been run. It had lasting effects and set the stage for the Big Red Horse's arrival!

When Secretariat stepped off the plane at Toronto International airport, for what I would later discover was his final race, he was greeted with a hero's welcome, complete with news journalists, photographers, and television cameras rolling. In those days it was very unusual for racehorses to travel by air. Even Secretariat had never been on an airplane before this trip. Horses usually traveled by truck or van. It was as if Elvis Presley had arrived. He stood on the runway like the real superstar—superhorse—that he was. The Big Red Horse seemed to understand he was the toast of the racing world and handled the plane and the press with ease—like visiting royalty.

The focus of horseracing had been switched from America to Canada to Woodbine and now to the Canadian International Championship. This was the moment I had dreamed of. It was the culmination of everything I had worked so hard toward for two and a half years since returning from Arlington.

The pressure was on, but I was ready for whatever came my way.

Once we had Secretariat on the Woodbine grounds, I put him in a prominent barn that was well secured and right on the roadway. We had access to it at all times and could control any situation that might occur. Press was flying in from all over to visit Secretariat in the barn, because we wanted to make sure the world knew what was happening at our track. Bruce Walker did a wonderful job with the onslaught of publicity.

The world knew, all right, because someone called in a threat to kidnap Secretariat. Naturally, we had to treat the call as a genuine threat. We immediately got the Royal Canadian Mounted Police (RCMP) involved as well as the Toronto police.

Toronto, however, is not known for high levels of crime. Saying there was a threat to kidnap Secretariat was akin to announcing that Jack the Ripper was on the loose downtown. It was so uncharacteristic in Canada.

We didn't know where the threat came from or whether it was real, but we couldn't take any chances. We had to pay attention to it.

We beefed up security and filled Penny in on what was happening. We did everything we could to ensure the safety of the horse. Luckily, that was the last we heard from the alleged kidnappers.

Crowds were coming every day to catch a glimpse of Secretariat. During his first morning there, a dense fog set in. Cars were lined up along the roadway. Families had come to see the horse breeze, but because of the mist they couldn't see the track just a couple of feet in front of them. Darrell Wells, the track announcer, sounded like God. Everyone could hear his booming voice from the booth, but no one could see him in the haze. It was brisk and chilly. We'd never had fog like this. I postponed the workout every hour, waiting for it to clear. The workout across the dirt track was compulsory. It was an Ontario Racing Commission rule that we endorsed and enforced. It was put in place to help familiarize visiting horses with navigating the crossing. Finally, we got a little break, and he breezed beautifully, giving everyone who stayed all that time a glimpse of the champion they had waited to see. The estimated crowd of mainly women and children was 3,500.

As the big race approached, Lucien wanted to do a short work with Secretariat. The Ontario Racing Commission rules say that all horses that race the Marshall Turf Course, which is what the course at Woodbine was called, have to cross over the dirt to the inside track to finish. Crossing over the dirt was a major complication for a lot of horses. They do it at Santa Anita in California going short distances, but it wasn't as controversial as it was on this course because the horses were dropping in elevation and turning and crossing, so some horses had a tendency to jump. The Ontario Racing Commission said that a horse couldn't start the race if it didn't work over this particular dirt strip.

Lucien convinced me to ask the Commission to waive the rule for this race because he thought it was unnecessary, but I couldn't get them to do it. Whenever you enter a celebrity horse in a race, it changes the dynamic. They think they should get everything they want. In this instance, he could have said he wasn't going to race if they didn't agree to waive the rule. As it was, we were still day-by-day, minute-by-minute with Secretariat. This was a real threat. The kind that caused as much nervousness for me as the threat we'd just had to kidnap that damn horse!

When the Commission said no, Lucien gave in and worked Secretariat for three-eighths of a mile across the dirt. He took it like the champion that he was.

A couple of days before the race, Ronny Turcotte, a native Canadian who rode Secretariat in all his races except one as a two-year-old, received a suspension due to a riding infraction in New York. It's a very big setback to lose or change your rider right before a big race, and this could have been a deal-breaker! It was late in the process to find another quality rider for the horse, but Lucien called upon Eddie Maple, another Meadow Stable regular, to handle Secretariat in his final start.

The race was set for October 28, the last Sunday in October—and the morning after the end of Daylight Savings Time. The forecast was lousy, calling for intermittent snow flurries. I was like a dog shitting razor blades.

It began to rain and sleet; the turf became heavy; the grass was long. The outlook was bleak. This would shorten daylight considerably. Concern orbited around the condition of the main track crossing if it were to become heavy mud. Would the horses navigate it without injury?

I caucused with Mr. Taylor and the OJC president, John Mooney. My recommendation was to dig out the Drumtop race of 1970 and play it over the internal system at least twelve times a day. Lucien's son Roger had trained Drumtop and provided a good reference of the crossing if Lucien needed to discuss it further. We had the option of rolling the turf tracks, provided we could get the heavy equipment on them without creating ruts.

"We might not run if the weather gets any worse," Penny kept saying to me. An owner with a horse in a stakes race can scratch right up until forty-five minutes before post time. They are not obligated to run in a race.

E. P. Taylor was on the phone asking for updates every hour.

"What's the latest? What are they saying?"

"They're talking about weather, footing, track conditions . . ." I reported everything I knew to E. P. and Mooney exactly as I knew it.

I was back and forth trying to keep everyone calm while doing my best not to show them I was sweating this, too.

There were other "chicken shit" complications that were interfering with my tasks as director of Racing and Operations. As a result of our tremendous racing accomplishments and rapidly accelerating global acknowledgements, there was a lot of petty animosity and jealousy within our operations. I had my suspicions when I was enrolled in a business course at York University, along with Doug Elliot, a junior executive assistant, that began the week leading up to and including the Championship weekend. The timing of the course couldn't have been worse! Then I was told to report for a lie detector test relative to checks I had approved for cashing in order to allow a well-known big bettor to wager. I had done this type of thing before as a favor to horsemen and big bettors who were close to our company. It was convenient on holiday weekends when big bettors ran out of cash, and I was the only executive working on those days. The old boys' club was clearly getting out of hand! I attended the York University course for one hour, then left the pile of books on "widget woes" in a heap on a desk before walking out. As for the checks, I spoke with John Mooney, who acted surprised about the lie-detector test and advised me to ignore the request until after Championship week. I also spoke with my good friend Jake Howard who was a senior partner in Blake Cassels and Graydon. He was equally shocked. He said it was an insult and to call him if the request persisted. I took his advice and carried on. Besides, I had a beautiful twenty-acre farm, mares and foals in the lush, rolling hills of King, Ontario, and, if that didn't piss my adversaries off, maybe my new BMW 530i did.

All the while, the track was getting wetter by the minute from the melting snow, making it spongy and yielding.

Penny was more than halfway certain she wouldn't allow her horse to run.

Wet grass is one thing, but crossing the dirt strip when it's muddy is another. It becomes a real obstacle. They didn't like the conditions at all. And to be fair, they were difficult to defend.

We couldn't move the first race up any earlier because we were running on a Sunday. The venue served alcohol, so by law the government wouldn't allow us to open before noon, which meant we would not only be running the Championship race in the snow, but we'd be running it into darkness too. The thought of suspending alcohol sales for the day would have been disastrous for us. We waited years to get the right to sell alcohol at the track and even longer to sell it on a Sunday. There wasn't a shot in hell we'd consider suspending the sale of alcohol, not even to run the race earlier. Now, add in a Triple Crown winner running that day and no booze available for our patrons? It would have been anarchy!

I suggested we walk the course on the morning of the race.

Penny put on her rubber boots; Lucien donned his. I was in my suit and tie, and we walked around. I had them roll the turf prior to our arrival to flatten it out.

When we got to the end, Penny turned to me and said, "We will do it."

The crowd was assembling in the grandstand as the weather continued to worsen. Even though she had agreed to run, she could still scratch.

In all of the haste around the decisions to race that day, no one had made arrangements for Penny and Lucien to have box seats. We were in the paddock area when she asked me where she should sit to watch the race—a slight omission that wasn't in my bailiwick.

The paddock scene was unbelievable. Security was doing their best to fend off the eager fans, some of whom had jumped over the iron barred fencing that encircled the walking ring.

It was ten minutes before post time.

"Penny, come with me." I grabbed her hand, as we channeled through to the trustees elevator and pushed up. I barged my way through the crowd that had gathered in the trustees room and brought her right to E. P. Taylor. We got there just as the horses were at the starting gate.

The snow was falling harder than ever.

It was getting pitch black.

I stayed with Penny because I knew I wouldn't make it down to the track before the start of the race.

When the gate opened, the horses all broke well, but Kennedy Road really took the top off. They were hammering down the backstretch on yielding grass, and the crowd was going crazy. Eddie Maple stayed up on him, but Avelino Gomez urged Kennedy Road, trying to get to where he could bump Secretariat.

I was looking through my glasses and thought, *You brazen bastard, Gomez!* He was trying to take a shot at Secretariat in the biggest theater in our history.

Kennedy Road stayed with him down the backstretch until Eddie let him widen across the Marshall turf course with no incidents.

I always hesitate to say there are smart horses and dumb horses, but if there are, Secretariat was one smart horse. Secretariat won the Canadian International by six and a half lengths, with Big Spruce closing to be second ahead of Golden Don.

One is left with a wonderful, lasting image from that late October day in Canada: Secretariat turning for home through light snow flurries, front legs pumping like powerful pistons with mammoth clouds of wind blasting from his nostrils.

Penny was jubilant with her win. She was hugging and kissing everyone.

It seemed like a half hour passed before making it across the main track into the center-field winner's circle. Everyone in the entire facility was celebrating this win, and it was downright thrilling. The crowd wanted Secretariat to win and cheered for him in his final victory. The pari-mutuel tickets wagered commemorated Secretariat with the words "BIG RED." Few were actually cashed.

Despite the snow, the darkness, the kidnap threat, and all of the other challenges, the race was flawless. I had a tremendous team that performed with great pride and dignity! The world knew about Woodbine, and Canada was finally seen as an important stop in Thoroughbred racing. I could breathe, perhaps for the first time in two years, because I felt my job here was done.

CHAPTER SEVENTEEN

After the success of Secretariat in the Canadian International Championship, we were able to bring in great horses for many years to come, including Dahlia, Youth, and Snow Knight. We also attracted stables owned by Nelson Bunker Hunt and the Phipps family. They owned Bessemer Trust, major steel companies and conglomerates, and were owners and contributors toward dominant U.S. pedigrees.

Woodbine became the epicenter for ground-breaking changes in racing. We allowed the controversial Lasix, a loop diuretic used to prevent bleeding through the nose during races for a year and then banned it. We were also the first racecourse in North America to build dormitories for women. Our policies, accommodations, and experience left no doubt in the world scheme of global racing.

We also became a high-stakes player on a global level. Our limousines were equipped with multilingual drivers who carried pictures of foreign dignitaries who were enthusiasts of racing and other VIPs who were scheduled to attend our races. They were assigned to every owner and trainer making the trip to Canada for fun—win, lose, or draw. Women of the racing world flocked to attend our show, where they were gifted with complimentary credit cards for Holt Renfrew (Canada's premier furrier) and other luxury-item retailers to keep them well dressed during their stay. Even stable help were presented with convenient trips to Niagara Falls and surrounding landmarks.

The Championship week encapsulated a world council of international leaders, including Jean Romanet, the director general of France's Société d'Encouragement and one of the most forward thinking men in horseracing; the Weatherbys of the General Stud Book of England and Ireland; Jockey Club members; and many other members of European racing royalty. We had eclipsed the Washington, D.C. International and the United Nations Cup and outrivaled New York and California on the foreign front. Our Canadian-bred stakes investment had paid off and was great for attracting and establishing pedigree and locals, but still was not considered an important race across the border or in comparison to contests of international interest and prestige.

To scout horses for the Championship for the fall meet, I started going to Europe, where I got to know Maurice Zilber, a great trainer who had won French, English, and Irish derbies. Maurice and I had our first chance meeting at John F. Kennedy airport, where I was coming from a meeting with Nelson Bunker Hunt in Lexington, Kentucky. He was on his way back to Europe, and I was flying there to expand our possibilities. I didn't know what he looked like, and he didn't know what I looked like. All I knew was that he was an Egyptian Jew who spoke seven languages. He was a very clever and talented horseman.

I know it seems strange, but I spotted a man at the airport who struck me as someone who might fit Maurice's description. He was in a hurry, running to catch his plane. I reached out, grabbed his arm, and when I did, his suitcase fell, opening and spilling his clothes and personal articles onto the floor.

"Are you Maurice?" I asked.

"Yes," he said gruffly, followed by a litany of foreign words that didn't sound especially friendly. While I helped Maurice pick up his underwear, I had the chance to say, "I have to talk to you about the Canadian International Championship and shipping horses to Canada. . . ."

By the end of the conversation, he started to pay attention to who I was and what I had to say.

"Come see me in my office in Chantilly," he said.

When I arrived in France, I made it a point to make his acquaintance in a more formal fashion. We talked about divisions of horses, especially three-year-olds and up, and where they would fit in Canada. I already knew Angel Penna, a world renowned Argentinian trainer who had won two Arc de Triomphes with three- and four-year-old fillies and who had a magnificent training yard there full of top horses owned by Daniel Wildenstein and Countess Betanye. He was a genius of equine strategy. We became fabulous friends and toured a great deal of Europe together accompanied by Artur and Madame Pfaff and Omar Sharif. They were heady times—but none so important as the late-night presentation of a gold medal lifetime credit card to the world famous Paris nightclub Chez Régine by Régine Zylberberg herself, one of the most fascinating and resourceful people I had ever met. These coveted cards were considered more prestigious than an American Express black card today. They gained you access to Régine's nightclub and all of the glamorous, rich, fashionable, and famous people who could be found there on any given night. If you possessed one of these cards, you were "in" with the "in" crowd. At the time, it meant a lot to score one of these golden babies.

I intensified our concentration on international racing, making multiple trips abroad each year, including a meeting with the Russians in Baden-Baden, Germany. But the latter development was thwarted by the height of the Cold War. I knew about training, riding, breeding, caring for horses, and anything else people wanted to know. I was a great frontman for the OJC and the racing association, which helped line up an arsenal of horses that would go long on the grass, especially those coming from Ireland, England, and France.

I headquartered at the Bristol hotel in Paris and the Park Lane in Piccadilly, London—boutique spots that were central both to aristocracy and the horse business. I got to know most of the European courses, the many celebrities who frequented them, and people, who came in groups of six, seven, and sometimes ten or more, for a variety of stakes. In building that arsenal, I became world renowned in the profession. I had become an expert in shipping horses overseas and handling everything else that went into assuring their safety and well-being.

As a result of my efforts to raise the quality of the horses racing during the development of the Canadian International, the Phipps family shipped several of their horses to race in Canada. Dinny Phipps was on the board of NYRA and, like his father before him, was destined to someday become its chairman. He saw what we were doing for Thoroughbred racing in Toronto. His trainer at the time, John Russell, and I were very close friends, and my efforts and contributions to the sport were gaining in esteem and popularity.

Around 1976, I hit what I felt was the glass ceiling at the OJC. I had emerged from a long-standing family of horsemen and racing officials, but because I wasn't a blue blood, I had gone about as far as I would ever go within the organization. These were somewhat stuffy and pompous folks who favored lawyers and other multidegreed relatives who went to high-profile schools. Knowledge of the sport and industry was considered nonessential above certain ranks. Many of them had a parking spot with their name on it and a full pension plan from day one. Most didn't even know where the track kitchen was, nor did they care. We were top-heavy with these guys who hadn't a clue where the backstretch was or about any of the people who worked there. They had never seen a dirt floor, and I found that terribly frustrating. I had a father and two uncles who had put in sixty years of officiating at OJC racetracks who never got a pension and were fired in the parking lot when they got too old. I thought that was shabby. I could see that I was headed in the same direction. I had been with the OJC for the better part of seventeen years as an executive with no talk of pension. Even though I had reached director of racing and operations, I wanted to become a vice president. I wanted to be in on board meetings on a regular basis, not just when they needed my help. They brought me in from time to time, and I knew I was well respected, but there was a ceiling for those who weren't like them. I couldn't go any further, and they as much as said so.

One of the trustees I got to know well was a gentleman named Bud Willmot, who was the chairman of Molson Industries. He was a very smart man who loved the game and was trying to ratchet up his breeding and racing business. He owned two Canadian Thoroughbred farms called Kinghaven Farms "One" and "Two" in King, Ontario, approximately twenty minutes north of Woodbine and five minutes from my farm where I was now living with Barbara and our four children. I had boarded twenty mares for Bud while Kinghaven Two was being constructed. They had some fine pedigrees and good racing stock.

Barbara and I had become friends with Bud's son David and his wife, Patti. He offered me the opportunity to come on board, even giving me the title of vice president of operations and an 11-percent stake in the farm and assets, an amount equal to his two sons' stake. Both of his sons were strong-willed fellows. David was in law school, and Mike was a budding stockbroker in the city. Bud was an excellent businessman and used psychology to get me to take the deal by giving me the same percentage as his own sons. He was clever that way.

His approach made it an easy decision for me.

I immediately said yes and spent the next year and a half building up Kinghaven. Bud Willmot was wonderful to me, spending a lot of that time mentoring me, offering fatherly advice and paying me lots of compliments for the work I was doing. He appreciated all that I brought to his operation and acknowledged my talents and skills. The changes and planning that I contributed during that brief time helped to precipitate Kinghaven's meteoric rise as the leading breeder and owner in North America. It was so gratifying to share in Bud's success. In that brief time, I personally trained Fairly Regal, a Northern Dancer filly, to a double stakes win and enhanced her value significantly. David was nearing completion of his law degree and would soon return to full-time work on the farms. I never intended to work with them for a long time.

After a meeting with Bud, David and I traveled to Miami, where we met with Mickey Taylor and Dr. Jim Hill, the owners of a two-year-old horse named Seattle Slew, who wasn't yet the extraordinary, historic horse he went on to become but, in my eyes, showed an awful lot of promise. I had become good friends with Jim and Mickey and had some inside knowledge about how good their colt was, though no one really knew at the time just how good. We offered $3.5 million for half of Seattle Slew. While we were politely turned down, the substance and meeting were indicative of what Bud was willing to invest in a good horse—on my recommendation—and where the farm was headed. It was a tremendous experience for all of us—especially years later, when we all watched Seattle Slew go on to win the Triple Crown. Isn't that the thrill of horse racing? It is a world of would haves, should haves, and could haves, for sure!

When Dinny Phipps heard I'd left the OJC, he had just become chairman of NYRA. After settling in, he made arrangements to have his new president, a fellow named Jim Heffernan, reach out to me. Heffernan was formerly the NYRA in-house counsel and was a good man. He was calling to gauge my interest in coming to New York to work for Phipps.

Barbara and I had just designed and built a beautiful new home in King with fifty feet of glass looking out onto the forest when I received a second call; I'd just poured myself a drink when the phone rang. Good thing, too, because this time it was Dinny Phipps himself on the line.

"Dave, you need to come to New York."

"Nice to talk to you, Mr. Phipps. Can you say that again?" I said.

Phipps reiterated that he wanted me to come to New York to work at NYRA.

"I won't come if I am going to be in the position that some of the NYRA people are in today, because they are just doormats. I am not a doormat," I said without any hesitation or remorse.

Phipps assured me I would never be a doormat with him, and I would always have whatever I wanted or needed in my new position as head of Horseman's Relations. The only condition was that he needed me to come to New York right away. He was eager to start his new position with his team in place.

Although the position I was being offered mirrored the one I had left at the OJC, it was extremely flattering to be asked to join such a prestigious organization as NYRA. And though Phipps had moved Jim Heffernan from the legal department into the position of president at NYRA, I felt he was a talented guy—one I could respect and work with and for. When I weighed the opportunity, it made perfect sense to say yes. NYRA had the potential to be the greatest racing operation in the world. Everyone knew it had become a mess, but I shared Dinny's vision for what it could become—again!

Barbara and I had been in our new home for ten days when I took the job, leaving her and the kids behind for a short while. I quickly bought a gorgeous home on two and a half acres in Old Brookville, Long Island, down the road from Phipps, on Wheatley Road. It had thirteen rooms! I figured I better make it a big upgrade if I were going to convince Barbara to move yet again with our four kids in tow.

I hit the ground running and became the number one shit-disturber-in-chief at NYRA from day one, and, true to his promise, Phipps never said no to me—not once. He was truly a man of his word. I had made a career out of watching NYRA for years, making a living out of its backstretch, hustling stakes horses, and befriending horsemen. I watched their stakes, monitored the horse population, and read their daily programs. I'd done a ministudy of their operation, not knowing I'd someday end up working there. I've always looked at the racing industry as a whole, and that's what made me such a valuable asset to everyone I ever worked for.

I was prepared for everything and anything.

When I arrived, NYRA was riddled with folks who had been there for a long time—people who were quite content to see things stay exactly the way they were.

The problem with that way of thinking was that the state of the business was on a steep decline. I didn't know the financial realities until I arrived, and they proved to be far worse than I originally thought. The organization had become decadent. The massive barn areas were in poor condition, lawless, and unsupervised. Packs of dogs ran unchecked; veterinarians complained about security and unfettered access to stables. The unions had taken it over. Thirty-four unions were embedded when I arrived, and they were demanding raises and more powerful changes at Belmont, Aqueduct, and Saratoga, the three tracks under our management. To oversee things more closely, I decided to live on the grounds in the backstretch. I did so for three months.

The new team quickly compiled a list of changes and started to cut and slash wherever we could justify our rapid-results decision-making. I was immersed in the job day and night. As a result, I moved up to director of racing within three months of being there. I was accumulating power with every recommendation and money-saving idea. I didn't want to be a total pain in the ass, but I was calculating the fastest path to get me to where I wanted to be in the hierarchy. We wanted to relinquish the stranglehold at each track as fast as we could. It was difficult to understand why there had never been departmental budgeting before and easy to see why they were in such dire financial straits.

Jim Heffernan was new to racing operations but was an expert on union activities. He was a quick learner and a good listener. We soon did an inventory and applied budgets to all departments. As a result of his open mind, in a very short time, he and I had become very good friends and allies.

According to our assessment, the expense line was going to intersect the revenue line before 1980. Jerry McKeon was the finance guru and had a good handle on the financial position.

My biggest foes were the unions. We bumped heads at every corner. We couldn't screw in a light bulb or rake a leaf or blade of grass outside the barns because the unions wouldn't allow it. We had weekly and sometimes daily meetings with their leaders, which started to affect some change, but then we'd butt heads again. The mutuel clerks expected constant increases, and they fought automation of any kind. Our whole team had identified what was wrong. But would we have the will to act? Was the timing right?

Dinny Phipps had grown up in a dynasty of great horses with great pedigrees. He was well versed in European racing traditions—their dedication, disciplines, and expectations of the sport. By comparison, I had grown up with turkey houses, dirt floors, billy goats, manes and tails, and exposure to the extreme, seedy side of a failed and neglected part of the industry. The Vanderbilt era had just come to an end at NYRA, and, although he had a great love of the sport, he still traveled the high road and ruled by cronyism. It was clear that he had turned a blind eye to the degeneracy that descended on NYRA. The vision of Off Track Betting when it was first offered by the state was shunned based on short-sighted misinformation put forth by lobbyists who predicted its illegitimacy and abortion in the state senate. Surprisingly, the state passed it in the dark of night. NYRA lived for years since then, threatened with the constant cannibalism of the ugly stepchild who trampled the sport and sapped on-track handles and attendance.

Phipps knew he had to assemble a stellar team to initiate the renaissance of American horseracing's crown jewels: NYRA.

Few understood those crown jewels or appreciated what the hundreds of acres of land covered by gigantic ovals, steel, bricks, and mortar represented. Even fewer of the talented and zealous assembly from far afield realized that the crown jewels, subject to mandate and penchant, were closely tied to Kentucky and the protection of America's equine treasure of pedigree. It wasn't just about New York. Dinny Phipps knew, and so did I.

Union conflicts took up many long hours in a NYRA day. Demands were generally made to perpetuate the coffers of the thirty-six hungry pariahs. Pari-mutuel sellers and cashiers represented over a thousand of the forty-five-hundred-person NYRA workforce. They had many cottage industries within the encampment that sold more merchandise than Sears did and hired people who held two jobs in many cases and were convicted several times of laundering money from illicit sources.

Its union was powerful!

With the threats of off-track betting (OTB) and dwindling on-track handle, the union became entrenched on key issues. They insisted on holding their numbers and were absolutely resistant to installing automated tellers.

Heffernan, a former Sylvania labor lawyer, was tall, tough, and well equipped for warfare.

Don Drew was trained in a totalizer environment.

McKeon was street-smart savvy.

Legal scholar Martin Lieberman left a prominent law firm in Texas to join us and was overzealous in his demeanor.

Newly hired John Keenan was formerly chief of detectives, fresh out of the New York City police force with the capture of David Berkowitz, the serial killer known as "Son of Sam."

I was in formidable company!

After long, perennial, and protracted engagements, the union demonstrated intractability, intransigence, and finally an outright militancy toward NYRA over its plea of disability to meet the demands of its growing overhead. They simply could not comprehend this reality's threatening conclusions. They missed their permissive cronies and were determined to defy every change NYRA's new team proposed. They called a strike, incorporating the sympathy of their other thirty-five union brethren.

Racing was being conducted at Aqueduct. The track had only a four-hundred-stall capacity in which to stable horses, so it was reliant on Belmont, whose two thousand stalls were only partially filled during the winter months. The unions knew they had a strong hand to go to war and had planned well. NYRA was a "long shot" to win, to put it in wagering parlance. We were up against the largest and strongest unions in the country.

Our team met and developed a plan for board approval, with the suggestion that the long-term existence of NYRA was germane and contingent upon the cuts, wage concessions, and automation we were proposing. It was a far different picture than the unions were used to.

There would be *no* capitulation beyond what we had offered, even facing shutdown.

Our plan was to begin the training of all nonunion employees and volunteers on the teller equipment we had. The workday changed for most of us.

Negotiations ground to a halt.

A total walkout occurred following a series of "sick-outs" and absenteeism.

We continued with a skeleton crew, adding new tellers as they completed their training.

I reported our position and predicament daily to the horsemen and prepared several contingency plans, including alternative training hours for horses, feed distribution, and additional safety requirements.

The horse vans had to traverse about a six-mile distance from Belmont Park to Aqueduct. But the additional concern was that "the van drivers were teamsters!"

Winter conditions prevailed, and we estimated that we had only a few more days before sympathy grew and the other unions would strike in solidarity, too. The Belmont main track was not maintained in winter, which left us with just the small and large training tracks at that facility. The horsemen at Belmont and Aqueduct were fortunately in solid sympathy with our stance and continued to enter for racing.

I stopped the large daily shipments of horse manure to the Pennsylvania mushroom growers and redirected those loads to be dumped into the large Belmont parking lot. We shaped the straw and manure into a twenty-foot-wide six-furlong galloping ring approximately twelve to eighteen inches in depth and continued to stockpile more to maintain a deep cushion. Because the organic material doesn't freeze easily, we knew it would create a suitable cushion on which to train. One by one, the union placed pressure on workers to stay at home. The picket lines were increasing in size at both facilities. Feed trucks ceased to cross those imposing lines in both locations. Finally, the electrical support teams left the premises, followed by carpenters, plumbers, and tractor drivers who manned the harrows and trucks maintaining the tracks. We continued to race, and the hostilities grew. The mutuel manager was run off the road on his way home from work, and I received life-threatening calls against Barbara and the children. My name appeared on a five-foot-tall, stuffed sack-cloth image, alongside two other sack-cloth figures intended to represent Phipps and Heffernan that were burned daily outside of the entrances to Aqueduct. Large spikes welded to flat steel plates were thrown in front of the horse vans at periodic intersections en route to Aqueduct, and many other attempts to cause damage were made on a regular basis.

The Unions were slowing us down, but they weren't stopping us. We functioned with a complete operation devoid of union personnel. They knew if they stopped the horses there would be no racing!

Keenan was sent an emergency order to form convoys of horse vans onto the Belt Parkway to evade the menacing attackers. (At the time, New York State law prohibited trucks on the beltway.) The police escorted the convoys. The horse vans were equipped with special shields placed on the truck rims, axles, and windshields.

The attacks intensified from the beltway overpasses with rocks, bombs, and metal objects being thrown in heavy bombardment. Helicopter escorts soon joined the convoys.

When the feed trucks wouldn't cross the picket lines, I made arrangements for feed to be flown into the facilities by helicopter on a daily basis. The crowds dwindled as bombs were also being thrown onto the grandstand tarmac at Aqueduct. A few hundred loyal fans still continued to attend, and we had OTB in New York City, as well.

As the loyal horsemen continued to enter, the horses continued to train and run, the vans continued to deliver, the threats got closer to home.

I came out of my house on the thirtieth day of the strike to find my two German shepherds dead in the driveway. Unfortunately, my children also saw them on their way to school.

We continued to work seven days a week and on into the nights. On the fifty-sixth day of the strike, the unions capitulated. The strike ended and so did an era! We couldn't continue to operate under their thumb. We couldn't live in that type of controlling environment. Due to the cooperation and determination of the winter horsemen, we had won our battle against the unions and we paved the way for a new and prosperous year, too.

CHAPTER EIGHTEEN

When I ran the numbers to see what the stalls were generating in revenue per horse—looking specifically at the number of races, handle, and stakes winners—I realized the facilities were significantly underperforming. The stall applications were yielding unreliable, inaccurate, and generally bad information. I realized if I could come up with a uniform system to index and extract accurate data by division, age, sex, distance, course-type, and racetrack, that information would become invaluable when plotting our income streams. It would also be fair to the deserving horsemen—I wanted the economics of the horse herd encapsulated into one concise formula so I could understand it. Once I had that information, even though it was created for NYRA and our three facilities, the formula could be used nationwide to assist every racetrack in the country. My secondary reason for doing this was to raise the quality of the horse herd we had in both winter and summer.

I had visions of grandeur—I wanted to raise the merit of our facilities and was intense about doing it. The only way I could compete more effectively with Santa Anita, Del Mar, Maryland, Kentucky, or Arlington was to know what they had. I couldn't walk into their facilities and order a stall list. The only way I could get that information was from the source that originated their horse herd.

The data I needed and eventually put together would provide us with the consolidated past performances of three thousand or more horses from NYRA and those from the national horse herd. Despite the progress we had made thus far, NYRA was still in a state of chaos and disability because it didn't know which horses they had on the grounds or the condition they were in.

Computers were still new to a lot of businesses and certainly unknown to racetracks.

I requested meetings with Bill Williams, president of the Daily Racing Form in Hightstown, New Jersey, where the eastern version of the daily paper was published. My idea of computerizing the entire horse herd was explained to Bill and John Hartley, who was in charge of their inventory. Over a series of meetings, we mapped out the required fields for the centralized computers and monitored our progress day to day. Williams wanted to know how they were going to get their money back if they satisfied my requests for the data. We estimated that the information would generate enough to pay them roughly $36,000. I sold it to Heffernan and Phipps, and we had a deal. In six months, I had a working model and a computer set up in my office. I digitized the stall applications for every race meeting. It was exciting and rewarding in every way, because, for the first time in racing history, there was an accurate compilation of our horse inventory instantly accessible.

My manual assessment was correct but still far from what real-time data allowed me to see. I could now tell that we were trying to fill races drawing from 30 percent of the working herd. We started each year with nine hundred unraced two-year-olds that were capable of just one or two races per month. The New York bred program was yielding 40 percent of our inventory and rising. The growing claiming category of the herd was eroding quality at a tremendous rate, which was compromising the handle. NYRA's dwindling pari-mutuel handle and attendance were threatened by a growing unproductive and diminishing qualitative percentage of the herd. The great thing about this information was that it made change immediately actionable.

The results were wonderful!

We opened Saratoga Race Course for training, housing most of the nine hundred two-year-olds we expected and wanted annually, without interfering with the most productive part of the horse herd. We negotiated an agreement to eliminate claiming races for New York-bred horses, offering them to run in open-claiming races to participate for a legitimate value of the individual horse. We created a cap on claiming values that penetrated and diminished and interrupted the normal allowance ranks and values. We reduced the illusion of "three-race meetings within one" with the diminution of beaten, optional claiming, and illegitimate allowance offerings.

It was a progressive system intended to enhance pedigree, handle, and the value of the individual horse, while accelerating the vertical ascent of stakes contenders and offering the wagering public a legitimate and understandable categorization of value.

It was a revolutionary and productive system that gave horse trainers and owners an improved method of assessing and setting new goals and objectives. When it was fully implemented, it resulted in increased handle and attendance and provided a comprehensible product for entertainment and handicapping. It proved to be the endgame!

The system eventually was shaped into Bris Net and other market products, but ultimately it formed the foundation for the Jockey Club's Equibase products.

My time at NYRA unfolded just as I thought it would. I was named vice president in 1980. It was an exciting time to be a part of what most people think of as the Golden Years of NYRA. Racing improved, and we reshaped the company to become one of the finest organizations in the industry for the rest of my tenure.

One of my last accomplishments during my time with NYRA was the continuing development of international racing, much like I had done for the Canadian International, for a new race called the Turf Classic. Phipps wanted NYRA to join the ranks of the best international events. Belmont Park had successful Triple Crown horses and was thought of as the pinnacle course for Triple Crown racing in modern times. There were nose victories, and it was always exciting to be a part of a big race at Belmont.

NYRA was back in full bloom, and our profits were rising. Expenses had been significantly reduced by the measures the new team took early on, and those measures continued to prove effective. It was a truly rewarding time in my career.

In preparation for the Turf Classic, I was spending a lot of time in Europe courting top trainers, owners, and their horses to come to America. Shipping internationally wasn't commonplace. It was expensive, and a lot of owners were averse to doing it because of the risks to their horses and interruption of the European schedule. The English didn't ship well, nor the Irish, nor the French. But our purses were much bigger!

Actor Omar Sharif was a drinking buddy of mine who was always in our company when I was in France talking to trainers and soliciting owners for the Turf Classic. Omar was a dashing man with fine features. His hair was like a horse's mane. He loved everything about horse racing, especially betting. He was what I would refer to as an advanced and eager high-roller gambler. We always got the best tables wherever we dined. And whenever we went to the clubs or to see acts, he was always in for the late nights. He was eager for horse-related conversations, and I loved to speak with him about the intricacies of the sport. Although he was a big, handsome movie star, he didn't mind fetching a cup of coffee for us if it meant he could be in the room when we talked business. He was the only man I ever have known who was "beautiful."

When it came to horses, I was the go-to guy. I was sitting in a bar at the Bristol hotel in Paris when Berry Gordy asked me for some advice. I didn't know who he was until someone told me that he was the founder of Motown Records. He was there to buy a horse called Argument for the Prix de l'Arc de Triomphe. I was a bit taken aback that he knew who I was and even more taken aback by the gorgeous Playboy playmate he had with him. I was giddy as hell to meet someone in a Playboy magazine. Gordy had the world in the palm of his hand and acted like it.

"Dave, let me ask you. Do you think this horse is worth the money?" Gordy was about to spend some serious dough and wanted to know my opinion.

I had been asked that before when I negotiated the sale of Fanfreluche for $3.2 million, the highest sum ever paid for a broodmare from John-Louis Lévesque to Bert and Diana Firestone.

I looked at the jewelry around his neck and the big gold rings on his fingers and thought, *Does it matter?*

But before I could give him my answer, a waiter walked over, tapped Gordy on the shoulder, and whispered in his ear, "There's a gentleman at the back door who would like to see you."

"Who is it?" he asked.

"A dark-skinned fellow with glasses on. He wants to see you, sir."

"Bring him in."

In walked Stevie Wonder.

"What do you want?" Gordy was friendly and welcoming.

"I need some money." Stevie was shy and soft-spoken.

I watched Gordy reach into his pocket, pull out a roll, and grease him some cash.

"Dave, this is Stevie Wonder," Gordy introduced us. I reached out my hand to shake his "hello." I didn't know who he was either or that he was blind. Gordy told him to go get some of his memorabilia for me and then sent him on his way.

He was a hell of a lot of fun to be around.

Nelson Bunker Hunt was another familiar face when I toured Europe. He was a heavyset guy who loved to eat large decadent meals. Whenever I flew to Europe for business, I either flew on the Concord or in first class. Bunker Hunt had a Lockheed Lonestar, which was a large private jet. Traveling with Hunt was fun. Despite his great wealth, he was a down-to-earth guy.

My final one last kick-in-the-ass strategy to lure Europeans to Belmont was to show them what a wonderful facility we had. I was able to sell the idea of racing at Woodbine because I had them all come there. But now that I was with NYRA, they weren't familiar with New York or the fact that this facility was far superior. It had a mile-and-a-half racecourse that was state of the art.

Dinny saw the value in this pursuit, as it was in keeping with his ancestry.

So we thought long and hard about what we had to offer. We contemplated how we could show them our value and what more we could do to accommodate them. We were determined to break into their sphere of old-world aristocracy.

Finally, I devised a scheme to send a race from Aqueduct via two satellites into a hotel room where a group of Arab sheikhs and dignitaries would convene for a black-tie dinner hosted by NYRA. A family of wealthy Lebanese real estate developers shipped a filly named Anifa to Aqueduct for the race. Our president Jim Heffernan traveled to London to host the event and watch it on television in a deal I brokered with Peter George, who was chairman of Ladbroke, the biggest bookmakers in the world.

This would become the first simulcast sporting event in history.

I had months of work ahead of me to get it arranged with the telephone company so that I could get the signal to Andover, Maine, and then uplinked from there to a BBC satellite, and from the BBC to the hotel room where the event was to take place. It had to go conduit, satellite, satellite, and back to a landline. It was detailed and expensive, but what an extraordinary presentation for the Europeans it would be. There were lots of hurdles, but somehow I got it done.

While Jim Heffernan was in London with the group viewing the race, I stayed in New York to oversee the operations trackside. I created a media room and the equivalent of a sports broadcast with jockey trainers Angel Cordero and Frank Wright, along with live shots from Aqueduct. There was a lot hinging on this broadcast. Everything had to go perfectly because it was the only opportunity I had to advertise what NYRA offered as a venue.

What I didn't realize was there was a bookmaker in the room with the sheikhs, who had bet on their horse. We couldn't bet because we didn't have state approval on the simulcast; however, the owners weren't bound by those same rules. Anifa went against a good field of horses, but the idea was to show off the facility, not break the bank.

Early on race day, a terrible storm blew the windows out of the clubhouse at Aqueduct. It was a storm of near hurricane strength. The stewards summoned me into a meeting and talked of canceling the races that day. Dinny Phipps was also in the room at their request.

"No way!" I proclaimed. "Let's weigh the evidence."

I had too much on the line. I only had the satellite feed for that one day. I couldn't postpone the event.

But the racing stewards were deeply concerned for the safety of the crowds and performers. The storms were too severe. People were running for their lives.

I had to think quickly. As a pilot, I had access to the aviation weather service, so I placed a call. According to the FAA, the storm cells were moving rapidly and would be well past the track by post time. I got the clear sailing from the weather service, which gave me the ability to convince the stewards and our chairman to postpone two races and resume them in an hour and fifteen minutes. What I was asking for was unprecedented.

I spoke to the jockeys, and they were willing to stay.

Next, I spoke to the trainers, and they, too, were willing to stay.

I told Dinny Phipps, who was very concerned about the safety of his guests, that we could make an announcement that the races were not being cancelled and that those who wanted to stay were welcome. Reluctantly, he agreed.

Thankfully, the sun came out, the skies cleared, and the race went off flawlessly. We only had about three thousand people in the stands that Saturday afternoon, but it didn't matter. The satellite signal was strong and clear.

Jim got on the phone after the race and was in full glee.

Anifa won the race at 42-1. They were delighted with the results.

"This is the best day of my life, Stevenson! The place looked great! I love this new concept!" Jim said.

It was a show, all right. They never even knew we had a storm or called off any of the other races.

When Jim came back from London, not only did people know how great our facilities were, they now knew we had the capability of broadcasting our races internationally. European owners could ship their horses over with the comfort of knowing our tracks were more than adequate, which meant I would have a much easier time bringing big-name horses in for the Turf Classic.

I also brought the English Derby and the Arc de Triomphe to Belmont from their respective countries via satellite and showed it at our racetracks. It was an experiment to see if developing international wagering was viable—to see how people would react to watching English racing in America. Even though the post time was early in the morning, around 8:30 a.m., the fans arrived on time and were all dressed up for the event. We drew three thousand five hundred people into Belmont just to watch the English Derby that day. Those special events showed me that international wagering could be done successfully in America.

There is a career in this, I thought. *And an awful lot of money and interest to be made.*

My decision to leave NYRA came at an opportune time. New management was coming in, and I had also received a job offer from Fasig-Tipton, the foremost Thoroughbred auction firm in America. They were working on a project in Fair Hill, Maryland, and offered me the position of vice president to run a training center they were putting together to complement their facility. They were struggling, and, because of my extensive expertise and experience, they thought I was the guy to spearhead it. I believed in the concept of yard-training horses, which meant not training them on a racetrack. It is more aligned with the European form of training, and I thought it would work better. The facility was large, with offices, stables, the training center, and several racetracks. It was unique to this country. I knew it wasn't going to be an easy project, but they offered me a very good salary, a high commission, and a fresh opportunity.

I told Jerry McEwan, who was then the president of NYRA, that it was time for me to move on. I left on very good terms with them, which was important to me because I had worked so hard to bring the organization back to its glory. I had done what I set out to do and felt good about the contributions I had made. It was a great team to be a part of at a time in racing history that I will never forget. I couldn't really go any further there, and deep down I knew it was time to do something else. Besides, my kids were getting older, and I wanted to get out of New York.

I took the job at Fasig-Tipton, and, though I made a gallant effort to get the facility off the ground, it wasn't enough to keep the business afloat. There was friction within management, and the cost of running the project was more than expected. The concept was exceptional, but it was premature. Although Fasig-Tipton is still very successful, that development eventually went broke and was put up for auction.

I didn't really mind the short-lived job with Fasig-Tipton. All the while I had the simulcasting idea still on my mind because of the success I'd experienced with the Aqueduct race. I saw technology rapidly changing. It was getting better. I knew we were going to have more opportunity ahead of us—not less. If I was smart and calculating, I could be at the forefront of it all. I foresaw the value in forming a company solely for the purposes of international simulcasting and knew I had to get involved.

CHAPTER NINETEEN

1988

Ater she spent decades devoting her life to raising our four children, who were all grown up now and living on their own, I decided it was time to do something nice for Barbara. She had lent me unwavering support over the years, quietly enduring the moves from one racetrack to the next, facing a plethora of dilemmas with me, and adjusting to a parade of more than fifteen houses. I wanted her to have a change of scenery and perhaps a dose of serenity. Now that we had shed the laborious farm in King, Ontario, and our marriage had endured two jobs in the brutality of Canadian winters, a calmer and more peaceful lifestyle sounded pretty good to both of us. We would spend a year on sabbatical, living in the Caribbean, where I thought I could use the time wisely, figuring out how to set up the offshore simulcasting venture I wanted to launch and also enjoying more quality time with Barbara and my sister.

Ginny was living on the island of St. Croix at the time, where she and her husband, Larry, owned and operated a full-service boat yard. They also ran a small dive shop featuring sea adventures in the vicinity of the salt river drop-off, part of the volcanically formed tectonic trench with depths of over 20,000 feet. I love to dive and had being doing so since the 1950s, when I began with an early developed J-valve tank in a papoose harness.

Diving in the Caribbean provided our family with camaraderies and many incredible adventures over the years. I vividly recall finishing a rather deep dive off of French Cap Island on the south side of St. Thomas. We had both blown off all of our air upon returning to the boat. My brother-in-law, Larry, had been using a sophisticated and expensive Nikon camera underwater to take some of the most incredible photos of the wildlife that lives under the sea. We were anchored in eighty-five feet of ocean. Upon climbing into the boat, the camera slipped from his arm, plunging quickly to the bottom. There weren't many words to describe the loss we both felt upon losing those images. They were gone! With no air left in either of our tanks, it didn't seem possible to retrieve it, yet it was too much to abandon. I hyperventilated several times and without explanation donned my mask and went for it. After two breathless attempts, I kicked straight for the lava formations below. Remarkably, I was able to find and carry the camera back from the ocean floor. Of course, we enjoyed those pictures for years to come.

As it turned out, fate colluded with the events of that day to help form and effect a host of important meetings and decisions forthcoming in my life.

Drinks were in order that night, and Larry was buying.

Ginny and Larry owned a beautiful home at the very top of a steep mountain road. Barbara and I bought a home close to theirs in Belvedere Estates, a little higher up on a lush hillside with sweeping views of both sides of the sea. It was a far cry from the pastures and rolling green farmland we'd gotten used to seeing every day at the barns and stables we'd been around for the past thirty-plus years together.

By this time, my father had become quite ill, suffering from the onset of Alzheimer's disease and the painful ravages of old age. He slowly stopped recognizing himself in the mirror, often telling stories about me that he believed were about him. My father would speak of when he won the Queen's Plate, the Cup and Saucer, and other grade Is as a young, virile jockey. I was pleased that those accomplishments brought him some pleasure in his deteriorating state, though it was an ironic twist of fate.

My father didn't like to take his medication, so whenever he'd visit with my daughter Rebecca, she'd slip his pills into his tea to make sure he'd get them anyway. He would sometimes fall into a state of delusion, thinking they were on a date. It was sad to watch him wander into and back out of reality. Even worse, he had become belligerent beyond any control toward my mother and, as a result, had to be institutionalized. It was the ex-wife of Bruce Naylor, the groom who took care of Canadian Champ, who looked after him there. She knew me and was happy that we could connect again even if it was under such dire circumstances.

I spent some time at the local racetrack in St. Croix, reacquainting myself with the owners and trainers and the few island breeders that I had supplied horses to for years. I figured these relationships would come in handy someday soon. Besides, despite being away from the daily grind, my heart and soul could never be too far from the place where I feel most at home.

Our island paradise and anticipated leisure time was soon cut short by the completely devastating arrival of Hurricane Hugo on September 17 and 18 of 1989. Every tree on the island had been stripped of its bark. There was also no more grass to be found on the ground. The canopy for the rain forest was gone, too. All of the roads were washed away. Even though I had access to two vehicles, a Land Rover and a Mercedes station wagon, the jungle and storm debris landlocked the roadways.

My sister and her husband were traveling in Europe at the time and our house was not completely finished, so we were staying at Ginny's to care for their dogs and cats. I couldn't go anywhere. It took me a day and a half armed with just a machete to cut a path so we could make our way up the road to inspect what was left of our home. I saw a few riders on horseback, with horses they no doubt stole from the local racetrack, toting machine guns amd machetes and swinging bottles of whiskey. That's when I realized I would need my shotgun for safety. It took me a day to get the gun and another to find my shells. If I was going down, by God, I was going down fighting.

For several days, we fought against elements we could never have imagined. The governor of the Virgin Islands was on CNN talking about the damage, having only surveyed St. Thomas and not St. Croix. Jesse Jackson was flying overhead in a helicopter. Rebels were looting, raping, and pillaging hotel guests at the resorts and killing kids in the ice line. It was total insurrection. Tourists were diving off the pier, trying to swim to the coast guard boats off in the distance. Prisoners were let out of jail, and no one knew how bad the damage really was where we were. We had a HAM operator on a sailboat, trying to get the word out that the prisoners and accompanying rebels had taken over the island. Rastafarians were on horseback with machine guns taken from the armory. When the coast guard tried to get close, they ran them off. The airport was closed, so no planes could get in or out. Reporters had no idea of the situation because they had no access to where we were.

I finally spoke to Sally Hill, a close friend in Miami, on a boat radio patched through Tortola, a neighboring island seventy miles away.

"Don't talk. Listen," I said. This was the first word we could get out about how dire things on the island really were and getting worse by the minute. Eleven hours over us, Hugo had wiped out every telephone, electric, or conceivable conduit to the mainland.

By this time, President Bush had called in the military and the U.S. Marshals to come from Puerto Rico, where there was an American base. I had also made contact with the U.S. Marshals to let them know the situation on the island. I desperately wanted to get Barbara off St. Croix as fast as possible. When the troops arrived, I was able to get a military plane to transport her back to San Juan, which was just sixty miles away. Once she was safely ensconced there, it was easy to make arrangements to get her to Miami, where our daughters Rebecca and Dianna were waiting for her.

I wasn't going anywhere because I had property to protect. I knew insurance adjusters would eventually find their way to St. Croix. I wanted to stay there until I got them to appraise the damage to our home and land. It was rumored that four insurance companies filed bankruptcy the day of the hurricane. Fortunately, I had coverage with a British company that was well funded. I'd had a steadfast rule in my life about never bribing anyone because once you do it, they'll expect you to do it all of the time. After seeing how bad things were in St. Croix, I knew it would take a bribe to get any appraiser to take action sooner rather than later, especially to get him to jump over a thousand huts to assess my property. The rule doesn't change, but the circumstances sometimes do. I wanted to get the hell out of there, too. Besides, for all of its beauty and serenity, Barbara didn't much like living in St. Croix. She missed our children. She wanted to move back to the States, where we could be closer to them and spend more time together as a family.

During that time, I received word from the Red Cross that my father had passed. Jack Kenney, president of the OJC, had learned of his demise. Somehow, in the midst of the chaos, they found me in St. Croix to let me know that he was gone. It would take a month of dealing with the rubble and wreckage in St. Croix before I was able to join Barbara and the kids back in Toronto for the funeral. We paid our respects, but Barbara and I didn't stay long. Neither of us ever really got over my parents' refusal to come to our wedding.

We officially moved back to Miami and into our winter home. We both loved Miami and had called it our second home for many years. S&A, our new entrepreneurial venture, was soon launched, and running out of our spare bedroom. The foundation of our business was simple: we wanted to sell live U.S. audio/visual signals to offshore clients who could wager on them. We would essentially take premier races such as the Kentucky Derby and send them by satellite to people in the Caribbean and other territories in South and Central America, but NYRA was our main client. We would have the ability to monitor the receivers, turn them on and off, and communicate with the uplink companies to control the access. We set up the business to make our money from the fees—not the bets. Typically, we would charge anywhere from $100 to $150 a day for each signal. Some shops would take five or more signals a day. Rebecca soon learned to keep spreadsheets of shops and signals and how much they owed. I'd collect fees monthly whenever I could, but it didn't always work out that way. If someone didn't pay, they would lose their signal because I had the ability to instantly shut them down. That was the only control I had to monitor fees aside from periodic trips in my new pressurized Aerostar, a pretty airplane that was fast but was limited to flying at 20,000 feet, just under the altitude necessary to clear the average thunderstorm.

Rebecca and—occasionally in the beginning—Dianna were my crew members, manning the phones and recording transactions and details required from the governing and regulatory bodies, while I wore every other hat to launch our simulcast horseracing and offshore betting business. It wasn't long after we got settled in Miami that I made my first deal with the Pang brothers to simulcast racing to Trinidad. Budsy Pang had been telexing entries and race results from England to Trinidad for a couple of years. His brother, Derek, was the bookmaker based in Trinidad. Together, they ran a very lucrative business on the island. They were the logical go-to guys to set up my first offshore simulcasting account with because they already knew and had the market for English racing via telex. Their business consisted of a guy standing with a ticker tape calling the live races from the U.K. as they were happening while people were wagering on it in their territory. We were introducing live pictures to their formula. Essentially, we agreed to take specific races and send them by satellite to boxes in various locations.

We kept track of who had what boxes and of any movement that took place. We not only delivered the boxes, but we controlled the signal. They agreed to handle the bets, of which we got a cut if they were pari-mutuel or a fee if they were not.

A lot of the islands were starting to get TV and would erect giant satellite dishes to receive signals from the satellites when we signed a contract with them. Satellites were few; they needed to be placed high; they had a limited footprint; and they could not yet reach all of the Caribbean. We constantly monitored the planetary movement of existing satellites and the new ones being launched. We managed complex mosaics of the celestial developments and the boxes necessary to absorb their signals.

For the tracks, it was found money. They had nothing to lose. We would negotiate each new contract and market the products, delivering them with faxed past performance to match each racing card. Every track I approached said, "Have at it." As long as I was bringing back money that they otherwise would never have been able to make on their own and I was guaranteeing payment, they were happy. That created a lot of early trust in what I was doing. Plus, they knew I would do it right and legitimately because of my reputation as a racing official. I made sure to check the licensing of every outlet, the requirements of every country, the needs of regulatory boards to make sure each of our clients were served and that we weren't dealing with any of the drug cartels. Bookmaking is legal in all of the countries I wanted to establish simulcast racing in. In the beginning I only worked with local bookmakers.

At first, I was doing all of the work, from the selling to the installations myself. I was loading the plane, flying to Trinidad, making the deliveries, and installing the boxes and faxes. If they wanted to receive the live broadcasts, they were responsible for getting their own satellite dishes. I'd send the basic requirements of what they'd need in advance of my arrival and cycled that information to them. Most of the time, the satellite dishes were shipped in from Miami or they were purchased second- and third-hand from the military or other sources. It was brand-new technology, and everyone had to learn from scratch.

Power was always a problem in the islands because of the outages and brownouts that are endemic in the Caribbean. We had diagrams with footprints of the satellites and could convey the information about size they needed and direction they should face. As we moved closer and into South

America, we sometimes negotiated a "double hop" requiring discussions with the Mexicans or Pan Am Sat, but those satellites were extremely high and demanded specific and technically detailed requirements.

Sometimes I'd find myself dealing with operators in a local bar or bodega, and other times I might be dealing with someone in a shack on the beach or in the jungle with nothing more than a cord tied to a tree. I was dealing with people who had little if any education in areas where there was often no electricity. Clearing customs and paying tariffs presented constant challenges, as bribes and payoffs—both customary and mandatory—existed everywhere. Once I arrived on the island with an airplane full of parts and tools, I'd find a local—usually someone with a little knowledge about electronics—who could learn how to install the boxes and connect the wires for me, so that if something went wrong after I left, I could rely on them to fix it. There were plenty of times when customers would lose a signal and one of my daughters—Rebecca or Dianna, who had now joined me as full-time employees of the company—had to talk a local tech guy through the troubleshooting process step-by-step until they regained a picture. The girls couldn't see what the techs were looking at on their television screen. All they could do was guide them through trial and error. They were very patient and resourceful! Dianna would sometimes have to make harrowing trips to Aruba, where she was mercilessly hit on by horny old men while installing preprogrammed fax machines. Many of our native clients were totally perplexed and astonished by the advent of fax machines. They marveled at all the new technology we were introducing to them.

At the time, there were only a few tracks in America that were simulcasting, including all of the tracks under NYRA. We did business with the bookmakers in Las Vegas, too, but the majority of other tracks of interest, like Churchill Downs, weren't taking the plunge just yet. I met Bob Strubb, owner of Santa Anita, and started them on the program. California allowed us to launch a night simulcasting program because of the West Coast time difference. On the islands where we set up business, crime was so bad, we had to invest a lot of time and make a lot of changes before those ventures fully succeeded.

Since this predated the Internet, we could only get a daily racing form put together two days in advance of a race. We would fax the fifty-page document daily to a woman named June in an office in Bermuda and to our contact Pang in Jamaica, who made copies and arrangements to have it delivered to all of our other outlets throughout the Caribbean.

In 1989, a fellow by the name of Hector Cruz met me in a restaurant in Miami Lakes and begged me to help him with a racetrack he was a part of in Costa Rica. He was about to lose it in a government auction because it had been foreclosed on by the banks. I didn't want the thing, but I told him I'd take a trip down and take a look at it anyway.

The racetrack was a small village track in Cartago, just east of San Jose, and I was afraid running it would take up a lot of my time. The more I thought about it, though, the more I liked the idea. NYRA liked the idea, too, because they thought that the track would be a catalyst for other signals throughout Central America. Manuel Estrada, a local veterinarian on staff for the government, who knew Costa Rican President Calderón very well, met me upon my arrival. He was very gracious, giving me a car and driver and all kinds of perks during my stay.

Calderón was a horse enthusiast who raised Thoroughbreds in Florida. He seemed eager to do the deal. Apparently, he owned a couple of shares in the racetrack.

The more time I spent looking at the opportunity, the more I realized there was potential because of its geopolitical positioning to South and Central America, so I bought the run-down track for $25,000. It took some time to assemble everyone's shares that I was buying to make it work from a legal standpoint, but I wasn't overly concerned. In retrospect, I probably should have been because I never asked whose shares I was actually buying.

The largest shareholder was a fellow named Norman LeBlanc. Norman was living in Costa Rica because he had fled Canada and the United States with Robert Vesco, the Kingfish who retreated to Cuba after he was accused of looting $250 million from investors in 1973. Norman was a business associate of Vesco's who was presumably on the run. He had a 707 he used for international travel and was involved with the cartels and organized drug trafficking. They were in Panama at the time but were in the midst of trying to find a new home when I showed up in Costa Rica and bought the track.

The track had a live volcano behind it that was a tourist attraction. Though it hadn't erupted in years, I wanted to use it as a way to bring people in. We started to look at how we could build up the horse herd. We also started to do demos so we could arrange to bring signals into Costa Rica. It was a real stretch because U.S. satellites were not compatible yet and did not include Costa Rica in the footprint.

During this time, I got to know Norman a little, as he had a horse farm in Costa Rica and because he owned Cabla Color, a major cable provider with a 100-foot dish. I told him what we were trying to accomplish with simulcasting throughout the country. We had a decree that was written by Calderón, making it racing law, so the stage was set. The decree stated that you had to have an operating track in order to conduct wagering in the country. Basically, no one else could come in with simulcasting unless they owned a racetrack. Since we owned a track and had the rights to conduct wagering in whatever form, we were pretty much competition-free. It was a lock because we essentially wrote the law. The rights also were written to include "simulcasting," a word that did not exist before then. When I told Norman about the plan, he was intrigued. He wanted to be helpful and introduced me to the operating managers of his company, Cabla Color. I salivated at the thought because I saw the 100-foot satellite dish that he had on the ground and knew it was unique. Because of its size, he could pick up lots of satellites. I instantly saw the possibility to reup the U.S. signals to South America, to link up with other commercial satellites, and to pick up the Costa Rican audience in the bargain.

"Can we test it?" I asked.

"Sure," he said.

I brought in decoder boxes from NYRA and Hollywood Park. We could reach both signals. It wasn't a perfect picture, but I had images clear enough to see from coast to coast in the United States.

In the meantime, the track needed work—lots of work. I made some changes, including resurfacing it and purchasing portable plastic rails. I also brought Jonathan and Betsy, a couple I'd met who answered an ad I ran in Miami, to live in Costa Rica and manage the track in my absence. They had never spent any time around a racetrack, but I needed people I could trust to keep an eye on things in my absence. They had college degrees, were down-to-earth hippie types, and despite the fact she was legally blind, I thought they were willing to embark on the adventure without freaking out. They were sail-boaters who loved the unknown. I thought I could teach them about racing and management. I trained them in the business for several months before getting them settled. I got them to the point where they had some concept of what they were supposed to be doing, even taking them on a couple of collection trips to Trinidad with me.

On one of the trips we took off, and although we had a clear weather report when we left, we encountered severe turbulence, large hail, high winds, and rain as we passed over the Cordillera Central, or Central Mountain Range. Lightning pierced through the cabin while we climbed through 16,000 feet in the direction of the Limon VOR. There was no en-route contact. The aircraft deicing equipment was not keeping up with the demand, and the airplane was heavily loaded with weight from passengers, luggage, and fuel. It was a lonely feeling. I consoled my two passengers with a radar prediction that we'd be out of danger in fifteen minutes.

Thankfully, we were! I had a lot of money on board because of our pick-ups in Guyana and Curaçao—bags and bags full. Because I was still concerned about the conditions, I decided to put the plane down in Curaçao, thinking it was friendly territory. Curaçao was known to be pretty neutral with respect to the acceptance of multiple currencies without asking a lot of questions. Many times, the money I carried had cocaine dust on it and/or contained counterfeit bills. There was always something odd. At the time, it was illegal for Trinidad and Tobago to bank American dollars. But we offered better credit to customers who came into a shop and bet with American currency. The shops encouraged it for that reason.

Bearing all these concerns in mind, I was looking for a bank to safely deposit the money in. We had researched and found one. I made a few advance phone calls, grabbed the bags, and told Jonathan and Betsy to follow me. When we walked into the bank, the management wouldn't take our money. They thought I was a drug runner. Despite my pleas to the contrary, they refused.

We stopped in Medellín, Colombia, where I had a meeting with a new proprietor who owned a shop that ran a wagering site. I wasn't supposed to be there, but he didn't mind. When I flew out of there, I had to patch into the American overseas controller.

"Where are you coming from?" he asked.

"Colombia," I said.

"Colombia?" There was silence. "You are out of Colombia? Do you have credentials to allow you to transit into the U.S?" His gruff voice matched the black and sinister night. There wasn't a hint of a light and no horizon as I stared into oblivion and leveled off at 18,000.

"Yes. They are in my ass pocket. See you later," I said in a smart-ass tone as I pushed on the throttles, dialed in the Panama City coordinates, and headed for Panama. Four hours later, as I left the outer marker and settled across the threshold at Tocumen airport, Panama, I thought, *Cash is a pain in the ass.*

We landed in Panama around 2:00 a.m., so we could refuel and get on our way to Juan Santa Maria airport in San Jose, DR. It was dark as hell. Betsy said she had to go to the bathroom.

"See that field?" I asked, pointing over to the tall grass on the right side of the airfield. "It's all yours," I said as I handed her my emergency flashlight. Yeah, I knew she was legally blind, but there was no way in hell I was going to hold her hand while she urinated in a field.

In the meantime, I staked the military boys fifty dollars apiece to get fuel. They called the fuel truck over, skipped customs, and got me loaded up to make the final leg of the trip to San José, Costa Rica. Jonathan and Betsy worked out for a while, but it turned out they became arrogant and uncooperative and had had enough of adventure. Who could blame them?!

I got to know Norman well. He looked like an accountant out of central casting. He wasn't brutal, but when he spoke, you understood he was sinister. He loved to talk about all of his business exploits and plans for the future. He spoke often about his work in Haiti with Baby Doc and his desire to build a Wall Street South. His dream was to own and control the island of *Île de la Gonâve,* an old pirate bastion positioned southwest of Port-au-Prince. Apparently, they had consented to that, but when they looked at the reality of it, there was too much clearing and no infrastructure, so he abandoned the idea and was looking elsewhere. We talked about his design for an air traffic control corridor that he developed with a computer model to move the navigation aids to circumvent the United States from Colombia to Mexico. The U.S. had invested heavily in closing and monitoring corridors going into the Bahamas and Caribbean and into Miami and Texas. It was then that I realized Norman was a genius but might not be the straight-up businessman he appeared to be. I knew the IFR (instrument, as opposed to visual, flight rules) corridors would be designed and used to guide drug traffickers.

We had a grand time exchanging stories, especially about flying. He was an experienced pilot, who owned many airplanes. He bragged about how his 707 was finer than Ronald Reagan's because it was better equipped and had more facilities and range. It was parked in Costa Rica in a clandestine strip where Ollie North's planes were parked while North was busy fighting the Sandinistas. He said he knew a little about the Kennedy assassination and thought that since I was Canadian, I'd find it especially interesting that the Montreal Mafia was instrumental in preparing Lee Harvey Oswald for the assassination. When I heard him say that, I was startled and taken aback. I remember the Warren commission saying there was no conspiracy, but he spoke with such certainty, beyond reasonable doubt, and put connectivity in his story. He said the gun had been delivered to Canada, where it was easy to reconfigure, and that is how they had access to the weapon. I didn't want to know the details, so I didn't probe any further. Norman was so forthcoming with information and seemed to know all of the right people. He sure loved to drop their names.

Norman eventually relinquished his U.S. passport and was made a citizen of Costa Rica so he could stay. With all of his political connections from Kennedy to Nixon to Reagan, he also managed to wire $325,000 to Calderón around the time he was made an official citizen. The Feds couldn't extradite him after that, despite the charges that were coming down the pike.

I finalized the purchase of the small racetrack in Cartago during a dinner at Norman's house, then returned to Miami. During that dinner, Norman told me he was planning a trip to London but that he wanted to meet again regarding Cabla Color's involvement in my simulcasting project upon his return.

Several days after my return, I received an evening telephone call from Don Luis Castro, a major coffee farmer, breeder, and owner of racehorses as well as a stockholder in the property I bought. Without a salutary greeting, Castro blurted out "Do you know who killed Norman? You were the last to see him?"

I was shaken.

"They are claiming it was a suicide. He was shot behind his left ear with his own pistol while sitting at his desk in the house," Castro carried on.

"No," I said.

I remembered Norman being right-handed, making a self-inflicted shot to the left side odd and highly suspicious.

"Is the deal done?" asked Don Luis.

"Yes," I replied.

The call ended without another word.

Two days later, I received a letter from Norman. The envelope and the letter were in his own handwriting. His letter was very upbeat and full of promise and plans for the future. It spoke of our last dinner and how much he enjoyed our time together and his desire to resume our talks about simulcasting the next time I was in Costa Rica. It certainly didn't sound like it was written by a man who was planning to take his own life—at least not to me.

With events happening as they were, and Jonathan and Betsy gone by now, it was important that I hire someone to look after my investment in Cartago again. Dianna had joined the business in 1991, taking over the organizational aspects from Rebecca so she could concentrate more on sales and collections and was free to start traveling with me. Dianna was someone we needed and could trust working in the family business.

One of my contacts in Costa Rica, Manuel Estrada, told me about a woman he knew in Del Mar who would be perfect for the job. Her brother ran Ora Flame, a cosmetic company, and she was quite rich. Barbara and I flew down to California to interview her and stayed at the L'Auberge Del Mar hotel near the beach in Del Mar.

As Barbara and I waited in the lobby of the hotel with high hopes, we saw our prospect drive up in a brand-new Rolls Royce.

"You are going to get *her* to work for *us*?" Barbara said as this five-foot-two woman emerged from the car smoking a cigarette and wearing too much makeup, sequins, and bright-red six-inch high heels.

"Buenos Días, mi llamo Susan. . . ," she said, holding out her perfectly manicured hand.

She spoke Spanish, was boisterous, had an infectious laugh, and in no time at all convinced us that she could manage the hell out of our little racetrack.

"You're hired!" I said after a few drinks and lots of cheer.

"Sí," Susan said, accepting the job.

Dianna flew to Costa Rica and spent a few days getting acquainted with the facility and working with Susan, who turned out to be a great hire. She loved to party, have a good time, and sing. She put on her red pumps, got on a table, and belted out Broadway tunes anywhere and anyplace she could. She was always dressed to the nines—frequently wearing an evening gown and her "fuck me" pumps, as she liked to call them. I was always walking around the table ready to catch her just in case she fell—but she never did.

Once we were able to add Santa Anita, a California track, to our roster of racing, we could get an evening or night signal, and that is when we doubled our business. We now had both a day and night signal and could meet the demands of the various time zones.

As we rolled out our simulcasting business, we eventually found ourselves dealing in nine different currencies—including those of Jamaica, Trinidad, Barbados, Bermuda, St. Kitts, Venezuela, Guyana, South America, and Colombia. We had a fifty-fifty deal on the money we brought back. The racetracks got half and we took half. There was no expense for the tracks, so it was a great deal for them because they didn't have to invest in the game; the money was guaranteed by their contract with S&A. It was all found money for them.

I was trying to get out of personally picking up fees on a monthly basis because I was focused on getting more tracks to provide us races. That's when Rebecca volunteered to take over collections. She kept perfect and precise accountings of what was due. She knew exactly how much money each vendor owed us. Oftentimes, they'd come with whatever money they could get. If they owed $2,000 they might bring $3,000 because they were able to get U.S. dollars. In theory, she was an ideal person to send because no one could argue with her about the amount they owed. She kept the books, and there was no question about just the amount she would be picking up.

I wasn't confident enough to let her go to the islands by herself, but since she was dating a bodybuilder who doubled as a bodyguard and had broken a few knuckles for some gangster wannabe in Palm Beach for a living at the time, I felt like she was in pretty good hands to make a run down to Trinidad and Tobago. This was before I had made contact with our bodyguard Raymond, who would later accompany us and was always well armed with more than just his fists.

Rebecca's friend Johnny was more like a steroid version of Johnny Bravo. He thought he was one tough son of a bitch. The two headed to Tobago on the lowdown. I didn't want anyone to know they were coming. There was only one shop there we were doing business with anyway. They would be in and out before flying over to Trinidad.

When Rebecca and Johnny arrived in Tobago, they spent the day on the beach, where they met a gigantic man who looked like a Russian bodybuilder. He was with a group of other bodybuilders.

"Come work out with us," they said to Johnny.

Not sure of what to do, he agreed. When he arrived downtown with them, he got a glimpse of where he was. He saw the poverty and the difficult conditions of the island while working out with people he didn't know. All of this made him terribly nervous and uncomfortable. Then he saw how and where we picked up money and the circumstances surrounding the transactions.

Panic-stricken, he wanted to bolt right then and there, but he stayed.

When Rebecca and Johnny flew to Trinidad the next day, they were met by one of the local bookmakers, who was trying to cut into our business and was refusing to pay certain bills. Rebecca had to deliver the news that we, in turn, were refusing to give him certain signals.

They checked into the upside down Hilton and proceeded with the usual protocol to collect cash. Johnny remained by her side, making sure everyone could see she had protection. Rebecca made arrangements to meet vendors in the lobby. Occasionally, they would prefer to slide paper bags into deposit boxes, or between the crack of the hotel door, because they didn't want to be seen carrying American currency. At this point, Johnny was becoming anxious about the exchanges and wanted to leave. Rebecca didn't find it unnatural to be carrying a briefcase or bag full of $50,000 in cash to dinner. She had done it a few times with me, but it sure seemed to make Johnny wet in the pants, and not in a good way.

"This is crazy. What the hell are we doing here? I am taking the next flight out," he announced. And he did.

Rebecca called me later that night.

"I have a dilemma," she said, explaining that her big bad friend had fled out of fear.

I was pissed Johnny didn't stay to do his job. I was paying him, and he left my daughter on her own with no one looking out for her.

There was only one pickup left to do. Rebecca assured me she would be fine to make it alone and to return home the next day. Under ordinary circumstances it wasn't safe for a woman to go out into the center of town where these shops were located on her own. It was especially not safe to do so while making collections. Rebecca was barely five-foot-three, and she's also quite a beautiful woman. I didn't want her to wander into downtown Trinidad. At that moment, I vowed never to let her go there again.

I told her to stay put at the hotel. I was painfully aware of how dangerous Trinidad could be.

I didn't dare tell her about the time I received a note under my door at the same hotel when no one else was supposed to know I was there. I purposely keep my location to myself, not divulging it to a single soul because you don't want people to know where you are when you're collecting huge sums of money. You're just asking to be robbed—or worse, to be killed.

I remember looking at the note as it was moving across the floor. I could see it was poorly written. I noticed a hand trying to shove it further inside the room, so I stomped my shoe on his fingers, slamming the shit out of him. When I finally took my foot off of his hand, he somehow managed to snatch the note back. I opened the door to see who it was. It was a turbaned individual—someone I didn't recognize.

Trinidad was a country of mixed population. There were Arabs, Syrians, blacks, and Chinese people—a real melting pot. There was great dissention between the various racetracks, bookmakers, and shops. They were territorial. They were always fiercely fighting over turf. We were the only supplier of signals, which caused even more dissention when we shut them off. In fact, whenever they lost their signals, they became downright hostile.

My only response was "we have an agreement. Pay your bills. I've got a business to run."

CHAPTER TWENTY

Lucien Chen was a very wealthy and powerful warlord who controlled most of the big gaming in Jamaica. He was a flamboyant and fascinating character who also dabbled in producing movies, including *The Marijuana Affair*, starring Bob Arum as a drug kingpin. He also promoted big-ticket boxing matches. One of his biggest was the so-called "Sunshine Showdown" between George Foreman and Joe Frazier on January 22, 1973. A crowd of 36,000 gathered at National Stadium to watch Foreman rip the heavyweight title away from Frazier. It was a surprise and savage beat-down that changed the face of heavyweight boxing. Without Chen's persuasive power and connections, that fight might have taken place at Madison Square Garden or Las Vegas and not in the tropical paradise of Jamaica, where Lucien Chen called home.

The fight was shown on closed-circuit television. No true fight fan would have missed the chance to see the bout between two of the hardest punchers in boxing history. Before the fight, Foreman predicted he was going to knock Frazier out cold. Technically, he never did. The fight was stopped without a count because Foreman turned to one of Frazier's trainers and said, "Stop the fight or I'm going to kill him." Only Foreman knows if he was serious or not, but Frazier has often described being in the ring that night and experiencing Foreman's punches as bullets whizzing past his head.

The moment most people remember from that night, however, is Howard Cosell's iconic commentary and the famous line, "Down goes Frazier!"

The other unforgettable image I'll never forget is Don King coming in with Frazier and leaving with Foreman. After seeing what a money-maker the Sunshine Showdown was for Chen, Don King was inspired to later stage his first heavyweight championship fight in a third-world country, as well. It was the infamous Rumble in the Jungle.

Lucien Chen was a little guy, about my height. He had a bad perm and wore fancy cowboy boots. When I met him for the first time in 1992, he was still involved in gaming, but he had diversified into horseracing. He had thousands of betting shops island-wide, but his main business was in Kingston at that time, the murder capital of the world.

Chen understood the concept right away. It was an easy sell because he already had the infrastructure in place to set up the boxes and was already handling daily wagering supplied by telex from England. In Jamaica, gambling is a way of life. The people there bet on everything.

There was just one issue: I was having a hard time getting Churchill Downs to come on board with providing their signal to us. Churchill Downs had always been a bureaucratic mess, so it was hard to get anything pushed through and approved. I knew Derek Pang was an excellent golfer, so we sent him to Kentucky to play golf with some of the executives from Churchill, thinking a little time and talk on the golf course might do the trick.

"I'll handle the signal problem," Pang said after 18 holes.

He'd become our man on the ground in Trinidad. He was the guy who collected most of the money and vetted it before pickup. We sent him programs, and he would disseminate the past performances with which to wager. He would get his share while his brother Budsy continued to run his bookmaking shop. It worked well for everyone.

Somehow Pang got Churchill Downs to say yes, and Chen started doing business with simulcast coordinator Ace Hazlip right away. The problem was that the faxed past performances from Churchill to Trinidad were costing hundreds of dollars more than signal fees. We ironed that out, and Churchill became a viable offshore account for us.

Jamaica was an even more hostile country than Trinidad. There were more killers per capita and a lot more violent crimes. Caymanas Park was the major racetrack in Jamaica. There was a lot of aggression between the tracks and the bookmakers. The bookies were very well established and had become experts in pirating U.S. signals. There were lots of them, and to some extent, they controlled the local tracks through politics. Betting in

Jamaica was largely illegal. Even so, it appeared everyone on the island was somehow in the business when I first went there.

The Gambling Law of 1899 defined "unlawful gambling" to include cockfighting and the act of betting or of playing a game for a stake when practiced in or upon any path, street, road, or place to which the public has access; in any spirit-licensed premises except in certain clubs approved by the governor; or in or at a common gaming house as defined under the law. The Courts had, over the years, decided that, in order for a transaction to constitute a bet or a wagering contract, it was essential that each party should either win or lose.

A transaction with a bookmaker constituted a bet or a wager, since, depending on the outcome of the events, either the bookmaker would lose or the person effecting the transaction would lose.

By contrast, where the transaction took place by means of a totalisator, the Courts held that such transaction did not, in law, constitute a bet or a wager because the owner of the totalisator could not win or lose, since his only benefit was his fixed predetermined percentage derived from the total amounts recorded by sales on the particular race. The transaction did not constitute a bet, and, therefore, no act of gaming, unlawful or otherwise, took place.

Therefore, there were few places in Jamaica where public betting could legally take place. One such place was at Knutsford Park in Saint Andrew, where horse racing was conducted. There were also a few offtrack betting outlets, which offered bets to punters unable to attend the races.

Cycle races, another very popular sport, were promoted every Friday night at Town Moor at the site at present called the National Heroes Park in Kingston. It was inevitable that illegal gambling would flourish in an environment where opportunities for gambling were few and beyond the reach of most people. Bookmaking had not yet been legalized, though this activity enjoyed popular support.

During the 1950s and the 1960s, two major developments occurred in relation to gambling in Jamaica. First, bookmakers expanded their business, and, second, there was a significant increase in the amount of money being spent on football pools and similar gambling promotions overseas. Thanks to us, and due to technological advances in television and satellites, by the 1990s we brought even more excitement to the island by introducing simulcast Thoroughbred racing from the United States to Jamaica.

Although we dealt with local bookmakers at first, we quickly figured out that Lucien Chen was the guy. Chen was both a shrewd businessman and an avid bettor. Whenever he was in Florida, he'd sit at Gulfstream Park every day and bet upwards of $40,000 to $50,000 or more. He looked like a refugee, but he always wore a nice sport coat. He had ex-wives and girlfriends everywhere. You never knew when or where one would show up. There was always a mention of him in the local paper whenever he came to town. Chen didn't like to keep a low profile. He enjoyed being in the limelight and being viewed as the high-rolling star that he was, even if he was smuggling money into the country left and right.

Doing business with Chen wasn't easy. He was as sharp a guy as you'll ever meet and very cunning. Despite his reputation, he didn't like to negotiate his contracts with Rebecca because *she* was too tough. Whenever he and I spoke, he'd ask if there was anyone else he could speak with to finalize his deals.

"Why?" I'd ask.

"I don't like to talk to your daughter, Dave. She always wants to negotiate with me."

Rebecca would turn off his signals for not paying his fees, which infuriated Chen.

"Do you know who I am?" he'd say to her.

"You should pay your bill, Mr. Chen," she'd calmly respond.

Chen would get very angry, but he and I actually became asshole buddies. I did tours around Jamaica with him whenever I was there. I felt bad for the guy whenever Rebecca played hardball with him because I knew he was good for the money, so she would turn off his signal and I'd turn around and switch it back on. Frankly, I was humored by the son of a bitch.

After a while, Chen didn't think he needed us.

"If it comes out of the sky, I will get it on my own," he said.

"Okay," I said.

I knew he was building his own decoder boxes and pirating my signals. And for a while that worked. All we had to do was scramble and change the codes. Rebecca was busy doing that all the time. When that happened, everyone who had bootlegged boxes went apeshit. We were in a constant cycle of changing things up to stay one step ahead of the pirating of signals that was occurring all over the island. And, if it was happening in Jamaica, it was happening on all of the islands where we were established.

"PAY YOUR BILL" was a standard answer from S&A whenever someone lost their signal. It was a pretty simple fix. If you don't pay, you can't play. It was as simple as that. No one was immune—not even Chen.

CHAPTER TWENTY-ONE

We grew the family simulcast business from a couple hundred thousand in the first year or two to a few million by year three at seventy-five dollars and hundred dollars a signal. The numbers don't sound big, but the business was starting to get lucrative. We had a constant flow of money in and money out.

I was happier than a pig in shit because I was finally doing something I loved almost as much as riding. I was flying my plane to exotic places that I really liked exploring, meeting with clients I mostly found interesting and exciting, and supporting an industry with a new technology that was only getting bigger and better with time and acceptance. I was at the forefront of a movement, leading the new frontier of horse racing by bringing a larger audience into my world of Thoroughbreds. All the while, I was able to support the cost of owning the airplanes of my dreams, and buying the fuel to fly them. I was also making new deals that supported my *entire* family.

I was never that guy who looked at how much money I was making. I was never that guy driven by the almighty buck. I didn't care about or place value on having money in the bank as long as I was doing what I wanted to do. In all fairness, while my stories are filled with many *wow* moments, there was never an excessive amount of cash laying around as a result of the simulcasting payouts. Most of it paid salaries and was put back into the buiness. The company grew exponentially as we continued to add shops or as we corrected and caught those who were not operating above board, but eventually it leveled off. In a way, it became more about policing the offshore business than creating new accounts because it was lawless in many places.

When we were first starting out, I had only been dealing with bookmakers throughout the Caribbean. I knew I'd taken the business as far as I could in the subterranean economic market. If I wanted to expand our business and increase our profits, I would have to infiltrate the Caribbean racetracks and add a pari-mutuel component to the existing bookmaking business. The seventy-five-dollar to one-hundred-dollar fee would no longer be applicable to a pari-mutuel client. I would get paid a percentage of the handle, making it a lot more lucrative for S&A.

Getting the racetracks interested was easy. They were mostly upscale track clubs that all knew who I was. The downtown tracks in Jamaica and Trinidad were more like top-of-the-line country clubs. The most important guy there was the man who unlocked the gate to let everyone in on race day because the culture loved racing. They looked forward to attending—it was the thing to do because they didn't have the same diversions we take for granted in the U.S. Going to the races is a weekly event like it is in England, Scotland, and Ireland.

Whenever I'd attend races there, I'd wear a suit and tie. I'd been going to races at their tracks for years, consulting for free, showing the operators and club management how to do things better at their facility, all for the love of the sport. Half the time, they didn't know they needed the knowledge I was offering. It was always a quandary trying to get the owners or managers of these tracks to understand why they needed to make the changes I was suggesting along the way. Their thinking was, "We have functioned just fine the way we've been so far. . . ." They'd think, "You've still got your own issues with U.S. horse racing, so don't come down here and tell me how to run *my* track." With that kind of pushback it was a real challenge to convince anyone that they needed to make changes or adjustments to function better, and yet I got no pushback when it came to wagering. *That* they understood.

Eventually, I became a guru of the sport to them. I would be in the turf clubs and I'd wind up eating with finance ministers, presidents, and vice presidents. I was appreciated for wanting to show them a better way. Suddenly, they were eager to know more about the things I knew, especially how to compete against the bookmakers, who were now cutting into their profits—big time. The bookies were an efficient operation compared to the tracks, and comparatively speaking, they had minimal operating expenses.

So it was those years of talking, getting to know the people, gaining their trust and respect that helped me to get those tracks on board and to secure a slice of the pari-mutuel betting pie. I understood that the racetracks supported themselves. They bet on their own product. The bookmakers took bets on local racing, and nobody ever said, "That cuts into our bets at the track." It didn't make sense that the bookmaker isn't paying anything to the track owner, who is relying on the same bet to stay afloat and is providing both the race and the venue. The bookmaker is underground—meaning he is moving his money through the subterranean economy. No one can account for it, so it doesn't really exist. Therefore, no one really gives a shit about it—not *even* the track owner—but they should, because that bookmaker is taking away their profit. As this reality became more apparent, the issue grew into something more contentious for everyone. It was the impetus for the knife-in-the-hand incident that day in Trinidad. The track owners had no clue how much money they were losing in the underground market. They were dinosaurs and they were dying.

Once I got in the door, had a few glasses of wine with them, and had the opportunity to explain how much money they were *really* losing—every day—it changed their perspective and the dynamic. I was able to show them how bringing American racing to them made sense. I was also able to show them how simulcasting—including Jamaican racing being sent to America as well as the other way around—could make them more money. After all, there was a large population of Jamaicans back in New York and Toronto— bigger than in Jamaica, who would love to watch feature races including the Red Stripe Derby. By doing this, the tracks in New York and Toronto could market their facility and develop a Jamaica Day. Ideas like this cemented my relationships with the authorities and the governments.

By showing the track owners how to compete with the bookmakers, we were able to help create a program to beat what the bookmakers were offering for odds. To support the tracks, we shut the bookmakers off from signals when local racing was occurring so it would force betting back to the tracks. I was literally able to tell the bookies to allow the tracks to have local betting on Saturdays and Sundays, the only days they raced, and the rest of the week would be theirs.

Although they weren't receptive to the idea at first, they eventually saw the logic and acquiesced. They all knew American racing was king, and they listened. Besides, they also knew we had the power to turn off their signal with the flip of a switch and no one wanted us to do that, so we had a few good years of a strong working relationship with both sides. It got testy from time to time. They were all cunning as hell, and there was a lot of politics in the expansion and going forward. Compromises were made and tempers flared, but for the most part, everyone understood the boundaries and adhered to them, so it worked.

Jamaica's economy became a concern for us when it all but dried up in 1996 to 1999. Jamaica experienced negative growth rates in GDP during that time, when unemployment rates averaged over 18 percent. The Jamaican government absorbed debts amounting to 44 percent of GDP in the wake of the financial sector crisis of 1995–96, one of the most crushing economic catastrophes in the world in terms of its effects on GDP. This crash was due to the poor regulation and management of the Jamaican financial sector. Although Jamaica was lucrative, they weren't paying us, because their currency was worthless. As a result, I no longer accepted Jamaican dollars.

Caymanas Park racetrack was partly government controlled, so they had to get special permission to get U.S. dollars to pay me. The books used black market currency, so it wasn't as difficult. They just had to shop for the best deal on the money. For several years, Jamaica would run out of U.S. currency in their treasury. In those instances we had to create a float in order to pay the U.S. tracks because I was contracted to give them their money whether my clients had delivered payment or not. At one point we were underpaid by roughly $3 million.

From time to time, I'd have to go to the racetracks and ask them to either accept TT dollars or wait for payment, which they would usually refuse to do because the amount of counterfeit money on the market was incalculable. Eventually, we set up our own bank accounts in Trinidad where our customers could take their TT dollars to the bank, make their deposit, and then send a copy of the deposit slip to Rebecca as proof of payment so we could credit their account. Rebecca would then ask the Trinidad bank to flip over whatever they could to U.S. dollars and transfer that money to us in Miami. This process allowed me to stop going to Trinidad as often to pick up the money because we had more control over the process at this point.

Even after we thought we had comfortably cornered the Caribbean market, others began to slowly creep in. Las Vegas wanted to disseminate to the islands, and they quickly became a competitor. As others joined the fray, Rebecca and I started to have lengthy conversations about the growing changes in the simulcast industry. Kenny Noe, a good friend and then the chairman and CEO of NYRA, called me asking for my input on how to handle large chunks of money coming out of the Caribbean through its pari-mutuel system. Kenny was primarily a "horse guy" and was far from proficient in the world of finance and wagering. I explained that we had knowledge of similar wagering transactions reported by Barkley Porter at Hollywood Park in Los Angeles.

"Get to the bottom of this, Dave," Kenny ordered.

Barkley Porter and Liz Bracken were two of the most honest and reliable simulcast directors whom we relied upon in our daily efforts to police and advise the industry. Barkley was without question the most experienced and proficient racing executive assigned to simulcasting in America. He was a very qualified horseman and extremely dedicated to the health of the horse-racing industry and was one of the closest allies S&A had.

After doing some research, we were able to assemble the details on the new tranches of incoming cash and narrowed it to St. Kitts and Nevis. We set a meeting with Kirk Brooks, the head of Racing Gaming Services (RGS), a registered Las Vegas company, to talk about his ADW, a telephone wagering system he had developed in St. Kitts.

Rebating had long been customary with bookmakers returning a percentage of large wagers, and in some cases excusing the debt of a customer suffering a bad term of luck on whatever sport he was gambling in. Experienced bookies were well aware of "churn," the steady amount wagered over a considerable length of time. Bookmakers have no takeout like the pari-mutuel industry does, which, provided by law, can take a percentage of the total handle for purses to horsemen, operating costs to run the racetracks, and even taxation. They know that when takeout is too high and "gimmicks" too plentiful, the "burnout" rate will soon "dry up" the customer.

The new and growing ADWs (telephone betting outlets) did not have to share revenue with racecourses and were charged a small percentage well below the 21.5 percent of the track's take. This formula, taking into consideration the bookmaker's knowledge of "burnout," gave the ADWs a legal profit that would allow for a "rebate" back to the bigger customers. And so it was. I met with Brooks over several days and found a meticulous operation on the island of St. Kitts. And well out of the jurisdiction of U.S. laws and taxation that would not license such an entity at the time. Their income tax records were all there for me to see. However, I deduced, RGS was suffering an identity and credibility crisis both at the same time and were soon to be facing a collective and insurmountable fit of rage from the industry. Brooks was unknown to all but the 90 boutique "whales" (big bettors) he had assembled mainly out of Las Vegas and to whom he applied his new formula. It was "genius," especially in comparison to the racecourse operators, very few of whom understood the complexities of takeout and "churn."

I reported the extent of my meticulous interview and inspection of the new St. Kitts entity to Kenny Noe and assured him of the legitimacy and credibility of the "new boys on the block." What I didn't disclose was that Brooks had the participation of his clients "throttled back" to about 20 percent of their daily capability. A 10 percent rebate to a big bettor extends his wagering life span to almost infinity in my estimation, impacted by his skill or ability to handicap.

The one thing no one else could do in the Caribbean that we could was police the decoder boxes—that's something that only we had the capability to do effectively. They didn't know where the signals were going and had no way to monitor it. Only we did.

Racetracks were trying to do it, and Autotote, a wealthy corporation that made their own decoders for this purpose, couldn't find the decoders. Rebecca did their work as they set up their new business. Another company that came along was Racing Services Inc., a rebating OTB firm owned by Susan Bala, a woman from North Dakota who, in my opinion, polluted the entire business.

Susan was a striking brunette, who was charming to talk to, always impeccably dressed, extraordinarily smart, and, who, from my perspective, turned out to be the devil in disguise. Whenever she'd see me, the first thing she did was rub my shoulders and in a very sexy, flirty voice say, "David, you've been working out!"

As a way to acquire information out of us, Susan feigned interest in buying S&A. She got cozy with us, pretending to be interested in our business from a financial point of view because we were lucrative and controlled the Caribbean. As I see it, Susan was a viper who wanted to take over the entire simulcasting business. When she walked into a room, people would rather see her than hear me. Okay, I get it. I am an ugly ex-jockey son of a bitch, and she was a glamorous smooth talker. Underneath that exterior, though, was someone who I believe turned out to be one conniving, manipulative, lying bitch.

When Susan got into the business, she ordered decoder boxes from us for her sites. We weren't providing signals to her. We were just renting her boxes. When we sell a customer a box or a signal, our contract states that we will prosecute any misuse of signals. We always took pirating of signals very seriously because this was our revenue stream. Sure enough, we soon found Susan selling our signals to customers in Trinidad using decoder boxes intended for domestic reception in the U.S. She was deliberately moving into our territory and undercutting the fee she should have been paying us. From where we stood, she didn't have an honest bone in her body.

What Susan didn't know was that we were very good at policing in those territories. Even so, the regulatory agencies urged me to go easy on her because they thought she was a nice girl just trying to do a good thing. I smelled a rat. I didn't like it one bit. Still, I let it go for the time being.

She allegedly got into bed with the Mexican cartel after she met us. We had heard through many that they agreed to finance her endeavors because she was funneling as much as $100 million in profits into Mexico, thereby avoiding state and federal taxes, not paying any of the racetracks, and pirating signals—which would eventually be proven in federal court charges brought against her.

A few of the racetracks forced us to service her Mexican facilities or they were going to cut us off from dealing with all of our other customers. They were going to violate our existing contract by taking away the signal from Santa Anita if we didn't sign with her. It was blackmail and it was ridiculous. I wanted to be in California, but under the circumstances I was being forced to sell my signals without curbing Susan's intentions. Susan, it seemed, had everyone in her pocket, with kickbacks and side deals everywhere from New York to Arizona. Suddenly the "pirates of the Caribbean" didn't seem nearly as bad as the "pirate of North Dakota."

When I took the evidence and Susan's story to Drew Kotu and the Thoroughbred Owners of California (TOC) at a meeting in Los Angeles, there was a Q&A from the legislature and regulators from the state government.

They thought I was making it up.

I predicted she would go to jail.

They questioned my integrity, which really pissed me off.

I was pretty sure there were two or three men in the gallery that were currently "intimate" with Susan. Why else would they be taking her side?

My pleas fell on deaf ears that day.

But it wouldn't be long before Susan's life of smoke and mirrors came to an end and she got what she deserved.

Susan was convicted in February 2005 by a jury in federal court in North Dakota on twelve separate crimes including charges of conducting an illegal gambling business, illegal wire transfer, and money laundering. The government claimed her company Racing Services handled $99 million in illegal gambling and held Susan personally responsible for $19.7 million. She was ordered to forfeit $19.7 million to the federal government and was sentenced to twenty-seven months in prison.*

The impact of Susan's conviction was devastating on my business. I became the bad guy because in the eyes of many, I took Susan down. She had everyone in her pocket including the TOC and Drew Kotu. He was Susan's lawyer, the Mexican cartel's lawyer, and he ran us out of California racing because we didn't want to play according to their rules. When she was taken to jail, he made it his mission to wipe us off the map and put me out of business.

By this time, our exclusivities in the Caribbean were eroding because many of the simulcast managers and some of the major U.S. tracks wanted to cut their own deals with our offshore clients. As they started to peel away the exclusivities, it eroded the collection process. When a client like Jamaica owes you $100,000 or more, as they did when we severed our ties there in 1998, we were pretty much left holding the financial bag. Jamaica was a slow burn until it finally came to a fiery and sad financial crash—thanks in part to Susan Bala putting an end to the simulcast era as we started it and creating the start of the rebating era that we clearly didn't want to be in.

As we pushed farther southward, the mainland racing companies were desperately competing and conspiring to take control of as much market share as possible and doing their best to eliminate the competitors. That included S&A. By 2006, "offshore" constituted several large wagering operations that were a mixture of very sharp newcomers that had extremely large handles from wagering clients, many of whom were day traders comprised of SOES Bandits and a combination of high rollers and whales from Las Vegas and around the nation. SOES bandits are individual investors who use Nasdaq's Small Order Execution System, SOES, for day trading. Their profits

---

*Editor's note: Susan Bala's conviction was overturned on appeal in 2009 for "insufficient evidence." She had served seventeen months in prison.

per trade are small, but they trade dozens or even hundreds of times a week. As a result, they are able to establish a position before most market makers have updated their quotes and can lay off their position at favorable prices through instinct. Despite having less information than market makers, they tend to be more profitable.

The Magna and Churchill Downs Groups formed a centralized simulcasting company in an attempt to create a higher mandatory pricing strategy using the Kentucky Derby and Magna's large market share of both southern coasts and winter racing. As a simulcast provider, if you wanted the Kentucky Derby, you had better play ball. That was the message on the street. The writing was on the wall, and S&A's strategy to grow a global wagering market to the benefit of horsemen and the industry became brand X. The notion of going global appeared to be unneeded. The simulcast operators were happy with the small slice of the pie they had. They had no interest in anything bigger. In the process of keeping things small, they cheapened racing. Fields got bigger with fewer quality horses. Racing across the board placed the A tracks in the same categories as the B and C tracks. Handles remained high as the domestic markets became saturated. Increasing the volume of gimmicks and races created a burnout far greater than increased takeout rates, and disposable income shrank. As a result, the overall quality of racing plummeted, and so did the attendance at racecourses.

When simulcast managers convinced track operators to lessen the quality of racing, it eroded the sport. Not wanting to take responsibility for their actions, the "newbies" blamed it on everything from the recession to a lack of interest in racing—but the reality is they alone sent domestic racing into this downward spiral they're still in. To this day they can't seem to comprehend what happened or why. Their lack of depth minimized their science because they didn't know what hit them!

S&A's depth of knowledge in the sport and industry became a natural for consulting. We had been doing it for years and up until that point for free. We had offered reams of detailed data, attended personal and group meetings with governments, horsemen, and racecourse operators, as well as informed the general public both domestically and abroad. It was time to change course, not drown with the beginners who were just starting to flounder in the deep end of the pool. We still had eighty contracts, had a bid on a large entity, La Rinconada racecourse in Caracas, had inspected an offer to simulcast live horse racing to Lima as well as in the jungle cities and villages of Peru. I wasn't about to let the changes in racing or the relationships I had with the domestic tracks take me down.

The simulcasting project presentation in Peru was a formal one from an assortment of people from government, horsemen, and the racetracks. I had first been contacted by a representative at our small village racetrack in Cartago, Costa Rica, during a race day.

Around the same time, a good friend, Eduardo Gaviria, a breeder of stakes winner Real Quiet and a well-known Colombian entrepreneur, asked if I would give him an analysis of Colombian racing and the facilities around the country to help project revenues. We were already sending signals to the Hipódromo Villa de Lava, a small track in the desert in Colombia, so it made sense to take a look at the rest of the country. While I was there, he asked if I would meet with horsemen and breeders in Bogotá, inspect and approve a site for a new racetrack in Medellín, and inspect a rather large racecourse in Cali, a city of 2.5 million people. Touring Colombia and inspecting the various landscape and facilities was beautiful, and dangerously tiring. I was aware that I was traveling into some of the most infamous drug trafficking areas in the world. I actually had to get special clearance from the cartels to meet in Cali. When we got there, I was frisked by the local Feds, who wanted to know why I was there. Everyone was on edge, including the Feds. Everyone was wearing fatigues, which made it hard to tell the good guys from the bad. I told the man rubbing up and down on the inside of my leg that I was there to inspect the racetrack facility on behalf of the horseman. I spoke in English unconcerned whether or not he could understand me. He motioned for another man to come over who translated what I was saying. Within minutes I was allowed to leave—with an escort from the local militia to the Cali racecourse.

When I got to the racetrack, it was in a state of disrepair and there were no horses at the track, which presented a big problem in my mind, as they are the most important factors when you are running a racetrack. I had no idea where all of the horses were, and frankly, I didn't ask. I was eager to get out of there as fast as I could. In my estimation, it would take at least $50–60 million to bring it back to being a functioning facility.

From Cali, we headed to the Hipódromo Villa de Lava, the small track in the desert we were already simulcasting to because I wanted to see it. I nearly got killed on a dirt bike at 8,000 feet while crossing a twenty-foot crevice on a two-by-four trying to get to our location. The scenery was spectacular—it reminded me of the Grand Canyon.

Next, we headed to Medellín. This portion of the trip turned deadly the night before my inspection of the potential track location in Rio Negro. When I got to the hotel the day before, the people I was there to meet insisted I have lunch in the dining room of the hotel. There was a waterskiing competition going on outside the large pane glass window of the dining room on the man-made lake on which the hotel stood. There was so much noise from the cheering crowd, it was hard to hear the people I was meeting with as they spoke throughout our lunch. I was exhausted and did my best to get through our meal before excusing myself and going up to my room.

I put the "Do Not Disturb" placard on the outside of my door, drew the curtains to block out the midday sun, and went to sleep. Much to my surprise, I was in a slumber until late that afternoon. I didn't want to sleep that long because I had planned to get some work done. When I awoke, I wandered the hotel. Oddly, there was no one there. It was eerie because it had been packed with people at lunch. I walked back into the kitchen looking for anyone who could help me get something to eat because I was hungry. Suddenly, I felt a hand reach up from under a counter and grab me. My reaction was to turn around and hit the guy. We got into a tumble until he was able to say in broken English, "Stop!" I was confused, but I could tell he wasn't going to hurt me. I asked him to make me a steak—which he did. I sat in the dining room, the same dining room where I ate my lunch, but this time, I was the only person there.

When I finished my meal, I headed back to my room. I still had no clue where everyone had gone. The next morning I was told that four of Pablo Escobar's generals were killed on the front doorstep of the hotel I was in. There were heavy weapons everywhere. Pablo Escobar was born in Rio Negro and was a well-known figure there. I had tea and toast with the people I was there to meet. We intended to tour the land for the potential racetrack before getting into three black Suburbans. It was during that breakfast when it was disclosed to me that the racetrack was going to be funded by Escobar's company. I never intended to be involved with the cartels or Escobar. I was paid a flat sum to go look at some land and pick out the best location for a track. I fulfilled my obligation based on the blueprints they showed me that day and never did any other consulting with them again.

Upon my return to Miami Lakes, I was scheduled to pick up Rebecca in Leonardtown, Maryland, for a meeting with NYRA at Belmont Park. We had been flying a new Mitsubishi-10 for a couple of years, which I loved to fly. That airplane gave me the ability to go longer distances—it allowed me to travel nonstop from Ft. Lauderdale to Caracas or St. Kitts, which was a joy.

The airplane had been in for repairs at North American Flight Services in Saratoga Springs, New York. The trip from Saratoga to Maryland was short and on time. Rebecca showed up at St. Mary's airport for our quick trip to Belmont only to find part of a smoking plane and a runway covered with cops and ambulances.

When I was coming in for the landing, I went through the usual procedure and thought everything was fine. Of course, it wasn't. When I put the plane down, all hell broke loose because I had no wheels. I knew when the undercarriage gave way that I had a hell of a problem because I was completely loaded with fuel. My main concern was keeping the aircraft straight in the slide and on the center of the runway because there was a twenty-foot drop. If I slid to either side and off the embankment, the airplane would have surely exploded. With no wheels, the only way to keep the airplane straight was to keep even power on the engines. I turned off all of the electric and shut the engines down so the props didn't hit the asphalt going 100 miles per hour. It was only toward the end of my slide that the plane took a slight turn to the left. In their investigation, the FAA said the nose gear pin sheared and somehow the main gear retracted. It was a fiery ride with metal hitting asphalt. Despite the smoke coming through the wheel wells and up through the pedals, I walked away without any injury. When Rebecca saw it was me standing on the runway, she drove her truck directly onto the runway.

"Should we call the meeting off?" Rebecca asked

"No way!" I said

I threw my stuff in her truck and we drove to Belmont and somehow managed to make our meeting on time.

With the airplane down for repair and unable to make pickups, I called Dr. Manuel Estrada, a veterinary friend of mine, and told him to meet me in Peru to take a look at their facilities and what it entailed. Together, I thought there were pieces we could make work. Manuel was a brilliant and dedicated doctor and extremely helpful on our Central and South American travels, where he gleaned information on herd sizes and conditions. This trip would set the stage for several more Peruvian and Brazilian trips in the future.

A few days after our arrival, I was escorted to the airport for a trip to the jungle to visit a very elaborate farm—or *finca*, as the Peruvians call it. I was there to assess the network that would funnel cash back as a result of wagering on simulcasting. When I arrived at the *finca*, I was presented with two large Spanish oil paintings of local scenes. I also attended an intense meeting about simulcasting with the local operators and members of the cartel. The meeting disclosed the demographics of more than thirty towns and villages and projected handle numbers and elaborate security apparatuses. The main challenge for my consideration was to arrange for a satellite dish with the capability to broadcast racing signals directly into the jungle region bypassing the Andes mountain range and Lima. This meant the dish had to be huge because the Andes Mountains are so high. One of the members at the meeting was introduced as Señor Vladimiro Montesinos, a very imposing and interested owner of several betting shops in Lima. The document that I was holding stated that the jungle area was particularly important because it was in possession of $2.3 billion U.S. narco cash annually and had nowhere to absorb it—meaning this was money that couldn't be put in a bank. This was the ultimate immersion of the subterranean economy in motion. This cash was kept in sheds, barrels in the ground, and various containers and was an annual sum to be disbursed under the radar.

At the time, I didn't realize who Montesinos was, but I would later discover he was the enforcer for Fujimora, the president of Peru, who later fled to Japan when his presidency imploded due to corruption. I left that meeting with more questions than answers although what I witnessed was pretty clear. Later that night in my hotel room, I read the documents they had given me again and again and pondered what I would do with all of this without getting involved in the narco portion of it.

For a lot of people, the temptation to wash $2.3 billion through the simulcasting business would have been great and easy—it would have changed the game. For me, it wasn't even a thought in my head. The only thing I was trying to figure out was how I could be involved without compromising my integrity. What could I implement without touching the narco dollars? The implications of getting my hands dirty were vast. I didn't want to go down like Susan Bala. I'd always been in this business for the love of the sport—never for the money. I wasn't about to risk it all now.

I had decided that Peru was not even a consideration because of my personal belief and what it would do to the racing industry. Although they had a different perception of the narco trade than I did, the morality and future of the horse racing business would not succumb to a horrific death and humiliation with my help. I had been witness to the destruction of close friends and relatives from drugs and could not rationalize any involvement. And in my mind, the horse racing sport and industry were too vulnerable and too greedy in its current state to even attempt any discussion of a deal with Peru. I wouldn't let it go any further. From my hotel room that night, I put the idea on a shelf and never brought it up to anyone ever again.

Many racetracks seemed to be in the real estate or other businesses and looking for a product other than horse racing for their lands and facilities. Simulcasting had become incestuous and unmanageable, and combined with rebating, Thoroughbred horse racing became indistinguishable and undefinable by S&A standards. If we were going to stay afloat, it was time to pick winners—that meant consultation became our new direction, not R&D.

We found ourselves advising clients on how to navigate the changing world of horse racing while facing hostile managements and bewildered but determined well-meaning alphabet groups, as I call them, which are the various industry organizations that are involved with the sport. S&A found itself in a bizarre, lucrative world of jealousy, contempt, and misunderstanding. The invasion of new faces, new money, and new applications had almost stricken the old establishment.

Our telephone was literally ringing off the hook! I found myself in Venezuela as a guest of President Hugo Chávez assessing a reconstruction of Venezuelan racing, advising his captains and generals on the benefits of a racing country, and presenting the trophy of the prestigious "Simon Bolivar," their richest and only graded stakes.

Getting to Caracas was an aviation challenge because it was under a military lockdown under Chávez. When you are his invited guest, however, you get carte blanche to land wherever he tells you, which was at the Miranda military base. As we taxied to the ramp of the Generalissimo Francisco de Miranda Military Air Base following a steep mountain approach that was initiated from a 12,000-foot mountain peak using a secret approach chart given to us by the Venezuelan military because a flight chart into the base is impossible to get, we encountered heavily armed combat troops everywhere.

I asked for permission to taxi the screaming MU2 to a remote place I spotted on the fortress tarmac.

"Why are you parking way out here?" asked my son Aaron, who had accompanied me on this trip.

"I want the airplane in one piece when we're through," I said. I had a hunch—a gut feeling this was the right thing to do. After all, we were in an active war zone at the time.

Four days later, the fuel dump and one truck were detonated into a dark black hole full of twisted metal. The "Mits" was safe, showing only traces of black soot and a few dents from flying nuts and bolts.

When I tried to pay my fuel bill and retrieve my plane to leave, I was confronted by the following demand.

"All cash," Captain Jesus Martinez said. He was a muscular man wearing a double strand of rounds to match the magazine of the old Russian Kalachnikov machine gun laying across the paperwork on his desk.

"I was told I could use an AvCard," I replied, but before he could answer I knew cash was the only acceptable form of payment. I threw the card and four one-hundred-dollar bills down and said "I only have four hundred in cash." The good captain reached for the cash, ran the card through an old rusty stamping device from the desk drawer, and handed it back. I held a straight and militant face and thought how glad I was that he hadn't chosen to frisk me because, of course, I lied!

We taxied out to the threshold of runway 11 in the midst of two receding lines of heavily armed combat soldiers.

"Was that worth it?" Aaron asked, knowing I had $5,000 in U.S. cash in my briefcase.

I didn't answer Aaron, but I thought to myself, *Fuck 'em. I didn't want to give that asshole the cash.* I'd spent a lifetime being shaken down.

I was deep in thought and glad that we were good to go. We were on our way to Jamaica to pick up some cash.

"So many ways to die," I muttered through the headset.

As I reflect on my life's work and where I came from, I think about all those who have shared my passion around the world. I recall the glint in the eyes and attentive smiles of the rugged people in Mongolian Gers deep in the Steppe Mountains—their bending and nodding to stories of great places and great races, remembering the prowess and world conquests of Genghis Khan. And the small groups huddled in a hotel in Ulan Bator listening and asking how to perpetuate the horse beyond their stunted and sturdy ponies. I can recall being in Beijing in 2005, dining with communist leaders eager to relive and return to the days when the horse was of great value, eager to show the world how its five-thousand-year history could serve to rekindle the hungry masses once again. The Thoroughbred horse is symbolic and resurging in most civilized populations of the world. But I quickly sadden at the realization that while the fiery image of the racing horse burns brightly in so many other global coliseums, its flickering majesty in America just barely floats above a sea of drugs. It is an emblematic scene of drowning glory.

I ponder why the "US AND THEM" cannot be "WE" in such a noble sport. And why so many quibble and clamor and defensively implement such condescending practices of mediocrity. At the brink of our most lucrative era, we find so many ways to denigrate the herd with selfish and uninspiring divisions of unbecoming class. Are there none left who will sacrifice their lot and pledge their minds to restore this noble game? Or are we so bent on driving all the memories of racing's origin into such far-gone obscurity that we can never reel it back?

I hope that there are those who will look beyond the creation of a welfare state and refuse to dwell in the self-deprecation of smaller minds. That there are those who will choose to raise up this national jewel that provides passion for such a gallant trade once more!

ACKNOWLEDGMENTS

There are many folks who impacted my career as a jockey and racing official in Canada and the United States. Without the guidance and inspiration from these remarkable individuals, there's no doubt my life would have been a lot different.

Frank Merrill, twice leading trainer of America even though he operated from his Canadian base in Toronto.

Bill Beasley, whose faith in me went far beyond a friendship.

Tony Simms, whose rigidity in the composure of a condition book taught me invaluable lessons in my transition from jockey to racing secretary.

John Sifton, of the *Winnipeg Free Press*, whose great friendship taught me the meaning of real fun when we went drinking with a Shetland pony hanging his head out the back window of his mother's Rolls-Royce.

A. E. "Bert" Blake, with whom I served in the stewards stand and racing department at Assiniboia Downs. The only man to sell his dog six times . . . and Lassie—yes, that was her name—always came home!

Dr. Jim and Sally Hill, for their warm friendship over forty years. We enjoyed a fabulous and fortunate ride during the "heady" Seattle Slew triple crown; many days and nights spent as guests at Sunninghill Farm, a true "castle on the hill"; and many holiday trips to exotic locations in sunny climes, where we held court and easily solved most of the world's problems with the help of many glasses of our favorite elixir.

Scotty Kennedy, GM, coach of the Winnipeg Blue Bombers, a very tough guy who could make something out of nothing.

E. P. Taylor, an industrialist whom I became very close to during Secretariat's Canadian International Championship win.

Chris Rogers, a mentor and the finest jockey Canada ever produced.

George Frostad, to whom I sold Viva la Zaca, Rouge Sangue, and Buckley Boy. We became close friends when I arranged for Viva to be the first horse ever to be transported by air in Canada.

John A. "Bud" McDougald, a reclusive man who became a fast friend through his fascination with Secretariat.

Jake Howard of Blake, Cassels & Graydon LLP, a serious and brilliant mentor to me over the years.

Eddie Gorman, who shared the stewards stand when we worked for the Ontario government; a great friend with a wonderful wife, Regina.

D. G. "Bud" Willmot, probably my greatest mentor, whose lessons were passed along primarily in the cockpit of my Aztec from Toronto to Muskoka.

David S. Willmot, past chairman and CEO of Woodbine Entertainment Group (previously the Ontario Jockey Club).

Ronnie Robinson, a friend and valet with whom I shared many great times.

Bill Galvin, a partner in the first backstretch magazine *Guineas' Gazette*, which was fun and successful, and was the forerunner of Bill's advancement to the Canadian Horse Racing Hall of Fame.

J. T. Smithers and T. Dunn, a special thanks to these two powerful but gentle men who perhaps saved my life and many broken parts during those grueling days of winter training on the Big Sink Pike in Versailles, Kentucky. They had a unique wisdom that only comes from practical experience in the school of very hard knocks.

Nelson Bunker Hunt, a true lover of horse racing and breeding. I shipped seventy to eighty Thoroughbreds to his yard in France on Christmas Day for years. We met in Paris at the Bristol Hotel, where I headquartered in Europe, and arranged to ship fifteen head to Woodbine for fall racing. Included in the shipment were Dahlia, Youth, and Hippodamia—all international Group 1 winners, helping Canada become part of the international tour.

Maurice Zilber, trainer of multiple Group 1 winners, a good friend with a great imagination.

Woody Stephens, Hall of Fame trainer of five Belmont Stakes winners. We worked together during the Woodbine meetings and later on a daily basis at New York Racing Association.

Angel Penna, Sr., trainer of two Prix de l'Arc de Triomphe winners, world-class trainer for European royalty, and good friend for forty years. I witnessed his deft hand of horsemanship with Pawneese at Ascot when she turned back a staunch male brigade in the G1 King George VI and Queen Elizabeth Stakes and when he rocked the sport in winning two Prix de l'Arc de Triomphes with fillies San San and Allez France. It was always warm and inspiring in the comfort of his company. His wife, Elinor, broke the mold when she was the first female correspondent to write a football column from an all-male press box. Angel always did well with fillies!

Penny Tweedy, who became a household name in the mid-1970s when she literally put words in the mouth of Secretariat, arguably one of the finest Thoroughbreds on the planet. But the gutsy lady pushed the envelope when she walked the Woodbine turf course on a cold damp fall day with Lucien Laurin and me in tow. We were friends for years, and I will never forget that day or her.

LeRoy Jolley, a Hall of Fame trainer of two Kentucky Derby winners, including Genuine Risk, one of only two fillies to win the Derby.

Marjorie Everett, a legendary and dynamic leader in the horse racing industry. She owned Arlington Park for Thoroughbreds; Washington Park for Standardbreds, which provided some of my best training ground and experiences of my career.

Ogden Mills "Dinny" Phipps, past chairman of the Jockey Club and Bessemer Trust who was lured to Canada with his father on a rare occasion to race horses in the Canadian International Championship during the renaissance of that event in the 1970s.

Ramón A. Domínguez, the first jockey to win nearly $26 million in a single year. One of the super stars, he is a gifted, gutsy man who knew the shortest way around a racecourse. A gracious and sensitive man and one of the most skillful and tactful jockeys that I have ever seen. We've been good friends for several years.

Jack Klugman, a well-known film and TV star who became a lover of Thoroughbred racing through his stakes-winning horse Jaklin Klugman. We spent many fun times together when Jack was in New York while I was at NYRA. He was as you saw him on stage and screen: just a damn nice guy to be around.

Jerry McKeon, the former president of NYRA who was a major supporter of our simulcast plan from the start.

I want to thank the Jockey Clubs in Brazil, Colombia, Chile, Peru, and Venezuela for their cooperation when we pioneered periodic satellite racing service to racing venues in the '80s, '90s, and beyond. The early efforts were costly but worth it.

Christopher Armond, who served as the CEO at race courses in Jamaica and Trinidad and as an announcer in Detroit and at Hialeah. He is also the past president of the West Indian Thoroughbred Racing Association. His lifetime of service to Caribbean horseracing has been untiring and unsurpassed in rather trying times.

Rodolfo Loria, who served us honorably in Costa Rica for over twenty years. His work with the political and labor requirements contributed considerably to S&A's business there, and we are extremely grateful.

Dr. Manuel Estrada, a master horseman, a lover of Thoroughbred racing, and a dedicated father. It was indeed a great pleasure to be in the company of Manuel during many of our international visits. I respect and appreciate his counsel and friendship. He is an impeccable and honorable individual having served his government, universities, and a great many of his fellow citizens in Costa Rica.

Susan Tessem, who provided a guiding hand while serving on our board in Costa Rica. Her bilingual capability during the racing seasons provided a great deal of harmony and much humor.

Eduardo Gaviria, an influential driving force during our trips to Colombia. We spent many pleasant hours in his home and in the company of his family.

I also want to thank the authorities and books in Antigua, Aruba, Bermuda, Barbados, Costa Rica, Dominican Republic, Grenada, Guyana, Curaçao, Margarita Island, Puerto Rico, U.S. Virgin Islands, Argentina, Brazil, Chile, Ecuador, Mexico, and Venezuela.

I thank the Japan Racing Association for its warm receptions and generous offerings during our many trips to that country. Most notable were our personal escorts who provided tireless detail and many history lessons regarding their horseracing, geography, and historic sites in many cities.

To our good friends Yoshi Kitahara and Shuji Inada, who became our close confidents and mentors during nine years of service together.

I would also like to express my appreciation to the governments, regulators, racing authorities, horsemen of England, France, China, Mongolia, and South Korea for their hospitality, freedom of movement, inquiries regarding their rules and customs related to horse racing, breeding, and wagering laws.

To the hundreds of incredible trainers I've met and learned from throughout my career. Their job is tedious and misunderstood, and those without imagination fail. It is a game of hope, and there are few shortcuts.

A heartfelt thank-you to all of the grooms, exercise riders, and hot walkers who are entrusted with billions of dollars of horseflesh. There is much love in these people but it is mostly expressed quietly and, sometimes, even silently. But if one watches closely, he might catch a slight smile that bubbles up from an image of contriteness that is generated from a scene or sound unknown to anyone who hasn't been around the track of a Thoroughbred.

When it comes to writing a book, I quickly discovered, it takes radical collaboration to go from telling stories on the golf course and around the dinner table to getting it all on the page. I must thank the following people for helping me make that happen in the most professional and enjoyable way.

To my good friends, Jerry and Marcia MacDonald. Jerry reveled in his handicapping skills and Marcia always enjoyed the stories and whirlwind elegance of the racing scene at Saratoga. They encouraged me to find a writer and go for it. I am deeply appreciative for their kindness and support.

Chef Kim Klopstock, Lilly, and the Rose catering of Saratoga Springs, New York, for providing us with a favorite watering hole and supplying us with rare and creative fare during our favorite visits.

Cot Campbell, who urged me to play golf after three solid years of thrashings on Saratoga's hard courts. I never won a game!

Hope Innelli, editor extraordinaire, who helped preserve the authenticity of the story while giving me guidance in the editorial process. Hope placed the book high up in her best reads, and we thank her for her insight.

Adam Mitchell, a young man who belies his years. He somehow managed to decipher two large bins of 50-year-old clippings and printed material. His job was not an easy one, akin to dealing with a foreign language. While the Q&A was extensive, he decoded the peculiar vernacular of horseracing into a bridge of learning.

To Becky Ryder and the Keenland Library, who offered valuable assistance in referencing charts and other data for the book.

Mel Berger from WME/IMG. One has only to experience a single audience with Mel to plumb the depths of wisdom and seriousness in his complex world of entertainment. I was fortunate to have had an hour with the man, bedecked in his office of global literature. A quietly pious man, you know whether you fit or you don't in the first ten minutes. I had the good fortune of his candor, survived his introspection, and came away cleansed and with the courage to continue. He's simply the best!

Laura Morton, a master in the literary world with nineteen New York Times bestsellers to her credit. She grasps detail and nuance in unusual substance and is prolific in expression of circumstances. Her ability to capture and expand on traumatic incidences, lexicon and diversity of this book was invaluable. She has become mentor and good friend to me.

To Skyhorse Publishing for believing in this story, especially Jay Cassell and Lindsey Breuer-Barnes. Thanks also to Kirsten Dalley for interior book design, and Tom Lau for the cover.

INDEX

Rogers, Jack, 24, 26, 49–50, 56, 64–66, 95, 97
Rogers, Joe, 24, 49–50, 54, 61, 64–66, 83, 95, 97
Rogers, Roy, 156
Romanet, Jean, 176
Ross, J. K. L., 2

S
Santa Anita, 170, 186, 207
Saratoga Race Course, 187
Saratoga Springs, ix–x
Scarlet fever, 15–16
Sea Biscuit, 101
Seagram, J. E. Frowde, 72
Seattle Slew, 179
Secretariat, x, 164–170, 174–175
Senator Jim, 115, 119, 123
Sewing, George, 99, 102
Shapiro, John, 167
Sharif, Omar, 177, 189
Shoemaker, Willie, 114
Silver, 58
Sledge, Olin, 100–102, 108
Small Play, 33–35, 38–39, 51–52, 58, 74–75, 79, 85, 95
Smith, Keely, 96
Smithers, J. T., 30, 44–46, 49–57, 59–61, 64, 66–67
Snow Knight, 175
Speak Free, 48, 55, 58–59, 67–68, 73, 83
Stafford, Jack, 119–120, 123, 125
Stakes horse, 137–138
Stanford Park, 17–18
Stephenson, George, 2
Steubenville Fairground, 38–39

Stevenson, Barbara, 151–154, 158–159, 179, 194
Stevenson, Charles, Jr. (father), 2, 5, 21–23, 77, 89, 195
Stevenson, Charles, Sr. (grandfather), 2
Stevenson, Charlie (uncle), 82
Stevenson, David, 156, 159
Stevenson, Dianna, 156, 197–198, 200, 206
Stevenson, Rebecca, 159, 195, 197–198, 200, 206–208, 213, 218–219, 226
Stevenson, Virginia Carol, 13, 15, 21–22, 194
Stevenson, Wilfred, 82
Strubb, Bob, 200
Suffolk Downs, 108–109, 114–115

T
Taylor, Elizabeth, 156
Taylor, E. P., 72, 115, 126–127, 141, 165–167, 171–172
Taylor, Mickey, 179
Telephone betting outlets, 219
Thistle Downs, 92–94
Thomas, Joe, 127
Thornecliff, 10–11, 17
Thoroughbred Owners of California (TOC), 221
Todmorden Mills, 4
Trainer, 136–137
Trigger, 129
Trinidad and Tobago, 203, 207–209, 217
Turcotte, Ronny, 171
Turf Classic, 188–189, 192